THE REVELS PLAYS

Former editors
Clifford Leech 1958–71
F. David Hoeniger 1970–85

General editors
David Bevington, E. A. Honigmann, J. R. Mulryne
and Eugene M. Waith

THE MAID'S TRAGEDY

MANCHESTER
UNIVERSITY PRESS

The Maides Tragedy.

AS IT HATH BEENE
diuers times Acted at the *Blacke-friers* by
the K I N G s Maiesties Seruants.

LONDON

Printed for *Francis Constable* and are to be sold
at the white Lyon ouer againſt the great North
doore of *Pauls Church.* 1 6 1 9.

THE REVELS PLAYS

THE
MAID'S TRAGEDY

FRANCIS BEAUMONT
and JOHN FLETCHER

edited by T. W. Craik

MANCHESTER
UNIVERSITY PRESS
Manchester and New York

*Distributed exclusively in the USA
by* Palgrave

Introduction, critical apparatus, etc.
© T. W. Craik 1988

The right of T. W. Craik to be identified as the editor of
this work has been asserted by him in accordance with
the Copyright, Designs and Patents Act 1988.

First published by Manchester University Press 1988

This edition published by Manchester University Press
Oxford Road, Manchester M13 9NR, UK
and Room 400, 175 Fifth Avenue, New York,
NY 10010, USA
www.manchesteruniversitypress.co.uk

Distributed exclusively in the USA by
Palgrave, 175 Fifth Avenue, New York,
NY 10010, USA

Distributed exclusively in Canada by
UBC Press, University of British Columbia, 2029 West Mall,
Vancouver, BC, Canada V6T 1Z2

British Library Cataloguing-in-Publication Data
A catalogue record for this book is available from the British Library

Library of Congress Cataloging-in-Publication Data applied for

ISBN   0 7190 3098 6   *paperback*

11 10 09 08 07 06 05 04   10 9 8 7 6 5 4 3 2

Typeset in Hong Kong
by Best-set Typesetter Ltd
Printed in Great Britain
by Bell & Bain Ltd, Glasgow

Contents

THE REVELS PLAYS

General Editors' Preface

Clifford Leech conceived of the Revels Plays as a series in the mid-1950s modelling the project on the New Arden Shakespeare. The aim, as he wrote in 1958, was 'to apply to Shakespeare's predecessors, contemporaries and successors the methods that are now used in Shakespeare editing'. The plays chosen were to include well known works from the early Tudor period to about 1700, as well as others less familiar but of literary and theatrical merit: 'the plays included,' Leech wrote, 'should be such as to deserve and indeed demand performance.' We owe it to Clifford Leech that the idea became reality. He set the high standards of the series, ensuring that editors of individual volumes produced work of lasting merit, equally useful for teachers and students, theatre directors and actors. Clifford Leech remained General Editor until 1971, and was succeeded by F. David Hoeniger, who retired in 1985.

The Revels Plays are now under the direction of four General Editors, David Bevington, E. A. J. Honigmann, J. R. Mulryne and E. M. Waith. Published originally by Methuen, the series is now published by Manchester University Press, embodying essentially the same format, scholarly character, and high editorial standards of the series as first conceived. The General Editors intend to concentrate on plays from the period 1558–1642, and may include a small number of non-dramatic works of interest to students of drama. Some slight changes have been forced by considerations of cost. For example, in editions from 1978, notes to the introduction are placed together at the end, not at the foot of the page. Collation and commentary notes will continue, however, to appear on the relevant pages.

The text of each Revels play, in accordance with established practice in the series, is edited afresh from the original text of best authority (in a few instances, texts), but spelling and punctuation are modernised and speech headings are silently made consistent. Elisions in the original are also silently regularised, except where metre would be affected by the change; since 1968 the '-ed' form is used for non-syllabic terminations in past tenses and past participles ('-'d' earlier), and '-èd' for syllabic ('-ed' earlier). The editor emends, as distinct from modernises, the original only in instances where error is patent, or at least very probable, and correction persuasive. Act divisions are given only if they appear in the original or if the structure of the play clearly points to them. Those act and scene divisions not in the original are provided in small type. Square brackets are also used for any other additions to or changes in the stage directions of the original.

Revels Plays do not provide a variorum collation, but only those variants which require the critical attention of serious textual students. All departures of substance from 'copy-text' are listed, including any relineation and those changes in punctuation which involve to any degree a decision between alternative interpretations; but not such accidentals as turned letters, nor necessary additions to stage directions whose editorial nature is already made clear by the use of brackets. Press corrections in the 'copy-text' are likewise collated. Of later emendations of the text, only those are given which as alternative readings still deserve attention.

One of the hallmarks of the Revels Plays is the thoroughness of their annotations. Besides explaining the meaning of difficult words and passages, the editor provides comments on customs or usage, text or stage-business—indeed, on anything judged pertinent and helpful. Each volume contains an Index to the Commentary, in which particular attention is drawn to meanings for words not listed in *OED*, and (starting in 1996) an indexing of proper names and topics in the Introduction and Commentary.

The Introduction to a Revels play assesses the authority of the 'copy-text' on which it is based, and discusses the editorial methods employed in dealing with it; the editor also considers the play's date and (where relevant) sources, together with its place in the work of the author and in the theatre of its time. Stage history is offered, and in the case of a play by an author not previously represented in the series a brief biography is given.

It is our hope that plays edited in this fashion will promote further scholarly and theatrical investigation of one of the richest periods in theatrical history.

DAVID BEVINGTON
E. A. J. HONIGMANN
J. R. MULRYNE
E. M. WAITH

Preface

I am grateful to Professor J. R. Mulryne for his help as a general editor of the Revels Plays with the preparation of the final version of this edition, and also to his research assistant Dr Janet Clare. My debts to previous editors are acknowledged throughout the volume: I here make special mention of Dyce, Daniel, Spencer, Norland, Gurr and Turner. When I was completing the late J. M. Lothian's edition of *Twelfth Night* a dozen years ago, Professor Turner was most generous in his help, placing his own unpublished edition at my disposal, and I have been glad to renew my correspondence with him about some of the new readings which I propose here, for which, of course, the responsibility remains my own. Professor Gavin Townend assisted me in discussing the classical names of the characters, Mr Hugh Shankland in translating Bandello and Professor Raman Selden in translating Valerius Maximus. For typing various parts of the manuscript I thank Mrs Margaret Crane and Miss Sandra Nicholson.

I gratefully acknowledge a research grant and a term's study leave from the University of Durham, and the permission of the Bodleian Library, Oxford, to reproduce the title-page of the first Quarto (1619) of *The Maid's Tragedy* (shelfmark *Mal 233(1)*). The Bodleian Library also supplied the microfilm photographs of the first and second Quartos from which I worked. The Glasgow Citizens' Theatre and the Royal Shakespeare Company allowed me to consult the promptbooks of their productions.

I dedicate the volume to Professor and Mrs A. R. Humphreys in recognition of their continual kindness and encouragement during more than thirty years, and also in recognition of Professor Humphreys's outstanding ability as a critical editor.

Durham, 1986   T. W. CRAIK

Abbreviations

1. EDITIONS OF *The Maid's Tragedy*

Baker   *Select Plays by Francis Beaumont and John Fletcher (Everyman's Library)*, ed. G. P. Baker (London and Toronto, 1911).

Brooke and Paradise   *English Drama, 1580–1642*, ed. C. F. Tucker Brooke and N. B. Paradise (Boston, Massachusetts, 1933).

Colman   *The Dramatic Works of Beaumont and Fletcher*, ed. George Colman the Elder, 10 vols. (London, 1778).

Daniel   *The Works of Francis Beaumont and John Fletcher, Variorum Edition*, ed. A. H. Bullen, P. A. Daniel, etc., 4 vols., unfinished (London, 1904–12).

Dyce   *The Works of Beaumont and Fletcher*, ed. Alexander Dyce, 11 vols. (London, 1843–6).

F2   *Fifty Comedies and Tragedies. Written by Francis Beaumont and John Fletcher, Gentlemen* (London, 1679). The second Folio.

Glover and Waller   *The Works of Francis Beaumont and John Fletcher (Cambridge English Classics)*, ed. A. Glover and A. R. Waller, 10 vols. (Cambridge, 1905–12).

Gurr   *Francis Beaumont and John Fletcher, The Maid's Tragedy (Fountainwell Drama Texts)*, ed. Andrew Gurr (Edinburgh, 1969).

Langbaine   *The Works of Beaumont and Fletcher* [ed. Gerard Langbaine the Younger], 7 vols. (London, 1711).

McIlwraith   *Five Stuart Tragedies (The World's Classics)*, ed. A. K. McIlwraith (Oxford, 1953).

Norland   *Beaumont and Fletcher, The Maid's Tragedy (Regents Renaissance Drama Series)*, ed. Howard B. Norland (Lincoln, Nebraska, 1968).

Q1   *The Maid's Tragedy* (London, 1619). The first Quarto.

Q2   *The Maid's Tragedy* (London, 1622). The second Quarto.

Q3   *The Maid's Tragedy* (London, 1630). The third Quarto.

Q4   *The Maid's Tragedy* (London, 1638). The fourth Quarto.

Q5   *The Maid's Tragedy* (London, 1641). The fifth Quarto.

Q6   *The Maid's Tragedy* (London, 1650 [? 1660]). The sixth Quarto.

Q7   *The Maid's Tragedy* (London, 1661). The seventh Quarto.

Q8   *The Maid's Tragedy* (London, 1686). The eighth Quarto.

Q9   *The Maid's Tragedy* (London, 1704). The ninth Quarto.

Q10   *The Maid's Tragedy* (London, 1714). The tenth Quarto.

Qq   Q1 and Q2.

Spencer   *Elizabethan Plays*, ed. Hazelton Spencer (Boston, Massachusetts, 1933).

Strachey   *Beaumont and Fletcher (The Mermaid Series)*, ed. J. St Loe Strachey, 2 vols. (London, 1887).

Theobald   *The Works of Mr Francis Beaumont and Mr John Fletcher*, ed. L. Theobald, T. Seward and J. Sympson, 10 vols. (London, 1750).

Thorndike *'The Maid's Tragedy' and 'Philaster'* (*The Belles-Lettres Series*), ed. Ashley H. Thorndike (Boston, Massachusetts, 1906).

Turner *The Maid's Tragedy*, ed. Robert K. Turner, Jr., in *The Dramatic Works in the Beaumont and Fletcher Canon*, general editor Fredson Bowers, vol. II (Cambridge, 1970).

Weber *The Works of Beaumont and Fletcher*, ed. Henry Weber, 14 vols. (Edinburgh, 1812).

2. OTHER WORKS

Arcadia Sir Philip Sidney, *The Countesse of Pembrokes Arcadia*, ed. A. Feuillerat (Cambridge, 1939).

Brereton J. Le Gay Brereton, *Marginalia on Beaumont and Fletcher:* I (*Sydney University Library Publications*, No. 3) (Sydney, 1906).

Chambers, *E. S.* E. K. Chambers, *The Elizabethan Stage*, 4 vols. (Oxford, 1923).

Deighton K. Deighton, *The Old Dramatists: Conjectural Readings* (London, 1896).

F1623 *Mr William Shakespeare's Comedies, Histories, and Tragedies* (the first Folio) (London, 1623).

Fleay F. G. Fleay, *A Biographical Chronicle of the English Drama, 1559–1642*, 2 vols. (1891).

Gurr (ed.), *Philaster* Francis Beaumont and John Fletcher, *Philaster, or, Love Lies a-Bleeding* (*The Revels Plays*), ed. Andrew Gurr (London, 1969).

Heath Benjamin Heath, 'Supplement to the new edition [i.e., Theobald] of Beaumont and Fletcher's works', *c.* 1750, British Library Additional MS. 31910.

Mason J. Monck Mason, *Comments on the Plays of Beaumont and Fletcher* (London, 1798).

Onions C. T. Onions, *A Shakespeare Glossary*, enlarged and revised by R. D. Eagleson (Oxford, 1986).

Oxford Classical Dictionary The Oxford Classical Dictionary, ed. M. Cary, J. D. Denniston, A. D. Nock, W. D. Ross and H. H. Scullard (Oxford, 1961).

OED The Compact Edition of the Oxford English Dictionary (Oxford, 1971).

Shakespeare Apocrypha The Shakespeare Apocrypha, being a collection of fourteen plays which have been attributed to Shakespeare, ed. C. F. Tucker Brooke (Oxford, 1908).

Shakespeare's England Shakespeare's England: an Account of the Life and Manners of his Age, ed. Sidney Lee and C. T. Onions, 2 vols. (Oxford, 1916).

Smith, *Dictionary* Sir William Smith, *A Dictionary of Greek and Roman Biography and Mythology*, 2 vols. (London, 1853).

Tilley M. P. Tilley, *A Dictionary of the Proverbs in England in the Sixteenth and Seventeenth Centuries* (Ann Arbor, Michigan, 1950).

Quotations from Shakespeare are taken from *William Shakespeare, The Complete Works*, ed. Peter Alexander (London, 1951); the titles of Shakespeare's plays are abbreviated as in Onions. Quotations from Beaumont and Fletcher are taken from *The Dramatic Works in the Beaumont and Fletcher*

Canon, general ed. Fredson Bowers (Cambridge, 1966–   ; in progress), apart from those from Gurr (ed.), *Philaster*, and those from Glover and Waller in Appendix B. Quotations from the plays of other dramatists are taken from Revels Plays editions when published in this series; quotations from Jonson's plays not published in the Revels Plays are taken from *Ben Jonson*, ed. C. H. Herford and Percy and Evelyn Simpson (Oxford, 1925–52).

Introduction

The first two editions of *The Maid's Tragedy* (Q1, 1619; Q2, 1622)
carry no statement of authorship; the play is first ascribed to Francis
Beaumont and John Fletcher[1] in the third edition (Q3, 1630). It
was included in the second Folio (1679), the first collected edition of
their plays.[2] That it was written by Beaumont and Fletcher in collaboration has never been doubted; the nature of their collaboration,
however, has not been exactly determined, either in this play or in
any other in which they worked together.

The seventeenth-century poetic tributes to the two writers as a
partnership commend their harmonious achievement: they had 'twin-
like Braines' and 'chiming Muses',[3] and were 'one Poet in a paire of
friends'.[4] One panegyrist, reporting that 'some thinke Your Witts of
two Complexions fram'd' (Fletcher inclining to comedy, Beaumont
to tragedy), denies it and declares 'you were Both for Both'.[5]

In each of two sets of commendatory verses William Cartwright
begins by saying that Beaumont assisted Fletcher by refining his
exuberance,[6] and the same idea is stated in John Aubrey's account
of the dramatists;[7] however, since Cartwright's principal theme is
that Fletcher's genius was not dependent on Beaumont and survived
Beaumont's death, and since Aubrey's informant may have been
influenced by Cartwright's verses, this tradition cannot be depended
upon.[8] The opening of Jasper Maine's verses indicates how little was
known, even in the dramatists' time, of their manner of working:

Great paire of Authors, whom one equall Starre
Begot so like in *Genius*, that you are
In Fame, as well as Writings, both so knit,
That no man knowes where to divide your wit,
Much lesse your praise; you, who had equall fire,
And did each other mutually inspire;
Whether one did contrive, the other write,
Or one fram'd the plot, the other did indite;
Whether one found the matter, th'other dresse,
Or the one disposed what th'other did expresse;
Where e're your parts between your selves lay, we,
In all things which you did but one thred see,

I

> So evenly drawne out, so gently spunne,
> That Art with Nature nere did smoother run.[9]

If the answers had been available, Maine would not have raised the questions.

In the nineteenth and twentieth centuries there have been attempts to assign particular parts of plays to Fletcher and his collaborators (including Beaumont) from internal evidence derived from versification and diction.[10] Fletcher made particularly frequent use of the feminine ending in his blank verse, he tended to make the breaks between sentences or their main units coincide with the ends of lines rather than fall in the middles of lines, and he preferred the form 'ye' to 'you' and such verb-forms as 'does' and 'has' to 'doth' and 'hath'. Such tests are not infallible. In the earlier works in which Fletcher had a hand, such as *The Maid's Tragedy*, he was still forming his style, and in the later works, where his style had become more mannered, it was easy for his collaborators to imitate it. Nevertheless, the relative conspicuousness of Fletcherian characteristics in four scenes of *The Maid's Tragedy*—II.ii, IV.i, V.i and V.ii—probably justifies the consensus of modern opinion that Fletcher wrote them.[11] This need not, and should not, be understood to mean that Beaumont had no hand in these four scenes and that Fletcher had no hand in any of the others; one may suppose that the authors worked over the whole play together at least once, and if Beaumont transcribed the whole text on two occasions, as will later be suggested, he may have made further alterations of his own.

2. DATE

It is agreed that *The Maid's Tragedy* was written in 1610 or 1611; this agreement is based on inference and not on any known facts as to its composition, licensing or first performance.[12] The upper limit of 31 October 1611 can be safely inferred from the name which Sir George Buc (or Buck), Master of the Revels, gave to another play, which he censored and licensed on that day by writing this note on its manuscript:

> This second Maydens tragedy (for it hath no name inscribed) may with the reformations bee acted publikely. 31 october. 1611. G. Buc.[13]

This shows that Buc knew (and had presumably recently licensed) *The Maid's Tragedy*. The first mention of a performance (which is also the first direct mention of the play) is dated 20 May 1613, when

John Heminges was paid for a number of plays, including *The Maid's Tragedy*, acted by the King's Men at court during the celebrations of the Princess Elizabeth's wedding to the Elector Palatine.[14]

The title-page of Q1 (1619) states that the play had been 'divers times acted at the Blackfriars'. The King's Men began playing there in the autumn of 1609.[15] Though there is nothing to rule out the possibility that its first performance was at the Globe, it is more likely that the play was written for the Blackfriars and received its first performance there, but probably not in the 1609–10 season because of the steady continuance of plague.[16]

If Beaumont and Fletcher wrote the play in 1610 or early 1611, it may reasonably be considered either the second or the third of the three plays in which their collaborative achievement is highest: *Philaster, A King and No King* and *The Maid's Tragedy*.[17] These three plays were written for the King's Men. Their earlier plays of single authorship, Beaumont's *The Woman Hater* and *The Knight of the Burning Pestle* and Fletcher's *The Faithful Shepherdess*, and their first collaborative play, *Cupid's Revenge*, had been written for boy actors.[18] Their new association with the King's Men, for whom (after Beaumont's marriage in 1613 and retirement from authorship) Fletcher continued to write throughout his life, put at their disposal the power and skill of Burbage and his fellows, and it is not surprising that they responded to the situation.

3. SOURCES

In their earlier collaborative plays *Cupid's Revenge* and *Philaster* Beaumont and Fletcher had drawn upon two prose romances, Sidney's *Arcadia* and Alonso Perez's continuation of Montemayor's *Diana*. Two stories from *Arcadia* were combined to form the plot of *Cupid's Revenge*; that of *Philaster* broadly follows one story from *Diana*, but treats it with more inventive freedom than the earlier play had shown, drawing also upon the character-types of *Cupid's Revenge*, and upon the emotional situations of *Hamlet*.[19] This advance in freedom is continued in *The Maid's Tragedy*.

Three incidents in the plot of *The Maid's Tragedy* have their sources in other works. One of these incidents gives the tragedy its title. As Dyce noted,

Aspatia fighting in male attire with Amintor has a sort of prototype in the combat between Parthenia and Amphialus: see Sir P. Sidney's *Arcadia*, Book iii.[20]

There can be little doubt that Sidney's romance provided the inspiration for Aspatia's death-scene (V.iii), though the circumstances of the two incidents are quite different. The story of Parthenia's death is told in *Arcadia* (1590), bk. III, chaps. 12–16. The situation is as follows. The King of Arcadia's two daughters are being held prisoners in the castle of Amphialus, their cousin, who is in love with the younger. The King besieges the castle; Amphialus challenges the besiegers to single combat, and overcomes several of them, where-upon the King sends for Argalus to champion the princesses. There is a poignant leave-taking between Argalus and his loving and anxious wife Parthenia. The combat, fought first on horseback and then on foot, results in Argalus' death, Parthenia arriving in time to receive his dying words. Shortly afterwards Amphialus is challenged by one calling himself the Knight of the Tomb and dressed in armour suitable to his name. The combatants almost immediately descend from their horses and begin a sword-fight in which the Knight of the Tomb for a while holds his own, but presently begins to suffer wounds and to lose strength. Amphialus offers to end the combat, but his offer is angrily refused, whereupon he in turn grows angry and fatally wounds the Knight. He pulls off the helmet of his adversary, and discovers that it is Parthenia. She dies, is universally lamented, and is buried with honour in her husband's tomb (see Appendix A). In *The Maid's Tragedy* Aspatia dresses herself as a young man, pretends to be her own soldier-brother, and in that disguise challenges her former betrothed, Amintor, to a duel for having deserted her. Neither disguised lady looks for anything but death. Parthenia can have no hope of killing Amphialus, and Aspatia has no wish to harm Amintor at all. What the two incidents have in common is that in both a heroine disguises herself and fights a duel in order to end her sorrows by death. The pathos of Sidney's narra-tion is akin to that of Beaumont and Fletcher's dramatisation. These resemblances of situation and of emotion are enough, in this instance, to make it much more probable that *Arcadia* is a source of *The Maid's Tragedy* than that it is not. The absence of verbal echoes is no argu-ment against this conclusion: *Cupid's Revenge*, which is undoubtedly based upon *Arcadia*, has no verbal echoes of the incidents which it dramatises.

The scene (V.i) in which Evadne kills the King, by repeatedly stabbing him after tying his arms to the bed while he sleeps, is derived from one of the *Novelle* (1554) of Matteo Bandello.[21] In this story (I, xlii) a rich young Valencian knight, Didaco Centiglia, secretly marries Violante, a young woman of humble birth, and secretly visits her for a year at her mother's house. He then openly marries the daughter of another nobleman. Violante, accosting him one day as he rides past the house, pretends to believe his excuses and invites him to spend the night with her according to his old custom. He gladly agrees. That night, as he sleeps after their love-making, Violante and her maid tie him up with a rope, gag him, and bind him in an upright position to a post which supports the main beam of the bedroom. Violante then makes him a series of reproachful speeches, in the course of which she cuts off his tongue and his fingers' ends, blinds his eyes, and after further mutilations plunges her knife into his heart two or three times. Next morning, when Didaco's servant and kinsmen inquire for him, she insists that she will speak only to the viceroy, and when he comes she tells him the whole story. She is subsequently beheaded along with her maid, who had steadfastly refused to leave her even though she had strongly urged her to do so after the murder.

The debt of *The Maid's Tragedy* to this story was noted by Wilhelm Creizenach, though his summary of the story is not fully accurate.[22] Fletcher certainly knew the story, for he based *The Triumph of Death*, one of the *Four Plays in One*, upon it, while complicating it with fresh plot-material of his own.[23] The verbal parallels between *The Maid's Tragedy* and *The Triumph of Death* are of twofold interest: they reinforce the ascription to Fletcher of the scenes echoed (II.ii, IV.i and V.i), and they reinforce Creizenach's statement that Bandello's story is the source of Evadne's murder of the King (see Appendix B).

Whether Fletcher was acquainted with Bandello's version of the story is uncertain. The story was re-told by Pierre Boaistuau (*Histoires tragiques*, 1559, fifth story), whose version was literally translated by William Painter in his *Palace of Pleasure* (1566: 1, xlii).[24] In this form the story, besides being diffusely narrated, is much altered. In Bandello the fatal invitation is offered by Violante from her window; in Boaistuau and Painter it is delivered to the knight at his lodging by the maid in a letter, and in *The Triumph of Death* she delivers it to him by word of mouth. In Bandello the victim's body is put into a basket and produced only after Violante's confession; in Boaistuau and Painter it is thrown out of the window into the street to be found the next morning; in *The Triumph of Death* it is produced, above, by the lady and her maid, after which the lady throws down first a written statement and then the victim's heart. The most important difference between Bandello's story and the version of Boaistuau and

Painter is that in the former the atrocities are all performed upon the living victim, whereas in the latter the victim is fatally stabbed in the throat by the lady as he lies asleep in bed beside her, his waking resistance being prevented by a rope tied to the bed at one side and pulled tight by the maid at the other, and the atrocities are all performed, with appropriate denunciations, upon his corpse. In *The Triumph of Death* he is not in bed at all (he has actually been trying to seduce a third lady in the presence of his original wife), nor is he bound, but is partially stupefied with a sleeping-draught, and instead of being mutilated he is repeatedly stabbed by the lady as is the King by Evadne. The question whether Fletcher made his revengers exultingly reproach their living victims because of his direct recourse to Bandello probably must remain an open question. Such exultant reproaches are an indispensable feature of tragedies of revenge, and he could hardly have failed to introduce them whether or not he knew that the Boaistuau-Painter version was an expurgation. But the fact that in *The Triumph of Death* the lady proposes to 'watch him till he wakes, / Then bind him, and then torture him' suggests that Fletcher was aware of Bandello's version of the story, though he refrained from staging its horrors. It is also worth noting that the name Violante is given to the heroine in *The Triumph of Love* by Fletcher's collaborator in *Four Plays in One*. This is Bandello's form of the name, which Boaistuau gives as Violente and Painter as Violenta. There are no verbal echoes of Bandello's version or of the Boaistuau-Painter one in either of the Fletcher plays.

The third incident in *The Maid's Tragedy* which can be ascribed to a source is the one (IV.ii) in which Melantius, having been accused by Calianax of soliciting his indirect assistance in a plan to murder the King, continues to solicit it in undertones while they are both in the King's presence, with the result that Calianax denounces him afresh and is disbelieved because of the improbability of Melantius' behaviour. W. D. Briggs drew attention to the origin of this incident in the collection of anecdotes made by Valerius Maximus, whose nine books of memorable deeds and sayings provided useful illustrations for rhetoricians and enjoyed popularity, in the middle ages and later, as a school book. The participants are Hannibal (corresponding to the King), Blassius (corresponding to Melantius) and Dasius (corresponding to Calianax), the occasion the Second Punic War (210 B.C.), and the issue the restoration of Salapia in Apulia to Roman control. The anecdote is quoted, with a translation, in Appendix c.[25]

Apart from these three incidents the plot of *The Maid's Tragedy* appears to be wholly original. The other influences upon the play affect either the detail of its language, or the way in which certain emotional situations are handled, or both.

Though there are no verbal parallels between Aspatia's death scene and the death of Parthenia in *Arcadia*, Sidney's romance is echoed on a few occasions elsewhere.[26] Beaumont and Fletcher echo other authors with whose work one would expect them to be as familiar as they were with Sidney's: Marlowe,[27] Donne,[28] Jonson[29] and Shakespeare.[30] The majority of the Shakespearean echoes are of *Hamlet*; particularly striking is the cluster towards the end of III.i, just when the play is moving from its 'discovery phase' to its 'revenge phase',[31] and Amintor is feeling the full weight of his moral and emotional burden. Philaster had himself a smack of Hamlet; so does the hero of *The Maid's Tragedy*. But the influence of *Hamlet* is not confined to the hero nor to verbal reminiscences. The scene in which Melantius confronts his sister with her guilt (IV.i) cannot fail to recall the scene in which Hamlet confronts his mother with hers (*Hamlet*, III.iv), and Evadne's decision not to kill the King in his sleep equally strongly evokes Hamlet's decision not to kill the King at his prayers (V.i; *Hamlet*, III.iii).[32] Calianax, in his roles of old courtier, unconscious buffoon and father of a pitiable virgin, re-enacts Polonius. It is also possible to compare the presence of the masque in *The Maid's Tragedy* (I.ii) with that of the 'mousetrap' play in *Hamlet* (III.ii), and to compare the function of the 'mousetrap' play with the King's attempt to catch the conscience of Melantius at the banquet in *The Maid's Tragedy* (IV.i).[33]

The prominence of revenge as a tragic theme in *Hamlet* and *The Maid's Tragedy* ensures that the associations between the plays are particularly strong, much stronger than any that can be established between *The Maid's Tragedy* and either *Julius Caesar* or *Othello*. The quarrel scenes, between Brutus and Cassius and between Amintor and Melantius, have a certain theatrical affinity in that the quarrelers are friends and that in both there is some reversal-patterning (Melantius challenges Amintor and later Amintor challenges Melantius; Cassius is angry and Brutus calm until the Poet's entrance, which angers Brutus and amuses Cassius), but because of the difference in substance the resemblance is rather technical than essential.[34] The same can be said of the murder scenes in *Othello* and *The Maid's Tragedy*: in both the focus is upon the bed in which a sleeper is awakened, charged with guilt, and murdered, but the essential differences outweigh this resemblance.[35]

One further Shakespearean source should be mentioned, *The Two Gentlemen of Verona*, in which Julia, serving her inconstant lover Proteus in the disguise of a page, is sent by him to Silvia to deliver her a ring and receive from her a picture. In a dialogue of dramatic irony Silvia interrogates the supposed page about Julia:

> *Silvia.* How tall was she?
> *Julia.* About my stature; for at Pentecost,
>   When all our pageants of delight were play'd,
>   Our youth got me to play the woman's part,
>   And I was trimm'd in Madam Julia's gown;
>   Which served me as fit, by all men's judgments,
>   As if the garment had been made for me;
>   Therefore I know she is about my height.
>   And at that time I made her weep agood,
>   For I did play a lamentable part.
>   Madam, 'twas Ariadne passioning
>   For Theseus' perjury and unjust flight;
>   Which I so lively acted with my tears
>   That my poor mistress, moved therewithal,
>   Wept bitterly; and would I might be dead
>   If I in thought felt not her very sorrow.
> *Silvia.* She is beholding to thee, gentle youth.
>   Alas, poor lady, desolate and left!
>   I weep myself, to think upon thy words.   (*Gent.*, IV.iv.153–71)

The emblematic aptness of the myth to the actual situation no doubt prompted its reappearance in Antiphila's needlework (*The Maid's Tragedy*, II.ii).[36]

4. THE PLAY

The plot of *The Maid's Tragedy* can be very briefly summarised. Thomas Rymer's abstract is faithful to the facts:

> *Amintor*, contracted to *Aspatia*, *Callianax's* Daughter, by the King's command marries *Evadne*, Sister to *Melanthius*, and expects to lye with her; but the Bride, mincing nothing, flatly tells him that he is but taken for a Cloak, that She indeed is a Bedfellow only for the King. The good man is perswaded to dissemble all, till his friend, *Melanthius*, extorts from him the secret, and thereupon hectors his Sister, *Evadne*, into repentance, and makes her promise to murder the King. Which she effects; in the mean time, by vexing *Callianax*, *Melanthius* prevails with him to deliver up the Fort wherein consisted the strength of the Kingdom, and so provides for his own security. *Lysimachus*, Brother to the murder'd King, succeeds on the

Throne, and pardons all. *Evadne* would now go to bed with her Husband, he refuses, she kills her self. *Aspatia* in mans habit kicks her Sweetheart, *Amintor*, duels him, and is kill'd; and now *Amintor* kills himself to follow her: at which sight his friend, *Melanthius*, would also take the same course, but is prevented.[37]

How may this plot have been devised? The three incidents which have been traced to sources—Melantius' confident behaviour in the face of accusation (IV.ii), Evadne's binding of the King's arms to his bed before murdering him (V.i), and Aspatia's disguise, challenge and death (V.iii)—are most unlikely to have been combined before, and it has never been doubted that Beaumont and Fletcher invented their own plot. Aspatia's death scene, though it gave the play its title, can hardly have been the starting-point. A more likely starting-point is Amintor's discovery, on his wedding-night, that his bride is the mistress of the King; this irreparable injury determines that the play must be a tragedy, not a tragi-comedy. Next may have come the question of developing and prolonging the action. What is to prevent Amintor from sweeping to his revenge? The answer is found in his conviction of kingship's sacred character; and since there is no reason why he should swerve from this, he can never be the revenger. Who then shall kill the King? At this point Melantius may have been brought in, and given his double motivation, as Amintor's friend and Evadne's brother, for revengeful action. But such action would be sure to reflect discredit on Amintor for his passiveness, so it was rejected (though in the writing of the play it gave rise to the quarrel scene). Next the dramatists' thoughts may have turned to making Evadne the revenger. There is no reason why she should spontaneously change her attitude to the King, but Melantius can put moral pressure on her: thus the King is killed, Melantius is fully involved in the action, and since the killing is done by a woman and not by another man attention is diverted from Amintor's failure to do it. Then came the problem of ending the play. That Evadne should return to Amintor, and that he should accept the situation and resume his marriage to her, was unthinkable. That he should reject her, thus precipitating her suicide, would settle her fate but would leave him and Melantius unaccounted for. At this point, perhaps, by a stroke of creative inspiration, Aspatia came into the plot as the betrothed whom Amintor was made to desert in favour of Evadne. Her introduction immeasurably improved the play: it solved the problem of Amintor's end (his unwitting killing of her would much more satisfactorily motivate his suicide than his horror at Evadne's killing of the King), and it greatly increased the original injury done by the King to Amintor. Since there is nothing for Aspatia to do in the middle scenes once the marriage-situation has got under way, her character and situation must be firmly established at the beginning of the play. Last of all, it may be, came Calianax her father, introduced partly so that his resentment could keep Aspatia's injury in our view, but principally so that another dramatic complication—Melantius' need to possess the fort, his steps to obtain it and his handling of his enemy's informing of the King—could be worked in.

Whether the plot did evolve in this way or in a quite different one, its combination of elements from Jacobean revenge tragedy and from Arcadian romance gives it a distinctive quality. The revenge element, set in motion by the King's misdeeds, reaches its climax in the first scene of Act V with his murder, an event which would have happened in the final scene if the play had been wholly a tragedy of revenge. The romance element dominates the final scene, especially in the pathos when Aspatia reveals her identity and dies. Evadne's suicide, and her confrontation with Amintor which has led up to it, is powerfully dramatic; by carrying the violent mood of the murder scene into this romantic scene it both acts as a contrast and contributes to the impression of unity which the play finally leaves.

It has long been agreed that the title *The Maid's Tragedy* does not accurately reflect the main tragic interest: Aspatia is not central to the plot as Vindice is central to that of *The Revenger's Tragedy* or D'Amville to that of *The Atheist's Tragedy*. Rymer declared that the play should have been called *Amintor*, 'and some additional title should have hinted the Poet's design', for the whole tragic action originates in Amintor's being 'false to his Mistress'. As for Aspatia, she 'comes in at the latter end, only, to be kill'd for company'. The moral drawn by Lysippus in the closing lines, he further pointed out, showed 'the dismal consequences of *fornication*', and if this was the authors' purpose 'then the Title of the Tragedy should have related to the King'. He argued that this difficulty in finding an appropriate title showed that 'the *Action* of the Tragedy is *double*', meaning that it lacked a single centre, a true focus.[38] Theobald, following up Rymer's criticism without his captious tone, commented on the concluding moral (V.iii.292–5) that it 'is in no kind to the Purpose' because 'the whole Distress of the Story' depends on Aspatia's being abandoned and Amintor's being grossly injured. He adds, '*Amintor* is every where, indeed, condemning himself for his Perfidy to his betroth'd Mistress; and inculcating, that the Heavens are strict in punishing him for that Crime; and so we have another *Moral* in the Body of the *Fable*'.[39] Later critics have endorsed these opinions.

Rymer's suggestion (a rhetorical rather than a serious one) that the play's title might have related to the King is obviously inappropriate. The King, though he is a powerful presence in the four scenes where he appears, is never allowed the centre of the stage. He is given no soliloquy. Even in his death scene it is Evadne who commands the spectators' attention. The weight of the moral interest falls on Amintor, Melantius, Evadne and Aspatia.

Of these four only two—Amintor and Evadne—are ever shown agonising over their course of action. Melantius, once he has discovered how his friend has been injured and his sister corrupted by the King, never wavers in his purpose of revenge, and, once he has seen Amintor die, is equally resolute not to outlive him. Aspatia, who from the opening of the play has been wishing for death, is quite certain that her indirect suicide is spiritually pardonable: a soliloquy of eight lines is enough to state her moral conviction of this.[40]

This is not to imply that Melantius and Aspatia are not tragic characters. Aspatia is very clearly tragic—the title of the play attests as much—by virtue of her sustained pathos and the ironical poignancy of her death. As for Melantius, he becomes tragic at the latest minute of the hour: hitherto, when he has shed tears, they have been tears of joy or of indignation but not of suffering.

But it is Amintor and Evadne who sustain the tragic burden and in whom the tragic interest is concentrated. Of the two Amintor is undoubtedly the more central to the play: 'he strongly engages our sympathy, and makes shipwreck of his life through weakness rather than crime'.[41] The two scenes of the wedding-night and the following morning (II.i and III.i) are, because of his soliloquy and asides, experienced by the audience largely through his emotions, and the quarrel scene with Melantius (III.ii) further displays his suffering; the latter parts of IV.i and of IV.ii continue to remind us of it; and in the final scene, killing himself between the bodies of Aspatia and Evadne, whose deaths he has respectively inflicted and precipitated, he symbolically occupies his central position. Evadne's tragic importance is slower in developing. In the opening scene (where Amintor is vividly characterised by Melantius) all we learn about her is that she 'strikes dead / With flashes of her eye'—an image which fixes itself in the mind. A vehement flaunting of her liaison with the King is her prevailing behaviour in II.i and III.i, and in IV.i she brazens out Melantius' accusation until he coerces her into repentance and a promise to kill the King. At this point she has her first soliloquy, which marks the transition to her repentant dialogue with Amintor. Her other soliloquy (V.i), as she prepares to kill the King, is a strange mixture of horrified and joyous anticipation. When he wakes, her ruthlessness ('I am a tiger') springs from her conviction that she can expiate her guilt by killing her seducer ('This steel / Comes to redeem the honour that you stole'); in her exit-line she even rises to moral generosity:

Die all our faults together! I forgive thee.

Her tragedy is that when she presents herself to Amintor as purged of guilt he can see only that she has piled a second crime upon her first. Therefore her suicide is her final attempt at expiation:

Evadne, whom thou hat'st, will die for thee.

It would be an over-simplification to say that Aspatia embodies the pity of tragedy and Evadne its terror (for Evadne is pitiable here), but there would be some truth in saying so.

A central question of the play, confronting Amintor, Melantius and Evadne, is whether the King shall die for his wickedness. Since it involves both murder and regicide it is both a moral and a political question. Yet it remains curiously separate from the characterisation, and hence from the tragic interest. Amintor and Melantius subscribe to exactly the same moral code, upholding honesty, loyalty, courage and chastity. Their one difference of principle is as to whether an injured subject is entitled to revenge himself on the king. They never debate the matter: each holds firmly to his own opinion (except for Amintor's sudden and brief abandonment of it near the end of IV.ii, which is not the result of persuasion but of provocation). Melantius' reasons in this particular case are clear: his family's honour has been injured, and he himself has been treated ungratefully. He never for a moment considers regicide to be a terrible crime (or indeed, in the circumstances, a crime at all, rather a duty and even a pleasure). For Amintor it is never anything but a terrible crime. Why he holds this view and Melantius does not is never explained, and there is no indication anywhere in the play that the one is right and the other wrong. In the final act regicide has to be admitted as a fact, but the treatment of it is (no doubt deliberately) evasive. Melantius, who persuaded his sister to kill the King, is reported as proclaiming from the fort 'the innocence of this act' (V.i.144). When the King's successor Lysippus goes to the fort he is told by Strato that the King's conduct provoked this revenge, and by Melantius that it demanded it. Under some pressure to avoid civil strife, he grants a pardon to the confederates at the fort. No one mentions Evadne. At the end of the final scene, when Evadne, Aspatia and Amintor lie dead and Melantius resolves to die too, Lysippus makes the closing speech:

> Look to him, though, and bear those bodies in.
> May this a fair example be to me
> To rule with temper, for on lustful kings
> Unlooked-for sudden deaths from God are sent;
> But curs'd is he that is their instrument.

The last line cannot refer to Melantius, whom Lysippus has pardoned and whose suicide he wants to prevent.[42] If it refers to Evadne, who 'was but the instrument' of her brother (V.i.139), it is making a morally inconsistent distinction between them. However, Evadne being by now conveniently dead, the generalisation has a sufficient specious plausibility, and it serves its main purpose, to assure the departing spectators that the dramatists do not condone regicide.

Political ideas are not important in the play, as they are in *Julius Caesar* or in *Bussy D'Ambois*.[43] Nor is the court of the play presented as corrupt, like the court of *Antonio's Revenge* or of *The Revenger's Tragedy*. Evadne, accusing the King, does indeed declare

> I was a world of virtue
> Till your curs'd court and you (hell bless you for't),
> With your temptations on temptations,
> Made me give up mine honour;   (V.i.79-82)

but this is merely a bit of local intensification.[44] Although Melantius, accusing Evadne, asserts that her loose living is common knowledge, her marriage to Amintor depends wholly on the court's knowing nothing whatever about her liaison with the King. Her soliloquy following Melantius' exit—

> Gods, where have I been all this time, how friended,
> That I should lose myself thus desperately,
> And none for pity show me how I wandered?   (IV.i.178-80)—

implies that those nearest to her neglected to rebuke her; but her brother at court, Diphilus, has to learn of her sin from Melantius, who learned of it from Amintor, who learned of it from Evadne herself. The gentlemen of the King's bedchamber know about the liaison (thus providing an ironical context to the murder), but Lysippus does

not, so that his apostrophe displays unconscious irony at the same
time that it suggests that the King did have some good qualities:

> Farewell, thou worthy man. There were two bonds
> That tied our loves, a brother and a king,
> The least of which might fetch a flood of tears.   (V.i.133–5)

The court of Rhodes is not Italianate but a hybrid of the Arcadian and
the Jacobean, as is the whole world of the tragedy. It is a background
for the passions of the figures who occupy the foreground.

The Maid's Tragedy is a play of strong passions and strong situations, an emotional play and not a reflective one. There has never
been any critical debate on this point. Criticism of the plays of
Beaumont and Fletcher, and of Fletcher's plays with other collaborators, has been chiefly concerned with two topics, their relation to the
ethos of the court of James I and their artistic value. The first of these
topics, though of great interest, is too large to be properly discussed
in the introduction to a particular play, but the second requires
consideration now.[45]

Beaumont and Fletcher have always been allowed, even by their
detractors, to be skilful in constructing a plot. Dryden, who admired
them, instanced The Maid's Tragedy, along with Jonson's Epicene and
The Alchemist, as a play in which 'you will find it infinitely pleasing
to be led in a labyrinth of design, where you see some of your way
before you, yet discern not the end till you arrive at it'.[46] The play's
five-act structure reflects the development of the action. The first act
is expository, though not in a merely functional way, as will presently
be shown. It introduces, either physically or by report, all the chief
characters, and it provides the necessary information about Amintor's
marriage—with the exception of the King's ulterior motive in arrang-
ing it. The wedding masque, to which the second scene is almost
wholly devoted, gives the marriage and the royal court substantiality.
It also delays the encounter of bride and bridegroom till the second
act. After that powerful scene, the longest in the play, we are given
a scene of lyrical pathos centred upon Aspatia, who will hereafter
disappear from the action until the final scene and therefore needs
to be impressed upon our minds. Like the masque scene, this scene
delays the next climactic scene to the next act.[47] This is the scene
on the morning after the wedding-night, in which Amintor and
Evadne are confronted by the King; it pulls tight the knot of the
action. In the second scene Melantius extracts from Amintor the
secret of the marriage, determines on revenge, and begins to negotiate

with Calianax for possession of the fort. Calianax's eagerness to tell
the King of this leads us to expect that the fourth act will open with
his doing so. Instead Evadne is confronted by Melantius, a situation
for which nothing in the previous scene has prepared us, and is
coerced by him into agreeing to murder the King. As in the second
act, a powerful first scene is followed by one of relaxed tension, in
this case the dramatic consequence of Calianax's informing against
Melantius. But at its end the action is driven onwards by the King's
sending for Evadne to his bed. 'She shall perform it then,' resolves
Melantius, meaning the murder, and in the first scene of the fifth
act this is done. The King's death, the first in the tragedy, fulfils
with great power the expectation that has been building up since
the revelation on the wedding-night. The following scene, in which
Lysippus pardons Melantius and his associates, again relaxes tension between two strong scenes. The final scene, like the fourth act,
opens with an unprepared event, the entry of Aspatia disguised as
her brother, and proceeds to her duel with Amintor and her fatal
wound.[48] This development so absorbs our attention that Evadne's
arrival with her bloody hands and knife comes as a shock. A feature
of the play is that Aspatia and Evadne become mutually exclusive,
and that when one is on stage we almost, or even entirely, forget the
other. Now the wounded Aspatia's groans punctuate Evadne's short
and passionate dialogue with Amintor, culminating in her suicide,
and the death of Aspatia and suicide of Amintor form the second
part of the scene's double climax. The conclusion is given dramatic
interest by the emphasis on Melantius' emotion.

   The play's construction does not depend upon a complicated
intrigue; it is easy to follow in the theatre, and easy to remember
afterwards. Yet *The Maid's Tragedy* leaves the impression of an
ingenious play. This is mainly owing to the way in which the situations are explored and exploited. The most striking instances are
Evadne's dialogue with Amintor in II.i and Amintor's dialogue with
Melantius in III.ii. In the former, Evadne's revelation of the truth is
drawn out to the fullest possible extent; and this protraction is not
achieved by such direct means as hesitations or long speeches, but by
a progression both tortuous and fluent. From the first ('If I should
name him the matter were not great') there are hints that she is
another man's mistress, yet Amintor is able for some time to cling to
the belief that her oath is a means of preserving her virginity; when
she exclaims 'A maidenhead, Amintor, / At my years?' his first
thought is that she must be mad, and seventy lines later he is still

pleading with her to convert his despair into joy by going to bed with him. Again, early in the dialogue, there is the complication and secondary climax of 'Why, who has done thee wrong? / Name me the man...', 'Wilt thou kill this man? / Swear, my Amintor, ...', and finally

> Why, it is thou that wrongst me, I hate thee,
> Thou shouldst have killed thyself.

Considered dispassionately, or with a prejudice against what may be considered Beaumont and Fletcher's outrageous stimulation, the whole dialogue is highly artificial, yet in the theatre Evadne's pronouns fall like hammer-blows. When the scene reaches its full climax, the word 'King' rings again and again in the verse. It has rung in the verse earlier;

> *Amintor*. I sleep and am too temperate. Come to bed,
>   Or by those hairs which, if thou hadst a soul
>   Like to thy locks, were threads for kings to wear
>   About their arms—
> *Evadne*.   Why, so perhaps they are.
> *Amintor*. I'll drag thee to my bed ...

Evadne's interjection forewarns us of what we are now ready to guess, and its impact justifies the florid expression used by Amintor, which so disgusted Rymer ('And did ever man huff with such a *parenthesis?*').[49] The whole encounter shows a remarkable control of dramatic speech. The repetition of words ('sworn', 'doubt') and phrases ('That I may show you one less pleasing to you'—which makes its crushing effect by being a complete line of verse) carries a strong emotional charge; 'the coyness of a bride', Amintor's explanation of Evadne's behaviour, is immediately retorted as exclamation, and then, fifty lines later, is reiterated with devastating finality:

> This is not feigned,
> Nor sounds it like the coyness of a bride.

The ingenuity of Amintor's encounter with Melantius (the quarrel scene, as it is usually called) is not a matter of delaying a revelation but of developing its consequences after it has been made. Melantius eagerly presses Amintor to reveal his cause of grief, and soon extracts it from him. He then challenges Amintor to a duel to the death for traducing his sister. Scarcely is he convinced of the truth of what Amintor has said than Amintor challenges him for proposing

to revenge himself upon the King, an action which would brand
Amintor with cowardice. Both challenges are abortive, and this fact,
together with the obvious symmetry of the action, lays this scene
open to the charge of theatricality. That it engages the modern
spectator's emotions far less than the wedding-night scene is partly
due to the degree of detachment that this theatricality creates. It
is also partly due to the content, the stress upon reputation, with
which a modern audience cannot sympathise as readily as it can with
Amintor's shock and disappointment on his wedding-night (though
the theme of reputation is present there also). The mutual challenge
is a good vehicle for actors, but it lacks the dramatic inevitability that
the play's other strong scenes appear to have. It may be argued that it
emphasises Amintor's courage; but this has already been convincingly
shown when he accused the King of tyranny in III.i. By contrast, the
complication at the end of IV.ii is thoroughly compelling. Amintor,
beside himself at the King's sending for Evadne, has thrown off his
scrupulous loyalty and is ready to go and kill him; Melantius, who
intends that Evadne shall perform the murder, exclaims 'He'll overthrow / My whole design with madness', and by reiterating the name
of King reduces Amintor to passiveness. The effect of this on our
opinion of Amintor might be damaging if it were felt to be the main
issue at the moment. The main issue, however, is whether Evadne
shall be allowed to kill the King or not, and to her killing him our
expectations and desires are thoroughly committed, so that we readily
accept Amintor's tractability, the more readily because his extreme
loyalty to the monarchy is by now an established fact.

   Despite the impression of ingenuity which we carry away from *The
Maid's Tragedy*, and of which we are perhaps made too conscious
during the quarrel scene, the play as a whole creates strong excite-
ment and deep involvement when read sympathetically or when seen
in a good production. The importance of IV.i can hardly be exaggerated. When Evadne swears to kill the King, the play, which has
hitherto been a tragedy of suffering (Aspatia's and Amintor's), begins
to change into a tragedy of action. Our consciousness that the King's
death is impending colours our reception of IV.ii, the banquet scene,
in which the King proves to his own satisfaction that Melantius has
no design on his life, in which the more Calianax insists on the truth
the less he is believed, and in which Melantius is so thoroughly
in control of the situation that he can continue to ask Calianax for
the fort. The scene is essentially a comic one, as the prominence
of Calianax ensures, and our sympathies are of course entirely with

Melantius in his moral ascendancy over the King; yet the presence of
Amintor and Evadne as guests of honour, the King's jocular remark
to them that they must be wishing to go to bed again (all three must
be conscious of the irony of this), and the unconscious irony of his
sympathetic comment on Calianax's supposed dotage ('we must be /
All old'—when he himself is presently to die), all add subtlety to the
mood.

Irony permeates the whole play. 'To speak generally, the situation
of Amintor, most miserable in the height of apparent happiness, and
of the King, slain in his amorous security, are examples of the contrast in which irony most delights.'[50] In the opening scene, Melantius'
commendation of Amintor ends by striking the first note of anticipatory tragic irony:

> His youth did promise much, and his ripe years
> Will see it all performed.[51]

With his very next words he unsuspectingly puts his finger on the
very act that has doomed Amintor not to fulfil his youthful promise.[52]
Aspatia enters and he salutes her:

> Hail, maid and wife!
> Thou fair Aspatia, may the holy knot
> That thou hast tied today last till the hand
> Of age undo't! Mayst thou bring a race
> Unto Amintor that may fill the world
> Successively with soldiers!

The universal embarrassment that follows his mistake is well caught
in the dialogue, and Melantius' comment when he learns that his own
sister is Amintor's bride—

> Peace of heart betwixt them!
> But this is strange—

lets us savour the ominous news, at the same time prompting
Lysippus' explanation:

> The King my brother did it
> To honour you, and these solemnities
> Are at his charge.

This is the third hint we have been given of the King's absolute
power, so important a factor in the tragedy.[53] The first time we read

or see the play there is enough here to make us uneasy; on reading or seeing it again we appreciate the full significance of the words.

The wedding masque in the second scene is full of irony when seen in retrospect from the wedding-night scene (II.i); 'the authors have seized on the assumptions of the traditional marriage masque—pre-nuptial chastity, bridal bliss and royal integrity—and contrasted them with a corrupt reality.'[54] At the time, however, it contains no obvious proleptic irony. The escape of Boreas, who raises a storm, introduces an element of alarm and disorder, but critics who regard it as deeply symbolic do not give due weight to its immediate context.[55] It is confined within the formal structure of the masque, and Neptune is confident of recapturing Boreas; the whole mythological imagery of sea-gods and wind-gods is appropriate to the fact that Rhodes is an island; and the escape of Boreas injects dramatic interest into a long masque which otherwise would lack it, while the storm he raises provides a dramatic reason for Neptune to return to the sea and for the other masquers to disperse. No critic suggests that the King has had the masque devised with meaningful intent (as Hamlet arranged for the playing of 'The Murder of Gonzago'). Nevertheless, though the ironies are retrospective, the misgivings aroused by the opening scene are bound to be maintained by the fact that the King is paying for the masque and presiding over it, and also by the sheer length and magnificence of it. The longer we are withheld from the encounter of the bridal couple the more we expect some great revelation when we reach it. Besides containing irony and creating suspense, the masque scene has other functions. It dramatises, near its beginning, the anti-pathy of Calianax for Melantius, and reiterates Amintor's desertion of Aspatia for Evadne. Moreover, once the stage has filled with persons and the long formal masque (uninterrupted by any asides from stage spectators) is under way, it serves as a foil to the intimate scene which follows, in which the reality of the marriage is to be shown.

With that scene the full glare of irony, veiled at first by Dula's levity and Aspatia's pathos, is allowed into the play. The control of mood is masterly, and Amintor's soliloquy after Aspatia departs and before Evadne re-enters brings the suspense to a peak:

> Something whispers me,
> Go not to bed.

It casts a chill across the scene:

> Timorous flesh,
> Why shak'st thou so? Away, my idle fears!

The immediate sequel is to show him how far from idle his fears were.

The two scenes of the wedding-night and the morning after it (II.i and III.i) form a continuous ironical whole, though for reasons of verisimilitude and dramatic contrast they are separated by Aspatia's pathetic interlude.

> When we walk thus entwined, let all eyes see
> If ever lovers better did agree.

Amintor's final couplet, with its glance at the actual theatre audience, fixes the irony of their situation in a tableau. Their re-entry in III.i to endure the boisterous jollity of Diphilus and Strato shows them still practising their enforced deception. With the arrival of the King, who knows the truth, the nature of the irony changes; and it changes again when Amintor plays his part so well as to make the King believe, wrongly, that the marriage has been consummated. It is a relief from the irony—though an agony to Amintor—when the three of them are alone and can speak freely.

From this point the irony is held in abeyance for some time. There are momentary flashes of it: Amintor says that Melantius will regret hearing the cause of his secret sorrow and Melantius denies it, only to break out in fury when Amintor reveals it (III.ii.122–36), and Evadne thinks that Melantius is about to pay her a compliment when he is really about to denounce her (IV.i.1–23). But in general these are scenes of passions directly applied to situations of which the participants are equally aware. Irony begins to resurface at the end of IV.i when the repentant Evadne tells Amintor that she will 'redeem one minute' of her life before she dies, and will not reappear in his sight

> Till she have tried all honoured means that may
> Set her in rest, and wash her stains away

—a resolution, if he only knew it, to kill the King, and, as such, a foreshadowing of her final encounter with her husband in V.iii.[56] With the banquet scene (IV.ii) irony becomes prominent once more: in fact, it is here the essence of the situation, and once Melantius has got the fort it continues to operate in his dissuading Amintor (who knows nothing of Evadne's promise to kill the King) from revenge.

The fifth act, bringing the death of the King in the first scene and those of Evadne, Aspatia and Amintor in the third, continues to make strong use of irony. Waking to discover that his arms have been tied to the bed, the King confidently assumes that this is Evadne's 'pretty

new device' to display her desire, and when she speaks metaphorically
of the 'physic' she has brought to abate his heat he wittily pursues it
as a sexual metaphor. Once she has drawn her knife irony gives way
to plain speaking, but after she has killed him and made her exit it
resumes, in a different tone, with the Gentlemen's prose dialogue.
They resolve to try their own luck with Evadne 'one of these nights,
as she goes from him', and comment

> How quickly he had done with her! I see kings can do no more that way
> than other mortal people.

What a neat stroke is in that colloquial use of 'mortal', and how it
underlines the fact that it was Evadne who had quickly done with the
King!

The duel between Aspatia and Amintor (V.iii) makes use of a
device frequent in comedy, the heroine's disguise as a young man,
to produce a tragic irony of pathos.[57] Aspatia's self-identification—

> When you know me, my lord, you needs must guess
> My business—

initiates the irony: he is now to know her as her brother, and her
business as revenge, but when he knows her as herself he will know
that her business was death. It is sustained in his expressions of
remorse—

>   yet, to enjoy this world,
> I would not see her, for, beholding thee,
> I am I know not what—

and in her reply:

>   Thus she swore
> Thou wouldst behave thyself, and give me words
> That would fetch tears into my eyes, and so
> Thou dost indeed.

After the duel, and the intervening action of Evadne's return and
suicide, a dialogue with its own violent irony ('Joy to Amintor, for the
King is dead!'), the poignant irony reasserts itself, and resolves itself
into the moving recognition:

> *Aspatia*. Did you not name Aspatia?
> *Amintor*.   I did.
> *Aspatia*. And talked of tears and sorrow unto her?
> *Amintor*. 'Tis true, and till these happy signs in thee

Stayed my course, it was thither I was going.
Aspatia. Thou art there already, and these wounds are hers.

One reason why the death of Aspatia is so moving is that it includes an element of subdued sexuality. Sexuality is important in
the play, contributing more to its emotional power than honour can
do. Considered in this aspect, the title *The Maid's Tragedy* is not
so inappropriate after all. The opening scene strikes the keynote,
with Melantius' mistaken greeting to Aspatia, 'Hail, maid and wife!',
implying that her marriage has taken place but has not yet been
consummated; before he is disabused of his error he proceeds to
wish her fruitful. That Aspatia's disappointment is sexual as well as
romantic is stressed when she wishes Evadne 'all the marriage joys /
That longing maids imagine in their beds'; as she laments,

This should have been
My night, and all your hands have been employed
In giving me a spotless offering
To young Amintor's bed

(though the epithet 'young' is a slight lapse, revealing the dramatists'
point of view rather than that of the speaker, who is at least as young
as Amintor). Her sexual disappointment is set against the wedding-
festivities' stress on sexual fulfilment, in the masque, in the King's
goodnight wishes, and in the preparation of Evadne for bed. In
Evadne's ensuing dialogue with Amintor sexuality is emphasised even
when she is most absolute in denying him her body:

I sooner will find out the beds of snakes,
And with my youthful blood warm their cold flesh,
Letting them curl themselves about my limbs,
Than sleep one night with thee.

After Aspatia's lyrical scene, in which her sexual disappointment is
not expressed directly but emblematically in her pose as the deserted
Ariadne, the directly sexual resumes in the morning visit to the
married couple. Amintor's asides picture the calm beauty—and the
desirability—of Evadne asleep. The King's questioning of Amintor,
in which he infers Evadne's sexuality from her black eye and red
cheek, and his questioning of Evadne, in which he adduces

the uncontrollèd thoughts
That youth brings with him, when his blood is high
With expectation and desire of that
He long hath waited for,

are thoroughly sexual in the images they evoke.

Thereafter, like irony, sexuality falls for a time into abeyance. In Amintor's scene with Melantius, and in Melantius' scene with Evadne, her 'whoredom' is stressed but (apart from Melantius' bitter taunt 'Y'are valiant in his bed') is not actualised; it is presented as an injury to the family honour and to Amintor. At the end of the latter scene Amintor's forgiveness, though sincere and accompanied by a hand-clasp and a kiss, shows how removed he is from sexual passion:

> My charity shall go along with thee,
> Though my embraces must be far from thee.

But in the banquet scene sexuality returns with irony. Amintor receives the bowl of wine from the King, drinks, and hands it to Evadne:

> Here, my love;
> This wine will do thee wrong, for it will set
> Blushes upon thy cheeks, and till thou dost
> A fault 'twere pity.

He is, of course, resuming his role as a happy bridegroom for which the King has cast him, and for which the King gives him appropriate cues:

> Be merry, gentlemen. It grows somewhat late;
> Amintor, thou wouldst be abed again.
> *Amintor.* Yes, sir.
> *King.*   And you, Evadne.

Evadne's murder of the King is framed by the lubricious remarks of the Gentlemen, so inappropriate to what she intends and accomplishes. Her soliloquy, as she ties his arms to the bed, fleetingly actualises their past embraces:

> I dare not trust your strength; your grace and I
> Must grapple upon even terms no more.

The waking King looks forward to 'embraces' such as would make the gods envious, and when she tells him that she has brought him physic, rejoins

> Prithee, to bed then; let me take it warm;
> Here thou shalt know the state of my body better.

This sexual imagery only adds to the irony, as does Evadne's fiercely ironic term 'love-tricks' for her fatal blows (as though they were slaps, pinches or bites).

In the next scene, between Melantius and the new king Lysippus, Evadne's whoredom reverts to a cause of family dishonour, but in the final scene the theme of consummation is reintroduced in two forms. Evadne bursts in upon Amintor fresh from murdering the King, tells him that she brings him 'joys' and that by her action she has made herself more 'fair' than she was at their wedding. When he repudiates her with horror, she continues to appeal to him to consummate their marriage:

> Forgive me, then,
> And take me to thy bed; we may not part.

She reiterates her appeal: 'Take me home'; 'Receive me, then.' Amintor, despite his anger and grief, is dangerously tempted:

> Thou dost awake something that troubles me,
> And says I loved thee once. I dare not stay.

Hereupon Evadne kills herself, and Aspatia comes out of the swoon into which her wound has thrown her. For a moment she feels herself reviving:

> I shall sure live, Amintor; I am well;
> A kind of healthful joy wanders within me.

But the glimpse of a second chance of happiness for her and Amintor fades again:

> My strength begins to disobey my will.
> How dost thou, my best soul? I would fain live
> Now, if I could; wouldst thou have loved me then?

The poignancy of these lines comes from their suggestion of marriage and its sexual consummation, now fated never to take place. She asks for Amintor's hand, and holds it as she dies.

The imagery of the masque—night, the sea, a storm and lovers' embraces—recurs elsewhere in the play, with some frequency, and there are other images, such as blood (violently shed or flowing healthily through the veins), disease, weapons, religious ceremonies and funeral rites, which spring readily to mind. Taken collectively, these images impart a sense of unity because they reflect the passions which absorb the characters. It is, however, easy and dangerous to over-elaborate their thematic relationships and use them to display patterns which are largely of one's own making.[58] To give this warning is not to acquiesce in Coleridge's and Eliot's charge (not made specifically against this play but generally against the whole Beaumont and Fletcher corpus) that the expression is merely accumulated and does not evolve continually from the imagination.[59] Again and again passages which may look contrived and unnatural when torn from their context look spontaneous and natural when restored to it. This is particularly true of declamatory speeches, of which there are many, such as Amintor's

> Is flesh so earthly to endure all this?
> Are these the joys of marriage? Hymen, keep
> This story, that will make succeeding youth
> Neglect thy ceremonies, from all ears (*etc.*: II.i.214–28).

Declamation has to be accepted as an integral part of the play's poetic medium. But only as a part; at other moments, the force of the expression lies in repartee (the opening of IV.i, where there are eight repartees in seventy lines, in the most striking example). When Amintor, Evadne and the King are on stage together in III.i, there is a particularly good instance of the rejoinder used dramatically. Amintor is expostulating with the King:

> But why—I know not what
> I have to say—why did you choose out me
> To make thus wretched? There were thousands, fools,
> Easy to work on, and of state enough,
> Within the island.

Before the King can reply Evadne interposes:

> I would not have a fool;
> It were no credit for me.

Amintor thereupon turns to Evadne and denounces her shamelessness, and then, still addressing her, adds

> But there were wise ones too: you might have ta'en
> Another.

This time it is the King who interposes:

> No, for I believed thee honest
> As thou wert valiant.

The impression that Amintor is trapped between the King and Evadne could not be more effectively created. His speech which follows is a cry of agony, as he sees how his very virtues have undone him.

The dialogue, here and elsewhere, is closely related to the stage action. The stage action itself is always visually expressive. How many readers have noticed that in the wedding-night scene Amintor is kissed by Aspatia but never touches Evadne until at the end of their dialogue they take hands in a loveless contract to deceive the world? Yet who could fail to notice this in the theatre? Even in the reading it is impossible not to visualise the stage action of III.i, with the business in front of the bedroom door, the entry of Amintor and his poignant asides, his double embrace with Melantius, the delayed entry of Evadne and her hostile aside to Amintor, the King's arrival, the dismissal of the other visitors, the King's questioning of Evadne while Amintor keeps his distance, and the brow-to-brow encounter in which both men lay their hands on their swords. The fact that in II.i and III.i the bridal bedroom is off-stage is no small token of the dramatists' art. The King's bed in V.i is, and should be, the first and only bed that we see.

The Maid's Tragedy is a play for the stage. This is obvious, but is often in danger of being forgotten. It is only in the theatre that its power can be fully appreciated.

5. STAGE HISTORY

The title-pages of the first and second Quartos state that *The Maid's Tragedy* was acted at the Blackfriars playhouse, the roofed 'private' theatre which was the winter quarters of the King's Men from 1609. It was probably also performed at their summer quarters, the Globe. The stage requirements do not point to either playhouse rather than to the other: an upper acting area is mentioned in I.ii and V.ii, though only the latter scene demands its use in the action (as the walls of the fort); a trap is needed for the rising and descending of Neptune and the sea-gods in I.ii; there is a 'rock' for Aeolus and the winds in the same scene; a banquet is brought on-stage in IV.ii, and the King's bed in V.i. The early scenes (I.i and ii, II.i) and the late ones (IV.ii, V.i–iii) take place at night, but no particular emphasis is laid on a stage effect of darkness.[60] The quiet-toned recorders required to play as a prelude to the masque (I.ii) would be more effective in the enclosed, smaller, Blackfriars theatre. But the staging would present no difficulty in either theatre, nor at court at its performance in 1613.[61]

Which actors originally performed the roles is unknown. Richard Burbage was still acting and was probably cast as Melantius. His successor John Lowin later played that part, and Stephen Hammerton Amintor.[62] It is notable that the part of Melantius has always been given to the principal tragic actor, though Amintor's part is only some twenty lines shorter and both he and Melantius appear in eight of the play's eleven scenes. The reason is probably twofold: whoever plays Melantius must have maturity and authority, both as Amintor's elder and as an experienced soldier, and he also has to be capable of the serio-comic acting required in the scenes with Calianax.

During the closure of the theatres from 1642 to the Restoration, a short comic interlude fitted for occasional performance at the Red Bull was extracted from Calianax's scenes and called *The Testy Lord*.[63] It is printed in Francis Kirkman's collection of such 'drolls', *The Wits, or Sport upon Sport* (1672, 1, 148–58), and would play for about twenty minutes. The 'argument' prefixed to it runs as follows: 'He is imployed near the King, in which office he exerciseth his Passion, and is as crosly dealt withal by another Lord.' The action begins with the opening lines of I.ii and ends with Calianax's exit in IV.ii. Cuts have been made in an attempt to detach the plot (such as it is) from the main action of *The Maid's Tragedy*, but its fragmentary nature is still obvious. The verse is printed throughout as prose.

In 1660 *The Maid's Tragedy* was in the repertory of a company of actors playing at the Red Bull, and in that of the newly formed King's Company under Thomas Killigrew.[64] Edward Kynaston, one of the last male actors of female roles, is said to have played Evadne.[65] During the next twenty years or thereabouts the principal actors and actresses were Wintersel (King), Mohun (Melantius), Hart (Amintor), Shatterel (Calianax), Mrs Marshall (Evadne) and Mrs Boutel (Aspatia). Pepys saw the play, in full or in part, at least five times, and on his first visit found the end (which was all he arrived in time to see) 'too sad and melancholy', but usually commented that it was 'a good play'. Rymer, while criticising the play severely as a tragedy, allowed that Hart and Mohun in the quarrel scene ensured its success in the theatre.[66] It was seen by Charles II in 1667 and by James II in 1687. By the end of the century Betterton was playing Melantius, which he continued to do till his retirement performance on 13 April 1710 (he died on 28 April). The other principal performers of this period were Wilks (first Lysippus, later Amintor), Mills (King), Norris (Calianax), Keene (first Diphilus, later King), Mrs Barry (Evadne) and Mrs Bracegirdle (Aspatia). In the next decade Pinkethman (Calianax), Mrs Knight (Evadne), Mrs Porter (first Aspatia, later Evadne), Booth (Melantius), Mrs Mountfort (Aspatia) and Mrs Thurmond (also Aspatia) joined the cast. The play continued to be acted, mainly with those named above, through the 1720s. The next recorded performances are in 1744 and 1745, with Quin as Melantius, Ryan as Amintor, Hale as the King, Hippisley as Calianax, Mrs Pritchard as Evadne and Mrs Bellamy as Aspatia. Thereafter *The Maid's Tragedy* ceased to be performed until it was revived in the twentieth century.

Before mentioning these revivals it is necessary to discuss two works based on *The Maid's Tragedy*.

The first of these is an alternative fifth act written by Edmund Waller (who died in 1687) and printed in two posthumous collections of his poems, published by Thomas Bennet and Jacob Tonson respectively, both in 1690. This fifth act, written in rhyme, converts the tragedy into a tragi-comedy. It opens with Evadne's decision, since it would be wicked to kill the King and since her oath to do so was taken upon compulsion, to spare him and to enter a convent of vestals.[67] She sends letters explaining this to Melantius and to the King (whom she asks to forgive her brothers 'if they return to their duty'). Melantius, his original plan having failed, tries to persuade Lysippus to join his faction and to take the throne which the King's death will give him; but Lysippus denies that the King deserves to die:

> Long may he live, that is so far above
> All Vice, all Passion, but excess of Love.[68]

He challenges Melantius to a duel, and they exeunt severally to make their preparations. The now remorseful King, who has overheard their talk, determines to fight Melantius himself: he sends for Diphilus and goes with him to the duelling place, where each pair of brothers opposes the other. Upon reflection, and impressed by the King's courage in volunteering a duel, Melantius ends by exchanging forgiveness with him, and returns to his loyalty. Meanwhile news comes that Aspatia and Amintor are both missing, '*And the Scene changes into a Forrest*', where Aspatia is about to end her sorrows by eating poisonous berries. Amintor arrives in time to save her by explaining that he was never really married to Evadne because she belonged to the King:

> You had my promise, and my Bed is free;
> I may be yours, if you can pardon me.

She does so. The King, with Lysippus, arrives and expresses his regret for what is past, which Amintor receives with gentlemanly urbanity:

Men wrong'd by Kings impute it to their fate,
And Royal kindness never comes too late.

Waller's fifth act receives mention in the play's stage history because of a tradition that in Charles II's reign the original play was temporarily prohibited and that Waller's version of the final act was written to provide an acceptable ending for performance. This tradition began in 1691, suspiciously close to the publication of Waller's version in 1690.[69] It was contradicted by Waller's editor of 1729.[70] Later discussion has never resolved the questions of when Waller wrote his fifth act, whether it was ever acted, whether he wrote it in response to a prohibition, whether there ever was a prohibition, and, if so, when it was made.[71] But we should probably regard Waller's fifth act rather as a contribution to English poetry and dramatic criticism than as part of the stage history of *The Maid's Tragedy*.[72]

The other work based on the play, *The Bridal*, does belong to its stage history; it is an adaptation of it to nineteenth-century taste, contrived by W. C. Macready, with assistance from the dramatist James Sheridan Knowles, as a theatrical vehicle for himself. It was finished in 1831, and acted in Dublin in 1834 and at the Haymarket Theatre, London, in 1837.[73] In his preface Macready writes that the original play's 'indelicacies of language, and strainings after effect' are only 'superficial blemishes' on a grand tragic subject. Knowles, who had at first decided that 'the beauties and deformities of the work were inseparable', was persuaded to write three new scenes and a speech when Macready proposed to change the ending of the play by introducing a development suggested by Byron's poem *The Corsair*. In this development Evadne kills the King (off-stage) in order to rescue Melantius from prison, into which the King has thrown him for challenging him to a duel. Other changes, equally sweeping, are made. Aspatia's match with Amintor has been broken off because the King falsely blackened her reputation; she disguises herself as her brother, not to be killed by Amintor, but to serve him as a page, in which capacity she gets her wound while saving him (off-stage) from assassination; and instead of dying she recovers and marries Amintor (for his bride Evadne, having killed the King, has taken poison, and dies in her brother's arms after assuring him that she did not buy his rescue with her dishonour).[74] Thus *The Bridal* is a tragedy with regard to the King, Evadne and Melantius (who, being disarmed, resolves to die in remorse at having partly caused his sister's death), but is a tragi-comedy with regard to Amintor and Aspatia. A surprisingly large amount of the original dialogue is retained, though it is so shifted about as to make *The Bridal* a kind of anagram of *The Maid's Tragedy*. There is no comic element: Calianax, instead of being Aspatia's father and a testy dotard, is her sensible and sympathetic kinsman, and his part is confined to the first act; all the business about the fort is omitted, and Melantius' bold response to a charge of treachery is transferred to a private confrontation between him and the King. *The Bridal* was successful on the stage, both in England and in America (where Macready played it in 1843–4).[75]

In the twentieth century Beaumont and Fletcher's tragedy returned to the stage. The Phoenix Society performed it at the Lyric Theatre, London (15 November 1921), with Sybil Thorndike as Evadne. *The Times* particularly praised her playing of the wedding-night scene, II.i: 'Miss Thorndike's experience at the Grand Guignol helps her to bring to tragedy a nervous agitation which intensifies the life of her part.' The 'richness and strength' of her performance was complemented by the 'dainty, fragile elegance' of Isabel Jeans's Aspatia. Ion Swinley (Amintor) and George Skillan (Melantius) played with 'the good elocution and the full-blooded style that Elizabethan characters demand', and Harvey Braban 'made a handsome voluptuary of the King'. Other players were George Hayes (Lysippus), Alfred A. Harris (Diphilus), Stanley Lathbury (Calianax), Silvia Young (Dula), Florence Saunders (Night), Mary Barton (Cynthia), Tristan Rawson (Neptune) and Cecil Melton (Aeolus). Though *The Times*'s review does not name the players of Antiphila and Olympias, their scene with Aspatia was evidently included, for it is stated that 'the revival gave the whole text, including the masque'.[76]

Four years later, to mark the tercentenary of Fletcher's death, *The Maid's Tragedy* was performed by the Renaissance Theatre at the Scala Theatre, London (17 May 1925). This time the Evadne was Edith Evans, of whom *The Times* reported: 'Her forced confession to Melantius and her repentance before Amintor are exquisitely done with a shaken anguish in which all Evadne's fears and griefs are reflected like images that appear and shift and are distorted in a ruffled pool. Her killing of the King, however, and her later demand for Amintor's approval of her deed require of Miss Evans a violence of attack that she does not accomplish without strain.' (In 1921, Sybil

Thorndike's suicide as Evadne had been called her 'least effective moment' because the dramatistis were too obviously 'getting rid of the heroine in the conventional way of every Elizabethan tragedy'.) Ion Swinley again played Amintor in a 'firm and vivid' manner, and Stanley Lathbury as Calianax brought out the 'simple nature' in the part (rather than exaggerating its absurdity). The Melantius was Baliol Holloway, playing with a lively vigour which ran some risk of falling into mannerism, and Marda Vanne was a distinctive Dula. Rose Quong was the Aspatia. The absence of any mention of the masque suggests that it was omitted.[77]

It was certainly omitted in Bernard Miles's production (2 June 1964) as part of the Mermaid Theatre's celebration of Shakespeare's quatercentenary, the other plays being The Shoemaker's Holiday and Macbeth, and all three being performed on a permanent setting designed by C. Walter Hodges. The Times considered that the effort to 'sustain a heroic style' had resulted in the loss of 'comedy and individual characterization', discommended the occasional 'graceless physical tussles', and reported that Evadne (Irene Hamilton) plunged her dagger into the groin of the King (Peter Halliday). The other principal roles were taken by David Weston (Amintor), Ronald Hines (Melantius), David Bird (Calianax), Hazel Penwarden (Aspatia) and Coral Atkins (Dula).[78]

All three of these productions of The Maid's Tragedy were costumed in the style of the Jacobean period.

There was also a production in New York at the Equity Library Theatre in 1972 of which no details are available.[79]

The two most recent professional productions have been by the Citizens' Theatre, Glasgow, and by the Royal Shakespeare Company.

The Citizens' Theatre production (16 November 1979) was adapted, designed and directed by Philip Prowse.[80] The principal parts were played by Mark Lewis (Melantius), Colin Haigh (Amintor), Pierce Brosnan (King), Steven Dartnell (Calianax), Julia Blalock (Evadne) and Angela Chadfield (Aspatia). Rupert Farley played Honour (a personification introduced by the director), 'a freshfaced youth' occupying an upper position on-stage, who 'hands weapons to those who need them for reputation's sake, and joins in unison with any line that treats of probity or esteem'.[81] The stage setting was opulent and symbolic.[82] The omission of some characters—Diagoras, Melantius' Lady, Dula, Antiphila and Olympias, Amintor's Servant and all the persons in the masque—led to some drastic expedients. Thus, at I.ii.76, Calianax was made to say 'Nay, I know you can

fight for that whore, your sister'; in II.i Dula's bawdry was given to
Aspatia as well as her own pathos which immediately follows; and in
II.ii, Aspatia being alone on the stage (though retaining her opening
lines addressed to her women), Calianax entered and abused her as
'you young lazy whore'. Besides the masque, the chief omission was
Amintor's brief impulse (at the end of IV.ii) to kill the King. At the
end of the last scene Amintor was denied his suicide and directed to
carry Aspatia to the front of the stage, where he remained, apparently
crazed with grief. Melantius, in his turn grieving over Amintor,
kicked Evadne's body when Diphilus directed his attention to it.

The Royal Shakespeare Company production (30 April 1980),
directed by Barry Kyle at The Other Place, Stratford-upon-Avon,
was in modern dress but in every other respect was less idiosyn-
cratic than that at the Citizens' Theatre.[83] The principal parts were
played by Tom Wilkinson (Melantius), Rob Edwards (Amintor),
John Carlisle (King), Raymond Westwell (Calianax), Sinead Cusack
(Evadne) and Domini Blythe (Aspatia). The text was given with few
cuts. The masque was included, though treated in the style of a
house-party charade: Neptune came on without his trident, which
had to be thrown on after him, and there was much by-play with a
large sheet and a snowbag full of 'petals'. This was consistent with
the small-scale staging required by the small-scale theatre. The stage
furniture (designed by Judith Bland) consisted of a bed for the King
in V.i (in IV.ii it had served as a covered table at the banquet), a
dozen lightweight gilded chairs (all of which, in the passion of the
final scene, Amintor hurled at Evadne), a drinks trolley, and in III.i a
piano which Strato briefly played at Amintor's line 'Is there no music
there? Let's dance.' A searchlight picked out Melantius on the walls
in V.ii. Instead of swords, sheath-knives were used for the fights.
The conviction with which the play was acted ensured the audience's
full attention, and perhaps the contemporary costume and *décor*
created a satisfying tension with the dialogue for some spectators.
Nevertheless, it would be interesting to see the play done (with the
same conviction) on a large scale, with Jacobean splendour, at the
Royal Shakespeare Theatre or at the National Theatre.

A non-professional production at the Guildhall School of Music and
Drama (26–9 November 1985), by students of the School directed
by Peter Clough, was one which deserved high commendation. The
director and performers believed in the play's ability to excite and
move an audience, and brought out its dramatic power. This was as
true of the masque as of the intimate scenes: rich velvet costumes,

expert choreography, and accomplished singing, dancing and playing made this a satisfying spectacle in itself as well as an appropriate embodiment of the King's power which is so important an element in the tragedy. The arrangement of the acting space, in traverse fashion between two facing areas of banked seating, both gave the masquers ample room and also made the audience feel like participants in the ceremony.[84]

6. THE TEXT[85]

There are two substantive texts of *The Maid's Tragedy*, the first Quarto (Q1) of 1619 and the second Quarto (Q2) of 1622. No other text has any authority.[86]

Q1 was printed with variant title-pages, some copies carrying Richard Higginbotham's name and others Francis Constable's. The copy had been entered to both these publishers in the Stationers' Register on 28 April 1619. The printer was Nicholas Okes, but only part of the work (sheets B to G) was done in his shop, the rest (sheets H to L, and sheet A) being contracted out to another, unidentified, printer.[87]

Q2 was printed, for Constable alone, by George Purslowe. Its title-page has the same layout as that of Q1 (which is reproduced as the frontispiece to this volume), but just above the woodcut are added the words 'Newly perused, augmented, and inlarged, This second Impression'. The claim made by these words is justified: Q2 contains about eighty lines (of undoubted authenticity) which are not in Q1,[88] it makes numerous verbal alterations to Q1, it corrects many of Q1's errors, and it frequently improves on Q1's inadequate punctuation. It is accordingly a better text than Q1. But it is not a wholly independent text. Though evidently based on a different manuscript from that on which Q1 had been based, it was not printed directly from this second manuscript but from a copy of Q1 over which someone (hereafter called the annotator), with the second manuscript before him, had worked. It frequently reproduces Q1's layout of text exactly, and also reproduces many of Q1's demonstrable errors.

Both manuscripts seem to have been authorial. Q1, though inferior to Q2, does not look like a 'bad' quarto (a memorial reconstruction of the text of a play), since it does not show the lapses of memory that bad quartos always show.[89] Neither Q1 nor Q2 looks like a text that has been prepared by the 'book-keeper' of the actors' company for stage performance: there are no anticipatory stage directions, the directions which exist are fewer than a promptbook would require, and the only one expressed in specifically theatrical terms could easily have been written by an author familiar with the stage.[90] Nor is there any reason for supposing that a professional scribe was employed: the manuscript copy for Q1 gave the compositors some trouble,[91] and the manuscript from which Q2's annotator worked cannot have been so clearly written that he was tempted to send it to the printer instead of marking up a copy of Q1 from it.[92]

Both manuscripts seem to have been wholly in Beaumont's handwriting, since Fletcher's linguistic preferences are not prominent either in Q1 or in the passages peculiar to Q2.[93] Whether the first manuscript was a late stage of foul papers (i.e., rough draft) or a fair copy which nevertheless had undergone considerable alteration is a matter of opinion.[94] There is nothing to indicate when the second manuscript was written. It may have been the result of further revision prior to the first production of the play. Possibly, however, the play was overhauled in readiness for its revival at court in Princess Elizabeth's wedding celebrations in 1613, the third choral song in the masque and the two solo songs for Aspatia and Dula being added on that occasion.[95] Beaumont composed his *Masque of the Inner Temple and Gray's Inn* for the same celebrations, so he may have revised *The Maid's Tragedy* at the same time. On the other hand, would he have made so many small alterations to the diction if the play was currently in the repertoire of the King's Men and the actors were familiar with their parts?

Beaumont died in 1616 and could have had no hand in the play's publication either in 1619 or 1622. Since Fletcher's linguistic preferences are not prominent in Q2, he can hardly have been the annotator. Who the annotator was, and why an inferior manuscript was sent to the printer in 1619 when a better one was available for the preparation of Q2 in 1622, are questions as yet unanswered.[96]

In view of this history of the text's transmission, involving the partial dependence of Q2 on Q1, I have, like all the most recent editors (Norland, Gurr and Turner) selected Q1 as the copy-text, and have adopted from Q2 all substantive variants except those which I consider for any reason to be suspect: for example, where the annotator may have misread his manuscript,[97] or where he may have altered the text on his own initiative without the authority of his manuscript,[98] or where he may have made a faithful annotation which the compositor misinterpreted,[99] or where the compositor may have made a simple error (such as omission) in setting his copy (whether this was an annotated or an unchanged passage in Q1).[100] Besides these liabilities to fresh error in Q2, there exists the certainty that uncorrected errors in Q1 persist as uncorrected errors in Q2.[101] An editor basing his text on Q1 and admitting superior readings from Q2 must be prepared to emend where both texts seem to be either unanimously or divergently in error. I have therefore taken into account the editorial tradition (beginning with Q3 and ending with Turner), and have considered, and where I thought proper adopted, its emendations. I have also proposed many emendations of my own, and in some instances admitted them to the text. All emendations that I have adopted are discussed in the commentary and are recorded in the collation, which also records all the substantive variants between Q1 and Q2. Additions to the stage directions of Q1 and Q2 are indicated by square brackets, and are not recorded in the collation except when some point of importance is in question.

All this edition's departures from the lineation of Q1 and Q2, and all variations in lineation between them, are recorded in the colla-tion, instead of being relegated to an appendix.[102] Though there are a few prose passages (such as the opening of I.ii between Calianax and Diagoras, and the dialogue of the two Gentlemen after the King's murder in V.i), these employ prose for obvious reasons of decorum,[103] and there can be no doubt that verse is the prevailing medium of the play. The lineation of Q1 (and of Q2, which, being set up from Q1, normally follows it in this) is often plainly wrong:

EVAD. A lies.   KING. A does not.
EVAD. By this light he does, strangely and basely, and
Ile prooue it so, I did not onely shun him for a night,
But told him I would neuer close with him.   (Q1, sig. F (III.i.185–8))

Here the correction is as plain as the error. But what of the following?

MEL. No, tis a iustice and a noble one,
To put the light out of such base offenders.
EVAD. Helpe?
MEL. By thy foule selfe, no humaine help shall help thee,
If thou criest, when I haue kild thee, as I haue
Vow'd to doe, if thou confesse not, naked as thou hast left
Thine honor, will I leaue thee,
That on thy branded flesh the world may reade
Thy blacke shame and my iustice, wilt thou bend yet?
                                    (Q1, sig. G4v.-H (IV.i.100–109))

The first two lines, and the last two, are evidently correct, but what should happen in the middle? Evadne's 'Help!' is extra-metrical. Thereafter all editors (except Gurr, whose old-spelling edition here reprints Q1's lineation) read, with Weber,

> By thy foul self, no human help shall help thee
> If thou criest. When I have killed thee, as I
> Have vowed to do if thou confess not, naked
> As thou hast left thine honour will I leave thee.

The first, third and fourth lines of this arrangement make accept-able verse, but it is beyond belief that Fletcher's ears would have recognized the second as one of his lines. We must try another arrangement:

> By thy foul self
> No human help shall help thee if thou criest.
> When I have killed thee
> (As I have vowed to do if thou confess not)
> Nak'd as thou hast left thine honour will I leave thee.

If the reader will suspend any prejudice he may feel against half-lines, and will scan the last line by stresses ('Nak'd as thou'st left thine honour will I leave thee') and not by syllables, he will hear characteristically Fletcherian verse, feminine endings and all. The emendation of lineation, it will be seen from this example, may go hand in hand with the emendation of diction: 'naked' (as *OED* confirms) can be a monosyllable, and (as II.i.2 confirms) can be read as such in this play.

It seems to me self-evident that, in a verse play, lines which defy an experienced ear to recognise them as verse constitute a *prima facie* case for supposing that either corruption or revision has occurred.[104]

The spelling and punctuation of the text have been modernised in accordance with the practice of the Revels Plays as outlined in the general editors' preface.[105] The division into acts follows that of Q1 and Q2, and of all subsequent editors: it is clearly authorial. Scene-divisions, which are not indicated in the quartos apart from '*Actus. I. Scæn.* I', have been supplied within square brackets. A new scene is marked, in accordance with the conventions of Elizabethan drama, whenever the stage is cleared of persons and a new phase of the action begins. It must be mentioned that in 1812 Weber wrongly thought it necessary to begin a new scene (which he marked V.ii) at V.i.12, and in this he was followed by many editors, with the result that scene-references in critical works need to be interpreted according

to whether the critic is reading a text with three or with four scenes
in Act V. Apart from this there is unanimity about where the scene-
divisions occur.[106]

NOTES

1 There is a good brief account of their lives and theatrical careers in
  Andrew Gurr (ed.), *Philaster*, pp. xx–xxiii. For further information see
  The Dictionary of National Biography.
2 The first Folio (1647) had contained only such plays as had not been
  separately published already. Both Folios include plays in which Fletcher
  had collaborated with other dramatists.
3 John Web, commendatory verses in the first Folio: Glover and Waller,
  I, xxxi.
4 Jasper Maine, *ibid.*, I, xxxvi.
5 John Berkenhead, *ibid.*, I, xli-xlii.
6 *Ibid.*, I, xxxvii–xl.
7 Oliver Lawson Dick (ed.), *Aubrey's Brief Lives* (Harmondsworth, 1972),
  pp. 184–5.
8 Aubrey's informant was John Earle, who was only fifteen years old when
  Beaumont died and who had also contributed verses to the first Folio.
  Cartwright's phrase 'wit / So overflow'd thy scenes' is echoed in Aubrey's
  'the overflowings of Mr Fletcher's luxuriant Fancy and flowing Witt'.
9 See n. 4 above.
10 Weber (1812) was the first editor to attempt to distinguish the contri-
  butors on stylistic grounds. Later discussions of the topic are in F. G.
  Fleay, *On Metrical Tests as applied to Dramatic Poetry: Part II* (1886);
  C. M. Gayley, *Francis Beaumont, Dramatist* (1914); E. H. C. Oliphant,
  The Plays of Beaumont and Fletcher (New Haven, 1927); Cyrus Hoy, 'The
  Shares of Fletcher and his Collaborators in the Beaumont and Fletcher
  Canon', *Studies in Bibliography*, VIII–IX, XI–XV (1956–62).
11 Hoy (see preceding note), XI (1958), 94; Norland, p. xiii; Gurr, p. 2;
  Turner, p. 3. For more evidence of Fletcher's authorship see Appendix B.
  On the numbering of the scenes in Act V, see below, p. 36. Gayley, *op.
  cit.*, pp. 108–9, notes that the ascription of V.i to Fletcher goes towards
  authenticating the anecdote in Thomas Fuller's *Worthies of England*
  (1662): the dramatists 'meeting once in a Tavern to contrive the rude
  draught of a Tragedy, Fletcher undertook to *Kill the King* therein; whose
  words being overheard by a listener (though his Loyalty not to be blamed
  herein) he was accused of high Treason, till the mistake soon appearing,
  that the plot was only against a Drammatick and Scenical King, all wound
  off in merriment.'
12 Norland, p. xi; Gurr, p. 1; Turner, p. 3.
13 Chambers, *E.S.*, IV, 45.
14 *Ibid.*, IV, 180. None of the performances can be dated: the wedding was
  on 14 February 1613, but the married couple remained at court till 10
  April (IV, 127–8).

15 *Ibid.*, II, 150.
16 Norland, p. xi. The King's Men practised privately for six weeks in order to entertain the court during the Christmas holidays of 1609–10. London was free of plague from 1611 to 1616 (Chambers, *E.S.*, IV, 351).
17 *Philaster* is assigned to 1609 by Gurr (ed.), p. xxxix, and *A King and No King* to 1611 by Robert K. Turner, Jr. (ed. in *Regents Renaissance Drama Series*, Lincoln, Nebraska, 1964), p. xi.
18 Gurr (ed.), *Philaster*, pp. xxi–xxii.
19 *Ibid.*, pp. xxix–xxxv.
20 Dyce, I, 313.
21 Matteo Bandello, *Le Novelle*, ed. Gioachino Brognoligo (Bari, 1928), II, 116–27.
22 'Thus Bandello has one story (i.42) of a woman who, after being faithlessly deserted by her lover, lures him back to her with treacherous endearments; then, when he is asleep, she binds him fast to the bed, wakes him, and, falling upon him with curses and maledictions, hacks his defenceless body with a knife till he dies in the most fearful agony. This story has been utilised by Beaumont and Fletcher in a scene in their famous *Maid's Tragedy*.' (Wilhelm Creizenach, *The English Drama in the Age of Shakespeare* (translated, London, 1916), p. 195). I am grateful to Dr T. P. Matheson for drawing my attention to this quotation, to which no editor of *The Maid's Tragedy* refers.
23 That the story is the source of *The Triumph of Death* is noted by Joseph Jacobs (ed.), *The Palace of Pleasure* (see following note), I, lxxv. He does not connect either the story or the play with *The Maid's Tragedy*. The date of *Four Plays in One* is not known (it was first printed in the Folio of 1647), nor is there any external evidence as to the authorship other than its inclusion in the Folio. Critical opinion unanimously ascribes *The Triumph of Death* and *The Triumph of Time* to Fletcher on the evidence of style, but is divided as to the authorship of the other two plays and as to the date of composition. For further discussion see Appendix B.
24 Pierre Boaistuau, *Histoires tragiques*, ed. Richard A. Carr (Paris, 1977), pp. 139–67. William Painter, *The Palace of Pleasure*, ed. Joseph Jacobs (1890), I, 218–39.
25 William Dinsmore Briggs, 'On the Sources of *The Maid's Tragedy*', *Modern Language Notes*, XXXI (1916), 502–3. Like Creizenach's, this observation has remained almost unnoticed: the only editors who refer to it are Brooke and Paradise (p. 760, in their introductory note to *The Maid's Tragedy*). This neglect probably arose because Briggs did not translate the passage from Valerius Maximus nor specify the scene in *The Maid's Tragedy*, and proceeded to speculate generally on possible areas of influence in classical legends about tyrannicide. Briggs's article is not included in *The New Cambridge Bibliography of English Literature*, I (Cambridge, 1974), 1715.
26 See notes on I.i.42–3; II.i.87–8; IV.i.222; IV.ii.231–2; V.iii.242. See also note 36 below.
27 See notes on I.ii.163, 278.
28 See notes on II.ii.7–9; V.i.104.
29 See notes on I.ii.38, 135, 204, 251; II.i.78–9.
30 See notes on I.i.15; II.ii.33; III.i.238–40, 270, 274, 283; IV.i.66–8, 85,

258; IV.ii.15; V.ii.2–3; V.iii.242.

31 The terms are H. Neville Davies's: 'Beaumont and Fletcher's *Hamlet*', *Shakespeare, Man of the Theater: Proceedings of the Second Congress of the International Shakespeare Association*, 1981, ed. K. Muir, J. L. Halio, and D. Palmer (Newark, N.J., 1983), p. 178.

32 'It is evident that Evadne does not wish to make the King's conscience active in order that he may die repentant, although the last scene of *Othello* may also have been remembered here: rather, she wishes him to die in torment, not to be rocked to another world.' (Clifford Leech, *The John Fletcher Plays* (1962), p. 125).

32 On the relationship between the two plays see H. Neville Davies, *op. cit.*, pp. 173–81. His view is that Beaumont and Fletcher are writing in emulation, not in mere imitation, of Shakespeare. On the influence of Shakespeare see also Daniel M. McKeithan, *The Debt to Shakespeare in Beaumont and Fletcher's Plays* (Austin, Texas, 1938, pp. 43–50), and Donald J. McGinn, *Shakespeare's Influence on the Drama of his Age studied in 'Hamlet'* (New Brunswick, N.J., 1938, reprinted New York, 1965, pp. 68–71).

34 *Julius Caesar*, IV.iii; *The Maid's Tragedy*, III.ii. Seward (Theobald, I, xxxvi–xxxvii), who points out that 'there is not such extreme *Dignity* of Character, nor such noble Sentiments of *Morality*, in either *Amintor* or *Melantius* as in *Brutus*', indicates the difference, namely that the whole scene turns on moral character in Shakespeare, whereas in Beaumont and Fletcher it does not. Seward also (p. xxix) drew attention to the reminiscence of *The Two Gentlemen of Verona*, mentioned below, p. 8.

35 *Othello*, V.ii; *The Maid's Tragedy*, V.i. The differences (in ascending order of importance) are that Beaumont and Fletcher reverse the sex of murderer and victim; that the King's guilt is real, Desdemona's illusory; and that Shakespeare's scene proceeds uninterruptedly to the tragedy's resolution in the enlightenment and death of the hero.

36 II.ii may also contain a further reminiscence of *Arcadia*, in Aspatia's desire that her waiting-women's demeanour shall reflect her own sorrow. The first encounter of Palladius with Queen Helen is described as follows: 'looking into the coach, he found in the one end a Lady of great beautie, & such a beautie, as shewed forth the beames both of wisdome & good nature, but al as much darkened, as might be, with sorow. In the other, two Ladies, (who by their demeanure shewed well, they were but her servants) holding before them a picture; in which was a goodly Gentleman (whom he knew not) painted, having in their faces a certaine waiting sorrow, their eies being infected with their mistres weeping.' (*Arcadia*, bk. 1, chap. 10, pp. 64–5).

37 Thomas Rymer, *The Tragedies of the Last Age consider'd and examin'd by the Practice of the Ancients and by the Common Sense of all Ages* (1678), quoted from J. E. Spingarn (ed.), *Critical Essays of the Seventeenth Century* (Oxford, 1908), II, 189–90. 'Lysimachus' is Rymer's error for Lysippus.

38 Rymer, *op. cit.*, p. 190. By 'some additional title' he presumably meant something like 'or, The Troth-Breaker'.

39 Theobald, I, 89.

40 V.iii.1–8. The functions of this soliloquy are (1) to identify the disguised Aspatia, (2) to strike the pathetic keynote of her encounter

with Amintor and (3) to reassure the audience as to the morality of her intention.

41 G. C. Macaulay, *Francis Beaumont: A Critical Study* (London, 1883), p. 135. This seems a more appropriate comment than Fredson Bowers's: 'The specific reason for his death is found in his broken betrothal to Aspatia: even at the orders of his sovereign, this was a crime which in tragedy could not go unrequited' (*Elizabethan Revenge Tragedy, 1587–1642* (Princeton, 1940), p. 173).

42 Norland (pp. xx–xxi) does not share this view: 'Melantius, whose sense of honor has provoked him to adopt the Machiavellian policy of his victim and to assume God's prerogative and "stand" as his "own justice", in the end is most cursed because, unlike the others tainted by the king's evil, he has not found release. Instead he is sentenced to live in a world that no longer holds any meaning for him.'

43 Beaumont and Fletcher choose a particular dramatic action 'because they are interested in the way in which it will develop towards its point of conclusion: ideas and attitudes will emerge from time to time, but intellectual argument will remain a side-issue.' (Clifford Leech, '*Edward II*: Power and Suffering' (*Critical Quarterly*, 1 (1959), 181–96).

44 Cf. Melantius' remark about courtiers as 'gilded things' (IV.ii.10–12, and n.).

45 Lawrence B. Wallis, *Fletcher, Beaumont & Company: Entertainers to the Jacobean Gentry* (New York, 1947), pp. 3–125, gives a comprehensive and well-illustrated survey of their reputation throughout three hundred years. This is supplemented by Denzell S. Smith, 'Francis Beaumont and John Fletcher', the first section (pp. 3–89) of *The Later Jacobean and Caroline Dramatists: A Survey and Bibliography of Recent Studies in English Renaissance Drama*, ed. Terence P. Logan and Denzell S. Smith (Lincoln, Nebraska and London, 1978). The most important modern study of *The Maid's Tragedy* in the context of Beaumont and Fletcher's other collaborative work and in the literary and social context of their period is John F. Danby's *Poets on Fortune's Hill: Studies in Sidney, Shakespeare, Beaumont & Fletcher* (London, 1952; reprinted as *Elizabethan and Jacobean Poets*, London, 1964). Danby sees Beaumont and Fletcher as social aspirers in the decadent world of the Jacobean court, adapting the literature of the Elizabethan great house (Sidney's *Arcadia*) and the drama of the Elizabethan theatre to the new age. Yet they do not do this cynically: Beaumont in particular is obsessed by the discrepancy between his royalist ideal and the corrupt reality, and this obsession is expressed in his heroes' self-division between the absolutes which conflict for their adherence. Danby stresses Beaumont and Fletcher's concern with wit, and compares their ingenious development of deceptive ambiguous situations with the metaphysical conceit; an instance of what he calls their 'moral puns' is Amintor's request (II.i.322–7) that Evadne will show him pity, not by returning his love and saving his life as a petrarchan mistress might do, but by literally killing him. There are errors of fact in Danby's account of *The Maid's Tragedy* (especially his statement that 'Melantius survives to preside over the fortunes and welfare of the future king'), but it is an acute and responsive one. Danby's views of Beaumont and Fletcher's relationship with their society, and of Beaumont's moral obses-

sion, have been questioned by some later critics (see Smith, *op. cit.*, for details). These are matters of opinion on which no definite conclusion seems possible.

46 *An Essay of Dramatic Poesy*, in E. D. Jones (ed.), *English Critical Essays: Sixteenth, Seventeenth, and Eighteenth Centuries* (Oxford, 1922), p. 169.

47 Though II.i is supposed to happen late at night (there is no suggestion that the masque has been in the early evening), II.ii is not presented as a night scene; far from being surprised to find his daughter and her women still up, Calianax crossly bids the latter get to their needlework. But there is nothing to connect it with morning either. This is a scene that is, in effect, free of place and time.

48 Aspatia's passive grief in I.i, II.i and II.ii is a false scent, by following which we never anticipate her active way of encompassing her own death.

49 Rymer, *op. cit.*, p. 201.

50 G. C. Macaulay, *op. cit.*, p. 110.

51 The recollection, earlier in the same speech, of Amintor as a boy handling Melantius' sword vividly dramatises the promise, and draws attention to the fact that Amintor has only just reached years of manhood—an important fact in the play.

52 After Melantius' tribute to Amintor, we might have expected Amintor's entrance at this point. The entrance of Aspatia, of whom we as yet know nothing, but whose relations with Amintor we immediately understand from Melantius' greeting, is an effective dramatic stroke.

53 The first was Lysippus' humorously hyperbolical 'The breath of kings is like the breath of gods: / My brother wished thee here, and thou art here' (I.i.15–16) and the second was Diphilus' explanation that he could not join his brother at the wars until the King allowed it (I.i.31–3).

54 Inga-Stina Ewbank, '"These Pretty Devices": A Study of Masques in Plays', in T. J. B. Spencer and S. W. Wells (ed.), *A Book of Masques in Honour of Allardyce Nicoll* (1967), p. 418.

55 See n. 58 below.

56 As a matter of fact, Amintor does see Evadne in IV.ii when they are the guests of honour at the King's banquet, but this is an inconsistency which passes unnoticed in the theatre.

57 There is often pathos in the comedies that use the device, e.g., Viola's dialogue with Orsino in *Twelfth Night*, II.iv. The situation in *Philaster* differs from those under discussion, since it is not known until the dénouement (at least, the first time that one reads or sees the play) that Bellario the supposed page is really a woman in disguise.

58 The danger is not altogether escaped by Michael Neill in his generally perceptive essay on the play, '"The Simetry, Which Gives a Poem Grace": Masque, Imagery, and the Fancy of *The Maid's Tragedy*', *Renaissance Drama*, n.s., III (1970), 111–35. In Aspatia's image of the sun scorching the fruit (II.ii.20–2) he finds an ironic reflection upon the King, who was called a greater sun in the masque (I.ii.279), 'and whose kiss has blasted the fruitfulness of Evadne's marriage'. The word 'die' in its sexual sense so obsesses modern commentators that one must insist that in Jacobean tragedy it usually carries its obvious meaning and no other. Neill extracts a double meaning not only from the King's 'O, I die!' (V.i.112) but also from Aspatia's 'There is no place so fit / For me to die as

here' (V.iii.104–5), seeing 'her absurd duel with Amintor' as 'an ironic literalization of the metaphorical battle of bride and groom'. On the significance of the masque Sarah P. Sutherland (*Masques in Jacobean Tragedy*, New York, 1983) adds nothing of importance to Neill's article, and her sexual interpretation of Boreas' escape is strained: 'Only the wedding night can determine whether the storm will be calmed, or whether the "proud charge should swell above the waste" and "ere day / Many a tall ship will be cast away." The *doubles entendres* are quite evident…' (pp. 68–9). Since her phrase for Boreas' escape, 'a sexual joke', originated with Clifford Leech (*The John Fletcher Plays*, London, 1962, p. 122), it is perhaps necessary to spell out that what Leech had in mind (wrongly, in my opinion) was the escape of wind from the bowels during the sexual act. William Schullenberger, in an unconvincingly Freudian and feminist article, says that 'Evadne's binding and murder of the King' reflects the 'chaining of Boreas' and that Evadne has 'the menacing power of the masque's dark goddess' ('"This For the Most Wrong'd of Women": a Reappraisal of *The Maid's Tragedy*', *Renaissance Drama*, n.s., XIII (1982), 131–6).

59 S. T. Coleridge, *Lectures and Notes on Shakspere and Other English Poets*, ed. T. Ashe (London, 1904), p. 446. T. S. Eliot, *Selected Essays*, 2nd edn, revised and enlarged (London, 1934), p. 155.

60 *Hamlet, Othello* and *Macbeth*, all written for the Globe, all include night scenes.

61 See p. 3 above. Other performances at court are recorded on 9 December 1630 and 29 November 1636 (G. E. Bentley, *The Jacobean and Caroline Stage*, Oxford (1941), I, 113).

62 James Wright, *Historia Histrionica* (1699), quoted by Bentley, *op. cit.*, II, 693. Wright states that Hammerton 'was at first a most noted and beautiful Woman Actor, but afterwards he acted with equal Grace and Applause, a Young Lover's Part'.

63 A. C. Sprague, *Beaumont and Fletcher on the Restoration Stage* (Cambridge, Mass., 1926), pp. 5–6.

64 For all information about performances and cast-lists in the period 1660–1745, see *The London Stage* (Carbondale, Illinois): *Part 1. 1660–1700*, ed. William Van Lennep (1965); *Part 2. 1700–1729*, ed. Emmett L. Avery (2 vols, 1960); *Part 3. 1729–1747*, ed. A. H. Scouten (1961). Entries relating to *The Maid's Tragedy* are listed under the name of Fletcher. Other information in this paragraph is from Sprague, *op. cit.*, pp. 7–39, and from Helen McAfee, *Pepys on the Restoration Stage* (New Haven, 1916), pp. 81–101.

65 Colley Cibber, *Apology* (1740), p. 100.

66 Rymer, *op. cit.*, p. 205.

67 So in Bennet's edition. 'But considering, that the Persons in this Play are suppos'd to be Heathens, who never admitted any but pure Virgins among their Vestals; he changed his design.' (Tonson's edition, p. 44). In Tonson's edition, accordingly, she embarks for foreign lands with her wealth, intending to dazzle 'Asiatick Kings' with '[her] shining Jewels, and [her] brighter Eyes' (p. 8).

68 Bennet's edition, p. 12. When Melantius insists on the King's death, Lysippus retorts, 'Tho more in years, you have a Mistress still, / And for

that fault would you your Soveraign kill?'

69 It was first stated by Gerard Langbaine (1691), whose account was repeated, with variations, by Charles Gildon (1699), Langbaine himself (1711), Giles Jacobs (1719) and Colley Cibber (1740). For quotations see Sprague, *op. cit.*, pp. 59–60, and Robert D. Hume, '*The Maid's Tragedy* and Censorship in the Restoration Theatre', *Philological Quarterly*, LXI (1982), 484–90.

70 Waller, *Works*, ed. Elijah Fenton (1729), p. lxxxviii (quoted by Sprague, *op. cit.*, and by Hume, *op. cit.*).

71 For a review of opinions see Hume, *op. cit.* His own opinion is that the play 'was quietly prohibited' during the Popish Plot and Exclusion Crisis of 1678–83, but that Waller's fifth act was probably written in or near 1664, when he was engaged in other dramatic writing, when couplets were fashionable (as they were not after 1680) and when alternative endings were also in vogue. He believes that the prologue and epilogues show that Waller intended his revision to be performed, but he thinks it unlikely that it ever was.

72 I remain sceptical of the prohibition story, and also of Waller's having intended his fifth act for the stage, where the juxtaposition of four acts of blank verse with a fifth act of couplets would be stylistically grotesque. I regard the two epilogues (one for a non-existent version where Aspatia and Amintor die, the other for the version that we have) as a *jeu d'esprit*, like the work as a whole, and though Hume gives strong arguments for a date *c.* 1664 I wonder whether Rymer's famous critique of 1678 may have provided Waller's stimulus. Rymer apostrophises Evadne: 'Did any force or philter overcome you? was not you as forward? did you not freely and heartily consent [to be the King's mistress]?'; and he objects to her being 'hector'd into a repentance so pernicious by her Brother' (Rymer, *op. cit.*, pp. 196, 197). Compare Waller, who points out through Lysippus that the King did not ravish Evadne but only 'compiy' with one 'fair, and not unwilling' (Bennet's edition, p. 12), and through Evadne that she was 'Compell'd by Threats, to take that bloody Oath' (*ibid.*, p. 4). A date contemporary with the Popish Plot and Exclusion Crisis would also be consistent with the favourable prominence given to Lysippus, the King's brother, and with the final lines in the Tonson version: 'This sacred Union has preserv'd the State; / And from all Tempest shall secure our fate: / Like a well twisted Cable, holding fast / The anchor'd Vessel in the lowdest Blast' (p. 42), an indirect compliment, as John Genest recognised, to the King and the Duke of York (*An Account of the English Stage*, 1660–1830, Bath (1832), I, 337).

73 The play was first printed in *The Acting National Drama*, ed. Benjamin Webster, vol. 1 (1837).

74 The dialogue between Amintor and the dying Aspatia is transferred to Melantius and the dying Evadne.

75 George C. D. Odell, *Annals of the New York Stage* (New York, 1928–31), V, 10–11, 17, 87. It was still being acted in New York in 1860, with J. W. Wallack, Jr., as Melantius (Odell, *op. cit.*, VII, 327).

76 *The Times*, 16 November 1921.

77 *The Times*, 18 May 1925. See also J. C. Trewin, *Edith Evans* (1954), pp. 39, 105, and Bryan Forbes, *Ned's Girl: the official biography of Edith*

Evans (1977), p. 93. The production was directed by Frank Cellier.

78 *The Times*, 5 June 1964. The information that C. Walter Hodges designed
the production and that Coral Atkins played Dula is from the programme,
'Shakespeare 400 at the Mermaid' (1964).

79 19–24 October 1972. Information supplied by the New York Public
Library (Performing Arts Research Center).

80 Promptbook at Glasgow Citizens' Theatre.

81 B. A. Young, review, *Financial Times*, 19 November 1979.

82 'In a dazzling opening, typical of Mr. Prowse's invention as a designer,
billowing curtains fall, a shower of glittering gold drifts over the frozen
actors and the play begins against a regal backdrop of black and golden
metals.' (Ned Chaillet, review, *The Times*, 21 November 1979).

83 Promptbook at the Shakespeare Centre Reference Library, Stratford-
upon-Avon.

84 See J. R. Mulryne, review, *Renaissance Drama Newsletter* (University of
Warwick, Coventry), VI, no. 2 (Autumn, 1985), pp. 14–15.

85 In the following account of the text I am particularly indebted to
Robert K. Turner, Jr., whose edition (1970) is the culmination of a
detailed textual study of the play begun with his unpublished Ph.D.
dissertation (University of Virginia, 1958). Turner has collated the six
extant copies of Q1 and the eleven extant copies of Q2 (the eleventh,
which appeared after the publication of his edition and is now in the
Library of the University of Wisconsin-Milwaukee, is described by him
in *Notes and Queries*, CCV (1980), p. 322). Full details of the press-variants
are given on pp. 133–5 of his edition.

86 The third quarto (Q3), printed for Richard Hawkins by Augustine
Mathewes in 1630, is a line-for-line reprint of Q2, but contains some
readings which are not in either Q1 or Q2. Neither the quantity nor the
quality of these suggests that Hawkins had access to an authoritative
manuscript, and it is probable that he introduced them on his own
initiative (Turner, pp. 4–5). The play was reprinted in seven more
quartos and in the second Folio of 1679. All these texts are derivative.

87 This other printer used a slightly different fount of type; he set the
speech-prefixes in italic, whereas Okes set them in small capitals; and he
abbreviated the prefixes for Calianax and Aspatia differently (*Call.* and
Aspat. instead of CAL. and ASP.). The spelling CALLIANAX in the list of
speakers establishes that he set sheet A (Turner, p. 6). Turner concludes
that Okes employed two compositors and the unidentified printer one; he
analyses the printing process in detail (pp. 6–9).

88 The chief of these (listed by Turner, p. 10) are I.ii.146–55, 240.1–54;
II.i.67–89; II.ii.7–10, 15–27; III.i.202–5; IV.i.80–5. Though some of
these passages (notably Aspatia's and Dula's songs in II.i and the dialogue
introducing them) must be the result of revision, other passages (notably
II.ii.7–10, 15–27, the omission of which spoils the metre) must be rein-
statements of material marked for omission (or believed by the compositor
to be so marked) in the first manuscript (Turner, pp. 10–11).

89 Turner, p. 15, lists the 'classical stigmata' of such texts as 'severe
abbreviation of the text, anticipation and recollection, gag, and echoes
of other plays'.

90 I.ii.52.1: '*Enter Calianax to Melantius*' (Q2). As Turner (pp. 18–19)

points out, this direction is wrong, because Melantius is still off-stage when Calianax enters. I think, however, that the manuscript may have read 'Enter Calianax, to him Melantius' (which would correctly describe the action), and that this was bungled either by the compositor or more probably by the annotator, who may have taken 'him' and 'Melantius' as synonymous.

91 Turner, pp. 12–14.
92 Norland, pp. xxv–xxvi, mentions the possibility that the annotator was working from the promptbook itself (which the King's Men would certainly not have allowed to go to the printer), but on balance he rejects this possibility.
93 Turner, pp. 17, 20.
94 Turner, p. 16, favours 'foul papers'; Gurr, p. 10, favours 'fair copy'.
95 The poem by Jonson which is a source for Aspatia's song (see II.i.78–9 and n.) was not published till 1616 in his Works, but it is thought to have been written much earlier, and it is probable that Jonson showed it to Beaumont, who, as his epigram 'To Francis Beaumont' shows, was among his closest friends.
96 Gurr (ed. Philaster, p. lxxvii, n. 2) observes: 'There is some possibility that the difficulties which the King's Men suffered in 1619, the death of Burbage and an attempt at restraining their activities at Blackfriars, can be linked with the publishing of several of their more popular plays between 1619 and 1622; three of them, Philaster, The Maid's Tragedy, and Othello, first appeared in versions which had subsequently to be revised.'
97 e.g., I.ii.52.1 (see n. 90 above).
98 As he did when he mispunctuated III.i.199–200. Turner (p. 23) is probably right in suggesting that he toned down the profanity at V.i.24 and deleted 'God' from 'God save you' at IV.i.1. But I doubt whether he meddled with metre by omitting words (Turner, pp. 23–4), since omissions are not uncommon compositor's errors in Q2.
99 eg., I.ii.160, 163; II.ii.68. Another instance may be I.ii.240.1 ('If not her measure' for 'Another measure'), though the misreading may have been the annotator's.
100 Examples are at I.i.6, 33, 36, 67, 127.
101 Examples are at I.ii.179; III.i.229; IV.i.221; V.ii.47–8; V.iii.45, 118, 156, 211.
102 As always in the early editions of plays, all speeches begin immediately after the speech prefix. It is a modern editor's responsibility to decide whether a short phrase should be considered as completing a line of verse or as extra-metrical. For example, at IV.i.9, 'I'll lock the door first. / Evadne. Why?' is treated as a line of verse in order to register the significant pause.
103 So does Evadne's speech at II.i.80–2, where she has a couple of sentences of prose to comment on Aspatia's song and to invite Dula's. The prose draws attention to the fact that Dula's song is rather a musical 'turn' than an expression of mood like Aspatia's.
104 Some (authorial) extra-metrical additions have been made in Q2 in the interests of clarification: I.i.13 ('to Rhodes'), I.ii.66 ('So near the presence of the King'), III.ii.270 ('to mine'); in Q1 and Q2, at IV.ii.126, 'things worthy' is, I think, an addition of the same sort. There also seems to

have been some expurgation in Q1 of certain passages expressive either of profanity (II.i.176–7; III.i.151–2) or of regicidal action (III.i.229–30; V.iii.145–7). Whether these cuts were made in a fit of caution by the authors or by the publisher is not clear; perhaps the latter, since in Q2 the passages are reinstated (though III.i.151–2 is reinstated in what looks like a toned-down form). This expurgation is distinct from the inferred expurgations by the annotator of expressions that had been allowed to stand in Q1 (see n. 98 above).

105 An exception to the usual practice has had to be made in the case of the word 'king'. When it refers specifically to the character in the play (as distinct from his office) it is printed with a capital K. This is necessitated by the fact that the King has no personal name in the text.

106 Daniel speculated whether a new scene should begin at III.ii.256, but he did not mark one, and neither has any later editor.

THE MAID'S TRAGEDY

SPEAKERS

KING.

LYSIPPUS, *brother to the King.*

AMINTOR, *a noble Gentleman.*

EVADNE, *wife to Amintor.*

MELANTIUS⎱
⎰ *brothers to Evadne.*   5
DIPHILUS ⎰

ASPATIA, *troth-plight wife to Amintor.*

CALIANAX, *an old humorous Lord, and father to Aspatia.*

CLEON ⎱
⎰ *Gentlemen.*
STRATO ⎰   10

SPEAKERS] *Q1, Q2.*   3. *a noble Gentleman.*] *Q3; not in Q1, Q2.*
9–10. *Gentlemen.*] *Q1; not in Q2.*

Qq 1 and 2 list only the principal characters in the play and the speaking ones in the masque; they do not include the minor speaking parts. This ed. retains the heading though including the non-speaking parts.

1. *KING*] Like the King in *Philaster*, he is given no personal name.

2. *LYSIPPUS*] the name of a sculptor, of Sicyon (4th century B.C.). His extant works include statues of Alexander the Great (Alexander III of Macedon), who 'allowed Lysippus alone to figure him because he preserved his lion-like and manly look as well as the turn of his neck and the softness of his eyes' (*Oxford Classical Dictionary*, p. 525).

3. *AMINTOR*] Amyntor is the name of an early mythological hero referred to by Homer, *Iliad* IX, 434; X, 266; Ovid, *Metamorphoses* VIII, 307; XII, 364, mentions him as taking part in the Calydonian hunt (Smith, *Dictionary*, I, 156). Aminta (i.e., Amintas) is the hero of Tasso's pastoral drama *Aminta* (1573).

3. *a noble Gentleman*] Cf. V.i.108.

4. *EVADNE*] 'Daughter of Iphis and wife of Capaneus, one of the Seven against Thebes. She burned herself on his funeral pyre' (*Oxford Classical Dictionary*, p. 353).

5. *MELANTIUS*] Melanthius is the name of a painter, of Sicyon (4th century B.C.). 'He wrote on painting, and said that works of art, like characters, should show a certain stubbornness and harshness (in contrast to Apelles' boasted "charm")' (*Oxford Classical Dictionary*, p. 554).

6. *DIPHILUS*] the name of a New Comedy poet (4th century B.C.) who admired Euripides and influenced Plautus (*Oxford Classical Dictionary*, p. 291).

7. *ASPATIA*] Aspasia (5th century B.C.) was the mistress of Pericles of Athens. Contemporary writers attest to her intellectual attainments (*Oxford Classical Dictionary*, p. 108).

7. *troth-plight wife*] engaged to be married.

8. *CALIANAX*] Callianax was a physician (3rd century B.C.) renowned for his severe remarks to his patients (Smith, *Dictionary*, I, 566).

humorous] 'moody, peevish, ill-humoured, out of humour' (*OED*, 3.b).

9. *CLEON*] the name of an Athenian politician (5th century B.C.) (*Oxford Classical Dictionary*, p. 201).

DIAGORAS, *a servant.*

ANTIPHILA $\left.\right\}$ *waiting Gentlewomen to Aspatia.*
OLYMPIAS

DULA, *a Lady.*

NIGHT   15
CYNTHIA $\left.\right\}$ *Masquers.*
NEPTUNE
AEOLUS

---

11. *a servant.*] *Q1; not in Q2.*

---

10. *STRATO*] the name of one of Brutus' men, who holds the sword for his suicide in *Caes.*, V.v. His character as drawn by Shakespeare provided some hints for that of this play's Strato (e.g., *Caes.*, V.v. 32: 'Strato, thou hast been all this while asleep', and V.v.62 (Strato to Octavius): 'Ay, if Messala will prefer me to you'). Plutarch's account of the death of Brutus mentions that 'he came first acquainted' with Strato 'by the study of rhetoric' (North's translation (1579), quoted by T. S. Dorsch, ed. *Caes.*, p. 165); cf. *The Maid's Tragedy*, I.i.5: 'Strato, thou hast some skill in poetry.'

11. *DIAGORAS*] the name of an athlete, of Ialysus in Rhodes (5th century B.C.). He was boxing champion twice in the Olympian games and was also victorious in the other three great athletic festivals (Smith, *Dictionary*, I, 999–1000). This may have a humorous reference to Diagoras's role in I.ii. Diagoras was also the name of an atheistic lyric poet, of Melos (5th century B.C.) (*Oxford Classical Dictionary*, p. 271).

a servant] Theobald adds 'to Calianax', but more probably Diagoras is employed about the court. Calianax's servants are at 'home', III.ii.40–1.

12. *ANTIPHILA*] a name apparently not attested in antiquity but formed from the common masculine name Antiphilus (which is the name of a character in Sidney's *Arcadia*). Antiphila is the name of a young woman beloved by Clinia in Terence's *Heautontimorumenos*.

13. *OLYMPIAS*] Olympias (4th century B.C.) was the wife of Philip III of Macedon and mother of Alexander the Great (*Oxford Classical Dictionary*, p. 621).

14. *DULA*] not properly a name but coined from *doulē*, the feminine of *doulos* (Greek), a slave.

15. *NIGHT*] Nyx (Greek), Nox (Latin), daughter of Chaos and one of the most aged deities. She appears in Spenser, *The Faerie Queene*, I, V, 20–44, and in Marlowe, *Hero and Leander*, II, 332–4.

16. *CYNTHIA*] the moon-goddess (Artemis, Diana, Phoebe), sister of Apollo the sun-god. She appears (as Cynthia) in Lyly, *Endymion*, and in Jonson, *Cynthia's Revels* and *The Masque of Blackness*, and (as Phoebe) in Drayton, *Endymion and Phoebe*.

17. *NEPTUNE*] originally the god of water, later identified with Poseidon, god of the sea. He appears in Marlowe, *Hero and Leander*, II, 155–226.

18. *AEOLUS*] god of the winds (a mortal in the *Odyssey*, X, a minor god in the *Aeneid*, I).

[Sea Gods ⎫
Winds   ⎬ *Masquers.*   20
Messenger.
Lady.
1 Gentleman ⎫
2 Gentleman ⎭ *of the King's bedchamber.*
Servant *to Amintor.*   25
Lords; Ladies; Servants; Guard of Soldiers.

The Scene: RHODES.]

19–20. Sea ... *Masquers.*] *Dyce* (Sea Gods), *Daniel* (Winds)*; not in Q1, Q2.*
21–6. Messenger ... Soldiers.] *This ed.; not in Q1, Q2.*   27. The Scene:
RHODES.] *Theobald; not in Q1, Q2.*

---

27. *RHODES*] the capital city of Rhodes, the most easterly island of the
Aegean Sea. By the 5th century B.C. it had colonies in Asia Minor and in
the western Mediterranean. Apart from a brief period of Persian domination
(355–333 B.C.) it remained independent and prosperous till its decline into a
second-rate power and ally of Rome in the 2nd and 1st centuries B.C. (*Oxford
Classical Dictionary*, p. 769).

The Maid's Tragedy
Act I

ACT I SCENE i

Enter CLEON, STRATO, LYSIPPUS, [*and*] DIPHILUS.

Cleon. The rest are making ready, sir.

Strato. So let them, there's time enough.

Diphilus. [*To Lysippus*] You are the brother to the King, my
    lord,
    We'll take your word.

Lysippus. Strato, thou hast some skill in poetry,   5
    What thinkst thou of a masque, will it be well?

Strato. As well as masques can be.

Lysippus.   As masques can be?

Strato. Yes, they must commend their king, and speak in

Act I Scene i] *Q1, Q2 (Actus. I. Scæn. I.).*   2. *Strato.*] *Q2 (Stra.);* LYS. *Q1.*
them, there's time enough] *Q1, Q2;* them./*Lysippus.* There's time enough
conj. this ed.   3–4. You ... word] *so Langbaine; as prose, Q1, Q2.*   3. the
brother] *Q2;* brother *Q1.*   6. thinkst thou] *Q1;* think'st *Q2.*   a] *Q1, Q2;*
the *Theobald.*   8. commend their king,] *Q2;* commend, *Q1.*

---

1. *The rest*] the other masquers (cf. l. 143).

2–4.] Q1's speech-prefix *Lys.* indicates that l. 2 was originally given to
Lysippus, and that its transference to the blunt Strato in Q2 was Beaumont's
afterthought. It can be delivered in a tone suitable to either speaker's character. The emphasis of Diphilus' speech will similarly vary according to
whether Lysippus or Strato speaks l. 2, making it either an agreement with
Lysippus or an indirect reprimand to Strato for interrupting before Lysippus
can answer Cleon; 'Lysippus, as the senior lord should, then soothes the
contention by asking for Strato's views on the notion of a masque celebrating
the wedding' (Gurr). But it is awkward that in Q2's text Lysippus never does
give his word that there's time enough (in performance he would have to nod
assent to Strato's remark). I conjecture that Beaumont intended the first three
words of l. 2 to be spoken by Strato and the last three by Lysippus. This
distribution would be 'in character' for both speakers, and would avoid
opening the play with a 'contention' that comes to nothing.

3. *the brother to*] For the idiom, cf. V.iii.40.

5. *Strato ... poetry*] Cf. SPEAKERS, l. 10 n. (*STRATO*).

6. *a masque*] i.e., the idea of celebrating the marriage with a masque. Strato,
in his reply, infers that the question is about the merit of the particular
masque; hence Theobald's emendation (not accepted by modern editors).

praise of the assembly, bless the bride and bridegroom in
person of some god: they're tied to rules of flattery.   10
Cleon. See, good my lord, who is returned.

Enter MELANTIUS.

Lysippus. Noble Melantius,
The land by me welcomes thy virtues home to Rhodes,
Thou that with blood abroad buyest us our peace.
The breath of kings is like the breath of gods: 15
My brother wished thee here, and thou art here.
He will be too kind, and weary thee
With often welcomes; but the time doth give thee
A welcome above his or all the world's.
Melantius. My lord, my thanks, but these scratched limbs of
mine   20
Have spoke my love and truth unto my friends

9. bridegroom] *Q2;* groome *Q1.*   10. they're] *Q2* (they'r); there *Q1.*
13–23. The land ... It ever] *so Langbaine (except ll. 17–19); all as verse,
Theobald; as prose, Q1 (to* it e-), *Q2 (to* it).   13. home to Rhodes,] *Q2;* home,
Q1.   14. blood abroad buyest] *Q2;* blowes abroad bringst *Q1.*   peace.]
Q2; peace at home, *Q1.*   17. too kind,] *Q2;* kinde; *Q1;* e'en too
kind, *Theobald;* too-too kind, *Daniel.*   18. welcomes] *Q2;* welcome *Q1.*
19. world's] *Q2;* world *Q1.*

---

13. *by me*] in my person as its spokesman.

to Rhodes] 'This reference, which creates metrical difficulties, was probably
added in revision to clarify the locale of the story' (Gurr). Otherwise the first
reference to Rhodes is at l. 38.

14. *with blood*] by shedding your blood in war; cf. *A King and No King,*
II.ii.87, where peace 'is not to be bought without our blouds'.

15. *The breath ... gods*] Cf. *R2,* I. iii.213–15. In *Philaster,* IV.iv.20–64, the
idea is treated with sarcastic scepticism.

17. *He ... kind*] Daniel's emendation 'too-too kind' is attractive, being
idiomatic (cf. *Love's Pilgrimage,* I.i.262: 'too too princely') and making a ten-
syllable line, but since the line is metrically defensible with the emphatic 'He'
as its first foot there is no obligation to emend, and since *Q2*'s 'too kind'
corrects *Q1*'s 'kind' it is unlikely that an intended insertion of 'too too' was
bungled by annotator or compositor.

18. *the time*] Gurr explains as 'The cause of his recall, the occasion of
Amintor's wedding to Melantius' sister. Melantius at this point is unaware of
his personal involvement with the wedding.' Alternatively 'the time' may refer
to the present peace and prosperity of Rhodes, due to Melantius' services (l.
14)

20. *these scratched limbs*] typical soldiers' self-disparagement: cf. *Coriolanus'*
'Scratches with briers' (*Cor.,* III.iii.51).

21. *spoke*] witnessed to.

More than my tongue e'er could. My mind's the same
It ever was to you; where I find worth,
I love the keeper, till he let it go,
And then I follow it.
Diphilus.　　　　　　　　Hail, worthy brother!　　　25
He that rejoices not at your return
In safety is mine enemy for ever.
Melantius. I thank thee, Diphilus; but thou art faulty:
I sent for thee to exercise thine arms
With me at Patria; thou cam'st not, Diphilus;　　30
'Twas ill.
Diphilus.　　　My noble brother, my excuse
Is my king's strict command, which you, my lord,
Can witness with me.
Lysippus.　　　　　　　'Tis most true, Melantius:
He might not come till the solemnities
Of this great match were past.
Diphilus.　　　　　　　　　Have you heard of it?　　35
Melantius. Yes, and I have given cause to those that here
Envy my deeds abroad to call me gamesome;
I have no other business here at Rhodes.
Lysippus. We have a masque tonight,
And you must tread a soldier's measure.　　　40
Melantius. These soft and silken wars are not for me:
The music must be shrill and all confused

32. strict] *Q2*; straight *Q1*.　　33. most true] *Q1*; true *Q2*.　　34. solemnities]
Q1; solemnitie *Q2*.　　36. Yes, and I] *This ed.*; Yes, and *Q1*; Yes, I *Q2*. that
here] *Q1*; that *Q2*.

---

24. *keeper*] possessor.
29. *exercise thine arms*] practise your military skill.
30. *Patria*] Patras, a port and fortified town in Greece (38.13 N, 21.45 E).
36. *and I have*] I retain the 'and' of Q1 since I think that the 'I' of Q2 was
intended as an insertion, not as a substitution; note that Q2 retains the comma
after 'Yes', instead of replacing it with a longer pause. 'I have' is to be elided to
a monosyllable.
37. *Envy*] grudge at. Probably here accentuated on the first syllable in the
modern way, though accentuation on the second syllable was still current in
the early 17th century.
gamesome] frolicsome, here with an implication of frivolity (as Brutus applies it
to Antony, *Caes.*, I.ii.28–9).
40. *measure*] stately dance.
42–3.] Cf. *Arcadia*, bk. III, chap. 15, p. 442, where the boastful warrior
Anaxius, presented with a serenade in his honour by Amphialus, tells him 'that

That stirs my blood, and then I dance with arms.
But is Amintor wed?
Diphilus.   This day.
Melantius. All joys upon him, for he is my friend.   45
Wonder not that I call a man so young my friend:
His worth is great; valiant he is and temperate,
And one that never thinks his life his own
If his friend need it. When he was a boy,
As oft as I returned (as, without boast,   50
I brought home conquest) he would gaze upon me
And view me round, to find in what one limb
The virtue lay to do those things he heard;
Then would he wish to see my sword, and feel
The quickness of the edge, and in his hand   55
Weigh it; he oft would make me smile at this.
His youth did promise much, and his ripe years
Will see it all performed.

Enter ASPATIA, *passing, attended by* ANTIPHILA *and* OLYMPIAS.

Hail, maid and wife!
Thou fair Aspatia, may the holy knot
That thou hast tied today last till the hand   60
Of age undo't! Mayst thou bring a race
Unto Amintor that may fill the world
Successively with soldiers!

Aspatia.   My hard fortunes

43. dance with arms] *Q2;* daunce *Q1.*   46. so young my friend] *Q2;* so
young *Q1.*   47. he is and temperate] *Q2;* he is *Q1.*   56. Weigh] *Q2;*
Weighes *Q1.*   58.1. *Enter* ASPATIA, *passing, attended by* ANTIPHILA *and*
OLYMPIAS.] *Q1 (subst.: Enter Aspatia passing with attendance.);* Enter Aspatia,
passing by. *Q2.*   58. Hail] *Q1;* Melan. Haile *Q2.*

for his part he liked no musick, but the neighing of horses, the sound of
trumpets, and the cries of yeelding persons'.
    53. *virtue*] power.
    55. *quickness*] sharpness, keenness (*OED,* 5).
    58.1.] I follow Q1 here because I suspect that Q2's direction may have been
abbreviated from that of Q1 in order to save space taken up in the second half
of l. 58 (treated as a separate line in both Qq) by Q2's superfluous and
unusually long speech prefix *Melan.* (The usual form is *Mel., Melant.* at
IV.i.1.1 being the only other exception.) The presence of Antiphila and
Olympias is theatrically important here because of the dignity that it confers on
Aspatia. It also prepares us for their presence in II.ii.

Deserve not scorn, for I was never proud
When they were good.   65
    [*Exeunt*]ASPATIA,[ANTIPHILA, *and* OLYMPIAS].
Melantius. How's this?
Lysippus. You are mistaken, sir, she is not married.
Melantius. You said Amintor was.
Diphilus. 'Tis true, but—
Melantius.   Pardon me, I did receive
Letters at Patria from my Amintor   70
That he should marry her.
Diphilus.   And so it stood
In all opinion long, but your arrival
Made me imagine you had heard the change.
Melantius. Who hath he taken, then?
Lysippus.   A lady, sir,
That bears the light about her, and strikes dead   75
With flashes of her eye: the fair Evadne,
Your virtuous sister.
Melantius.   Peace of heart betwixt them!
But this is strange.
Lysippus.   The King my brother did it
To honour you, and these solemnities

65.1. *Exeunt* ... OLYMPIAS] *This ed.; Exit Aspatia Q1, Q2.*   67. mistaken,
sir,] *Q1* (mistaken sir,); mistaken, for *Q2.*   74. hath] *Q2;* has *Q1.*
75. about] *Q2;* aboue *Q1.*

---

67. *sir*] Q1's reading is consistent with Lysippus' politeness (the speech is
rather impolite without it), and it marks off the factual statement 'she is
not married'; Q2's 'for' may be the compositor's accidental substitution,
influenced by 'for' in the same position and with the same punctuation three
lines earlier (l. 64).

69. *Pardon me*] i.e., for contradicting you.

75. *That ... about her*] who carries the light on her person (*OED*, about, 4).
The phrase is obviously parallel with 'and strikes dead / With flashes of her
eye' (ll. 75–6, where the metaphor is from lightning-flashes), so Dyce's
interpretation that Q1's 'above her' means 'above Aspatia' is ruled out (as it
also is by metre, since 'her' cannot carry a stress and would require one for this
sense). The meaning is debatable. *OED* does not record 'light' as a synonym
for 'lightning'. The sense 'sunlight' (*OED*, 2) might be applicable to 'shining,
golden hair' (Norland, who reads 'above' with Q1): cf. IV.i.181, 'in the
compass of the light', where 'the light' is perhaps used for the sun itself.
Alternatively the whole phrase refers to Lucifer (Latin: 'light-bearer'), not as
the name of the rebel archangel but as that of 'the morning-star; the planet
Venus when she appears in the sky before sunrise' (*OED*, 1).

Are at his charge.   80
Melantius. 'Tis royal like himself; but I am sad
　　My speech bears so infortunate a sound
　　To beautiful Aspatia. There is rage
　　Hid in her father's breast, Calianax,
　　Bent long against me, and 'a should not think,   85
　　If I could call it back, that I would take
　　So base revenges as to scorn the state
　　Of his neglected daughter. Holds he still
　　His greatness with the King?
Lysippus.   Yes, but this lady
　　Walks discontented, with her wat'ry eyes   90
　　Bent on the earth. The unfrequented woods
　　Are her delight, and when she sees a bank
　　Stuck full of flowers she with a sigh will tell
　　Her servants what a pretty place it were
　　To bury lovers in, and make her maids   95
　　Pluck 'em and strow her over like a corse.
　　She carries with her an infectious grief
　　That strikes all her beholders; she will sing
　　The mournfull'st things that ever ear hath heard,
　　And sigh, and sing again; and when the rest   100

81–2. 'Tis ... sound] *so Theobald;* Tis ... himselfe, / But ... sound *Q1, Q2.*
82. infortunate] *Q1;* vnfortunate *Q2.*   85. 'a] *Q1;* he *Q2.*   86. If I could]
Q2; Could I but *Q1.*   87. So] *Q2;* Such *Q1.*   88–93.] *so Langbaine;* Of ...
king? / *Lis.* Yes ... walkes / Discontented ... earth: / The ... delight, / And
... flowers, / Shee ... tell *Q2;* Of ... daughter. / LIS. O t'were pittie, for this
Lady sir, / Sits discontented ... earth, / In vnfrequented ... delight, / Where
when ... flowers, / Then she will sit, and sigh, and tell *Q1.*   91. earth.] *Q1*
(corrected) (earth,), *Q2;* ear *Q1 (uncorrected).*   96. her over] *Q2;* them ouer
her *Q1.*   100. sigh] *Q2;* swound *Q1.*

---

80. *at his charge*] 'Not only at his command but at his expense' (Gurr, who
points out that Beaumont's *Masque of the Inner Temple and Gray's Inn* (1613)
cost over £5,000).
　81. *royal*] generous, munificent (*OED*, 9).
　82. *infortunate*] unfortunate, inauspicious.
　85. *'a*] he.
　90. *wat'ry*]) tearful.
　96. *strow*] strew. It was not unusual to carry corpses to burial in open coffins
strewn with flowers; cf. *Wint.*, IV.iv.127–32, and Ophelia's burial in *Ham.*,
V.i.212–44. Aspatia's wish to be strewn with the flowers growing on a bank is
anticipated by Bellario's in *Philaster*, IV.vi.2–6.
　98. *strikes*] afflicts, like a disease (*OED*, 45.b).

Of our young ladies in their wanton blood
Tell mirthful tales in course that fill the room
With laughter, she will with so sad a look
Bring forth a story of the silent death
Of some forsaken virgin, which her grief   105
Will put in such a phrase that ere she end
She'll send them weeping one by one away.
Melantius. She has a brother under my command
Like her, a face as womanish as hers,
But with a spirit that hath much outgrown   110
The number of his years.

Enter AMINTOR.

Cleon.   My lord the bridegroom!
Melantius. I might run fiercely, not more hastily
Upon my foe. [*Embracing him*] I love thee well, Amintor;
My mouth is much too narrow for my heart.
I joy to look upon those eyes of thine;   115
Thou art my friend, —but my disordered speech
Cuts off my love.
Amintor.   Thou art Melantius:
All love is spoke in that. A sacrifice
To thank the gods Melantius is returned
In safety! Victory sits on his sword   120
As she was wont: may she build there and dwell,
And may thy armour be, as it hath been,
Only thy valour and thine innocence!
What endless treasures would our enemies give
That I might hold thee still thus!

---

101. our] *Q2;* your *Q1.*   102. fill] *Q2;* fils *Q1.*   112. fiercely] *Q1, Q2;*
more fiercely *conj. Coleridge;* fiercelier *conj. Daniel.*   113. *Embracing him*]
This ed.; not in Q1, Q2.

---

101. *wanton blood*] frolicsome spirits.
102. *in course*] in turn.
103–7. *she . . . away*] The syntax is irregular, but the sense is clear, and the
rhythm is well calculated to convey the sorrowful mood.
112. *fiercely*] more fiercely. The context makes the elliptical expression clear.
121 *build*] i.e., like a nesting bird; Victory is visualised as winged.
122–3. *And . . . innocence!*] And may thy valour and thine innocence
continue to be a sufficient protection to thee! Cf. Jonson, *Poetaster*, V.iii.61–
7: 'A iust man cannot feare . . . ; / His innocence is armour' gainst all these.'

Melantius.   I am poor   125
    In words, but, credit me, young man, thy mother
    Could do no more but weep for joy to see thee
    After long absence; all the wounds I have
    Fetched not so much away, nor all the cries
    Of widowed mothers. But this is peace,   130
    And that was war.
Amintor.   Pardon, thou holy god
    Of marriage bed, and frown not I am forced
    In answer of such noble tears as those
    To weep upon my wedding day.
Melantius. I fear thou art grown too fickle, for I hear   135
    A lady mourns for thee, men say to death,
    Forsaken of thee, on what terms I know not.
Amintor. She had my promise, but the King forbade it,
    And made me make this worthy change, thy sister,
    Accompanied with graces all about her,   140
    With whom I long to lose my lusty youth

125–7.] *so Theobald;* That ... thus. / MEL. I am ... man / Thy ... see thee
Q1, Q2.   127. could do no] *Q1;* could no *Q2.*   128. have] *Q1, Q2;* gave
Daniel.   133. those] *Q2;* these *Q1.*   135. fickle] *Q2;* cruell *Q1.*   140. all
about her] *This ed.;* about her *Q1, Q2;* aboue her *Q3;* far above her *Theobald.*

---

    125. *still thus*] i.e., for ever pinioned.
    126–7. *thy mother ... joy*] Not even thy mother could shed more joyful
tears.
    128–30. *all the wounds ... mothers*] Melantius insists that he wept fewer
tears of pain at his wounds or of sympathy at bereaved mothers' outcries.
Daniel's emendation 'gave' (in order to make him stoical about his own
wounds) makes him improbably sentimental about the wounds of his enemies,
for, to make sense in the context, the tears must be those shed by him.
    131–2. *thou ... bed*] Hymen.
    132. *I am forced*] because I am forced.
    133. *those*] those of yours.
    140. *Accompanied ... her*] a defective line in all the Quartos. Q3, whose
emendation 'above' has no authority, changes the line's sense to involve a
contrast with Aspatia and ruins its metre ('*a*-bove *her*'): editors following Q3
have usually restored the feminine ending by further corrupting the line ('far
above her'). My emendation draws its image from the episode in Spenser's
Faerie Queene, VI, x, 10–16, in which 'the Graces, daughters of delight, /
Handmaids of Venus' are seen encircling Colin Clout's beloved amid a troop of
dancing maidens; cf. also *Love's Pilgrimage*, V.iv. 64–5: 'Methought a
thousand graces met / To make you lovely.'
    141–2. *lose ... arms*] i.e., consume my youthful energy in sexual pleasure.

And grow old in her arms.
Melantius.   Be prosperous!

Enter Messenger.

Messenger. [*To Lysippus*] My lord, the masquers rage for
    you.
Lysippus.   We are gone.   [*Exit* Messenger.]
Cleon, Strato, Diphilus. [*To Lysippus*] We'll all attend you.
                Exeunt LYSIPPUS, CLEON, STRATO, [*and*] DIPHILUS.
Amintor.   We shall trouble you
    With our solemnities.
Melantius.   Not so, Amintor.   145
    But if you laugh at my rude carriage
    In peace, I'll do as much for you in war
    When you come thither. But I have a mistress
    To bring to your delights, rough though I am;
    I have a mistress and she has a heart,   150
    She says, but, trust me, it is stone, no better;
    There is no place that I can challenge in't.

142.1. *Enter* Messenger.] *Q2; not in Q1.*   143. *Messenger.*] *Q2;* AMINT. *Q1.*
143–4. We are ... trouble you] *This ed.;* LIS. We are gone, / Cleon, Strato,
Diphilus. / Exeunt Lysippus, Cleon, Steat [*sic*], Diphilus. [S.D. *centred*] /
AMINT. Weele all attend you, we shall trouble you, *Q1, Q2 (without S.D.)*
143.1. *Exit* Messenger.] *This ed.; Dyce (at l. 144.1); not in Q1, Q2.*
147. peace] *Q2;* sports *Q1.*   152. challenge in't.] *Q3;* challenge gentlemen,
Q1; challenge: *Q2.*

143–5.] The original version of this passage (Q1) ineptly postpones
Amintor's urgent message. The revised version (Q2) removes the ineptitude by
introducing the Messenger. The consequent *Exeunt* was inadvertently omitted
in Q2.
    143. *rage for you*] are impatient (*OED*, 7) for your presence.
    144. *We'll all attend you*] These words must have been meant to be spoken
by Cleon, Strato and Diphilus, whose names were meant as speech prefixes
and not as part of Lysippus' speech as Qq print them. Amintor is to be a
spectator of the masque in which Lysippus and his companions are taking
part, and should be attending on his bride rather than on Lysippus.
    146. *rude carriage*] raw behaviour.
    152. *There ... in't*] I think Q3's emendation restores the original line. I take
Q1's 'challenge gentlemen' to be an expansion of what the compositor misread
as 'challenge gent'; in the copy for Q2 the correction was indicated but only
partly performed ('gentlemen' was deleted but 'in't' was not inserted). The line
in Q2 would still be defective if 'There' were interpreted as 'in her heart' and
stressed accordingly.
    challenge] claim (*OED*, 5).

But you stand still, and here my way lies.

Exeunt [severally].

[ACT I   SCENE ii]

Enter CALIANAX *with* DIAGORAS.

Calianax. Diagoras, look to the doors better, for shame: you let
in all the world, and anon the King will rail at me. Why,
very well said! By Jove, the King will have the show i'th'
court.

Diagoras. Why do you swear so, my lord? You know he'll have   5
it here.

Calianax. By this light, if he be wise, he will not.

Diagoras. And if he will not be wise, you are forsworn.

Calianax. One may sweat his heart out with swearing, and get
thanks on no side. I'll be gone, look to't who will.   10

Diagoras. My lord, I shall never keep them out. Pray stay, your
looks will terrify them.

Calianax. My looks terrify them, you coxcombly ass, you? I'll
be judged by all the company whether thou hast not a
worse face than I.   15

153.1. *Exeunt [severally]*.] Theobald; Exeunt. Q1; Exit. Q2.

0.1. *with* DIAGORAS] Q2; *and Diagoras* Q1.   2. rail at] Q2; be angry with
Q1.   3. i'th'] Q3 (i'th); i'th the Q1, Q2.   5–6.] *so Weber;* Why ... Lord, /
You ... here. Q1, Q2.   9–12.] *so Q2;* One ... get / Thankes ... will. /
DIAG. My Lord ... out, / Your ... them. Q1.   9. may] Q2; must Q1.
sweat] Q1; sweare Q2.   his heart out] Q2; out his heart Q1.   11. Pray stay]
Q2; *not in* Q1.   13. ass, you?] Q2 (asse you,); asse, Q1.   14. judged] Q3;
iudge Q1, Q2.

153. *But ... lies*] 'But I detain you, and neglect my own engagement'
(Colman).
   here] (two syllables) A natural stress is thus thrown on 'my'.
   2–3. *Why ... said!*] Well done! That's right! cf. Onions, *Shakespeare
Glossary*, 'well said!'
   4 *court*] courtyard (*OED*, 1).
   5. *swear so*] swear that he'll have it there.
   here] in the hall.
   7. *By this light*] (a frequent asseveration) by this daylight.
   13. *coxcombly*] foolish.
   14. *all the company*] everybody here, i.e., the theatre audience (not the stage
audience of ll. 31–2); cf. *Tw.N.*, I.iii.53–4, where Sir Andrew says to Sir
Toby, of Maria, 'By my troth, I would not undertake her in this company'
(they are the only three characters on stage).

Diagoras. I mean because they know you and your office.

Calianax. Office! I would I could put it off! I am sure I sweat
   quite through my office. I might have made room at
   my daughter's wedding; they ha' near killed her amongst
   them. And now I must do service for him that hath for-   20
   saken her. Serve that will!   *Exit* CALIANAX.

Diagoras. He's so humorous since his daughter was forsaken!
                                             Knock within.
   Hark, hark! There, there! So, so! Coads, coads! What
   now?

Melantius. (*Within*) Open the door.   25

Diagoras. Who's there?

Melantius. [*Within*] Melantius.

Diagoras. I hope your lordship brings no troop with you, for
   if you do I must return them. [*Opens the door.*]

18. through my] *Q2;* through in my *Q1.*   20. And] *Q2;* But *Q1.*
22.1. *Knock within*] *Q1, Q2 (after l. 24).*   23. There, there!] *Q2;* whose
there, *Q1.*   So, so!] *Q2; not in Q1.*   Coads, coads!] *Q1 (codes, codes,),
Q2.*   25. *Within*] *Q1, Q2 (above door).*   26. Who's there?] *Q2;* Who i'st.
Q1.   27. *Within*] Weber; *not in Q1, Q2.*   28. troop with you] *Q2;* troop *Q1.*

---

16. *your office*] your official position. Calianax appears to be Lord
Chamberlain of the Household; cf. *H8,* I.iv, where the Lord Chamberlain
organises the spectators' seating and ushers in the masquers at Wolsey's
palace, and V.iv, where the Porter and his Man are keeping back the crowd
outside the royal palace at Princess Elizabeth's christening, and the Lord
Chamberlain superintends them.

17–18. *Office! . . . office*] Calianax, wilfully or obtusely, misunderstands
Diphilus as referring to his gown (as sign of his office; *OED* does not record
this use of 'office'; Daniel compares Prospero's 'Lie there my art', *Tp.,* I.ii.25).
Coleridge notes the word-play: 'The syllable *off* reminds the testy statesman of
his robe, and he carries on the image' (*Literary Remains* (1836–9), II, 293,
cited by Dyce).

18. *made room*] cleared the way, acted as usher; cf. l. 104.

21. *Serve that will!*] Let him (i.e., anyone) serve that chooses!

22. *humorous*] moody; cf. the description of Calianax in the list of SPEAKERS.

23*There . . . so!*] either equivalent to 'All right! I hear you!' or spoken as he
pushes the door closed against would-be intruders.

Coads] not recorded (in any spelling) in *OED,* but evidently a 'corrupt or
minced' form of 'God's' (*OED,* God, 14: 'Cods' and 'Cuds' are the closest
analogues). A very mild oath, as it is used by the over-scrupulous Widow in
The Puritan, IV.ii.26–7: 'Coades? What doe you meane, Gentlemen? fie, did
I not giue you your answeres?' (*Shakespeare Apocrypha,* p. 242).

28. *troop*] company; cf. 'the King's troop', l. 32, but possibly alluding in a
humorous-complimentary fashion to Melantius' position as a general (in which
case the notion of repelling an army suits Diagoras' present sitution).

Enter MELANTIUS *and a* Lady.

Melantius. None but this lady, sir.   30

Diagoras. The ladies are all placed above, save those that come
in the King's troop; the best of Rhodes sit there, and
there's room.

Melantius. I thank you, sir. [*To the Lady*] When I have seen you
placed, madam, I must attend the King, but, the masque   35
done, I'll wait on you again.

                          Exit MELANTIUS [*and the*] Lady [*at the*]
                              other door [*,which Diagoras opens*].

Diagoras. [*To those within*] Stand back there! Room for my lord
Melantius! Pray bear back! This is no place for such
youths and their trulls. Let the doors shut again. Ay, do
your heads itch? I'll scratch them for you! [*Shuts the door.*]   40
So, now thrust and hang!

                          [*Knocking within*]

Again? Who is't now? I cannot blame my lord Calianax for
going away. Would he were here! He would run raging
amongst them, and break a dozen wiser heads than his own

---

29. *Opens the door.*] Weber; *not in* Q1, Q2.   33. and there's room] *Q2; there
is no roome* Q1.   36.1.] *Q1 (Exit Melantius Lady other dore.); not in* Q2.
which Diagoras opens] *Dyce (subst.); not in* Q1, Q2.   39. again. Ay, do] *Q2
(agen: I, do); agen, no; do* Q1.   40. them for you] *Q2; them* Q1.   *Shuts the
door.*] *Weber; not in* Q1, Q2.   41.1 *Knocking within*] *Weber (subst.); not in*
Q1, Q2.   43. going away] *Q2; giuing way* Q1.   44. wiser heads than his
own] *Q2; heads* Q1.

---

29. *return them*] send them back again (*OED*, 15).

31–3. *The ladies ... there's room*] Diagoras here indicates the upper area
'above' the stage. It seems that some of the actors, dressed as ladies, are
stationed there already. Later (V.ii) it serves as the walls of the fort.

33. *there's room*] up there there's room.

36.1. *other door*] i.e., the door through which they did not enter. This is
also the door through which Calianax departed (l. 21). When Melantius enters
again he uses the original door (ll. 51–5), Calianax re-entering by the other
(l. 52.1). The phrase '*other door*' implies that only two stage doors were
required in the original staging.

37–8. *Stand ... bear back*] Cf. Jonson, *Cynthia's Revels*, V.iii. 17–40:
'Who's there? beare backe there. Stand from the doore ... Make place. Beare
backe there.'

39. *trulls*] wenches.

39–40. *Ay, do ... you!*] i.e., Are you asking to have your heads cuffed?

41. *hang*] be hanged.

in the twinkling of an eye. [*To those within*] What's the 45
news now?

[*A Voice*] *within*. I pray you, can you help me to the speech of
the master-cook?

Diagoras. If I open the door I'll cook some of your calves'
heads. Peace, rogues! 50

[*Knocking within*]

Again? Who is't?

Melantius. (*Within*) Melantius.

Enter CALIANAX.

Calianax. Let him not in.

Diagoras. O, my lord, 'a must. [*To those within*] Make room
there for my lord! 55

Enter MELANTIUS.

Is your lady placed?

Melantius. Yes, sir, I thank you. My lord Calianax, well met!
Your causeless hate to me I hope is buried.

Calianax. Yes, I do service for your sister here,
That brings mine own poor child to timeless death; 60
She loves your friend Amintor, such another
False-hearted lord as you.

Melantius. You do me wrong,
A most unmanly one, and I am slow
In taking vengeance, but be well advised.

Calianax. It may be so. [*To Diagoras*] Who placed the lady
there 65

---

47. *A Voice*] Dyce; *not in Q1, Q2. within*] *Q1, Q2 (above* the speech).
50.1. *Knocking within*] *Weber (subst.); not in Q1, Q2. 52.1. Enter*
CALIANAX.] *Q1; Enter Calianax to Melantius. Q2. 55.1. Enter* MELANTIUS.]
Q1; not in Q2. 61–2. She . . . you] *so Theobald; as prose, Q1, Q2. 64.* but
be] *Q2;* be *Q1. 65–6.] so Brereton; as prose, Q2.*

---

45. *twinkling*] instant (*OED*, 3: the time taken in winking the eye).
47. *help . . . speech of*] allow me to speak to.
49–50. *calves' heads*] fools' heads (*OED*, calf, 1.c).
54. *'a must*] he must (come in).
60. *timeless*] untimely (*OED*, 1).
65. *It may be so*] not an admission that he may be at fault, but a grumbling
retort equivalent to 'That's all very well'.
the lady there] that lady.

So near the presence of the King?
Melantius. I did.
Calianax.   My lord, she must not sit there.
Melantius.   Why?
Calianax. The place is kept for women of more worth.
Melantius. More worth than she! It misbecomes your age
     And place to be thus womanish. Forbear!   70
     What you have spoke I am content to think
     The palsy shook your tongue to.
Calianax.   Why, 'tis well
     If I stand here to place men's wenches.
Melantius.   I shall quite forget
     This place, thy age, my safety, and through all
     Cut that poor sickly week thou hast to live   75
     Away from thee.
Calianax.   Nay, I know you can fight for your whore.
Melantius. Bate me the King, and be he flesh and blood
     'A lies that says it! Thy mother at fifteen
     Was black and sinful to her.
Diagoras. [*To Melantius*]   Good my lord—
Melantius. Some god pluck threescore years from that fond
     man,   80
     That I may kill him and not stain mine honour!
     It is the curse of soldiers, that in peace
     They shall be braved by such ignoble men

66. So near the presence of the King?] *Q2; not in Q1.*   70. thus] *Q2; so Q1.*
72-6.] *This ed.; as prose, Q1, Q2.*   72. Why, 'tis] *Q2;* Tis *Q1.*   73. I shall
quite] *Q1;* I shall *Q2.*   77. Bate me] *Q1;* Bate *Q2.*   he] *Q2; of Q1.*

66. *So near ... King*] This phrase, added in revision, gives Calianax some
ground for objecting to what Melantius has done, while his main purpose of
spiting Melantius remains clear.
70. *womanish*] like a woman (derogatory); here, petty-minded.
77. *Bate me*] make an exception of (*OED*, 6.b: strike off, deduct).
78. *'A lies*] i.e., I will give him the lie. To do so would lead to a duel. At this
early stage of the play Melantius regards the King as being out of reach of such
redress.
79. *to*] compared with.
80. *threescore years*] Since Melantius can hardly be younger than thirty, this
makes Calianax well over eighty years old. Melantius, in his anger, is speaking
hyperbolically.
     fond] idiotic (*OED*, 3).
83. *braved*) defied (*OED*, 1).

As, if the land were troubled, would with tears
And knees beg succour from 'em. Would that blood,   85
That sea of blood, that I have lost in fight,
Were running in thy veins, that it might make thee
Apt to say less, or able to maintain,
Shouldst thou say more!—This Rhodes, I see, is nought
But a place privileged to do men wrong.   90
Calianax. Ay, you may say your pleasure.

Enter AMINTOR.

Amintor.   What vile injury
Has stirred my worthy friend, who is as slow
To fight with words as he is quick of hand?
Melantius. That heap of age, which I should reverence
If it were temperate, but testy years   95
Are most contemptible.
Amintor. [*To Calianax*]   Good sir, forbear.
Calianax. [*To Melantius*] There is just such another as yourself.
Amintor. He will wrong you, or me, or any man,
And talk as if he had no life to lose,
Since this our match. The King is coming in;   100
I would not for more wealth than I enjoy
He should perceive you raging. He did hear
You were at difference now, which hastened him.
Calianax. [*To those within*] Make room there!
Hautboys play within.

85. that blood] *Q2;* the blood *Q1.*   88. or] *Q2;* and *Q1.*   91. say] *Q2;* talke
Q1.   vile injury] *Q2* (vilde iniurie)*;* vilde wrong *Q1.*   93. hand] *Q2;* hands
Q1.   94. *Melantius.*] *Q2;* CAL. *Q1.*   100. coming] *Q1 (corrected), Q2;* come
Q1 (uncorrected).

87–9. *that ... more*] Melantius 'is as slow / To fight with words as he is
quick of hand' (ll. 92–3), a typical honest soldier (cf. ll. 82–5). If Calianax had
Melantius' blood in his veins he would have these good qualities. In a more
general sense, Melantius is declaring that Calianax has the querulousness and
impotence of dotage.
88. *maintain*] uphold (with weapons).
90. *privileged ... wrong*] given the special freedom to insult people with
impunity.
94. *heap of age*]) Cf. *2H6*, V.i.157 (Clifford to Richard): 'Hence, heap of
wrath, foul indigested lump, / As crooked in thy manners as thy shape!' This
comparable use of 'heap' suggests that Calianax is bent with age.
104.1. Hautboys] oboes.

Enter KING, EVADNE, ASPATIA, Lords *and* Ladies.

King. Melantius, thou art welcome, and my love   105
    Is with thee still; but this is not a place
    To brabble in. Calianax, join hands.
Calianax. He shall not have mine hand.
King.   This is no time
    To force you to't. I do love you both.
    Calianax, you look well to your office,   110
    And you, Melantius, are welcome home.
    Begin the masque.
Melantius. Sister, I joy to see you and your choice.
    You looked with my eyes when you took that man;
    Be happy in him.

                                    Recorders [*play*].

Evadne.   O my dearest brother,   115
    Your presence is more joyful than this day
    Can be unto me.

105. *King.*] *Q2*; *not in Q1.*   my] *Q2*; thy *Q1.*   106. thee] *Q2*; me *Q1.*
115.1. *Recorders play.*] *Weber*; *Recorders Q1, Q2.*   116–17. than this day /
Can be unto me.] *so Theobald; as prose, Q2*; then this day, *Q1.*   117.1. *The
Masque.*] *Q2 (The Maske.)*; *Maske. Q1.*

104.4. Enter ... Ladies.] 'Perhaps the entrance of Lysippus, Diphilus,
Cleon and Strato is not marked because they assisted in the performance of the
Masque' (Dyce).
    106. *still*] always (*OED*, 3).
    107. *brabble*] brawl.
    114. *You ... man*] Cf. *MND*, I.i.56: 'I would my father look'd but with my
eyes.' Melantius not only approves Evadne's choice but also loves her
husband.
    115.1.] The recorders, being the musical introduction to the masque, do not
play 'within'. They are probably played 'above'.
    117.1. *The Masque*] The best short account of the masque is still P.
Simpson, 'The Masque', chap. XXVI of *Shakespeare's England*, II, 311–35.
'Masques were always staged with considerable scenic elaboration, particularly
for entries and exits. In this masque a trap is used for Night and Neptune to
arise from, and for Neptune and the Sea Gods to leave by, and a rock covers
one entrance, for Aeolus to emerge from. Cynthia and the dancers presumably
enter normally' (Gurr). I agree with Gurr as regards the stage setting, though I
think that the Winds and the Sea Gods consistently make their entrances and
exits through the rock and the trap respectively. The manner of Cynthia's
entry and exit is debatable (see ll. 127.1 n., 283 n.). Aeolus' cave could be
moved into position between scenes i and ii; its use as an ordinary door at ll.
21, 36.1 and 52.1 would add realism and in the last instance humour (when
Calianax emerges blustering from it).

The Masque.

NIGHT *rises in mists.*

Night. Our reign is come, for in the raging sea
         The Sun is drowned, and with him fell the Day.
         Bright Cynthia, hear my voice; I am the Night,   120
         For whom thou bear'st about thy borrowed light.
         Appear; no longer thy pale visage shroud,
         But strike thy silver horns quite through a cloud,
         And send a beam upon my swarthy face,
         By which I may discover all the place   125
         And persons, and how many longing eyes
         Are come to wait on our solemnities.

---

118. come] *Q2;* now *Q1.*   raging] *Q2;* quenching *Q1.*   126. and how] *Q2;*
that haue *Q1.*

117.2. in mists] That Night's mists were made with smoke (Gurr, *The
Shakespearean Stage,* 1574–1642 (Cambridge, 1970), p. 120) I think very
improbable: I know of no evidence that smoke was ever used for mist or fog in
the period of the play, and real smoke would be hard to control. More
probably Night's mists were made of fine linen or cotton, dark in colour, and
either loosely attached to her costume or stretched over a light framework to
look like clouds and so pushed up through the trap as she rose. Cf. Marlowe,
Hero and Leander, I, 189–91: 'And Night, deep-drench'd in misty Acheron, /
Heav'd up her head, and half the world upon / Breath'd darkness forth (dark
night is Cupid's day)'. In *Love's Pilgrimage,* V.i.16, Beaumont and Fletcher
have 'A mist as thicke as ever darknesse was'.
    118. raging] Turner argues that since 'quenching' better fits the sense of l.
118, and Boreas has not yet broken his chain, 'raging' is a memorial error of
Q2's compositor. This is doubtful because (1) he was here printing from Q1,
where 'quenching' is conspicuous in the first line of the speech, and (2) if he set
the pages in the usual order (whether beginning with the outer or inner forme)
he could have set nothing about Boreas' escaping (B3v) or his raising a storm
(B4) before the present passage (B2)—only perhaps ll. 180–96 about Boreas'
roughness in general (B3). So it is safer to regard 'raging' as an authorial
change.
    sea] (pronounced to rhyme with 'Day').
    127.1. Enter *CYNTHIA.*] 'Qy "Descend"?' (Dyce). This is possible: cf.
Cym., V.iv.93: '*Iupiter descends* ...' (F 1623), *Tp.,* IV.i.74: '*Iuno descends.*'
(F 1623). Both were Blackfriars plays like *The Maid's Tragedy.* But the '*Enter*'
of Qq 1 and 2 weighs against a descent here. Cynthia's costume in Jonson's
The Masque of Blackness (ll. 214–16) is described as follows: '*Her garments
White, and Siluer, the dressing of her head antique; & crown'd with a* Luminarie,
or Sphere of light'.

Enter CYNTHIA.

How dull and black am I! I could not find
This beauty without thee, I am so blind.
Methinks they show like to those eastern streaks   130
That warn us hence before the morning breaks.
Back, my pale servant, for these eyes know how
To shoot far more and quicker rays than thou.

Cynthia. Great queen, they be a troop for whom alone
One of my clearest moons I have put on;   135
A troop that looks as if thyself and I
Had plucked our reins in, and our whips laid by,
To gaze upon these mortals, that appear
Brighter than we.

Night.   Then let us keep 'em here,
And never more our chariots drive away,   140
But hold our places and outshine the Day.

Cynthia. Great queen of shadows, you are pleased to speak
Of more than may be done; we may not break
The gods' decrees, but when our time is come
Must drive away and give the Day our room.   145
Yet whilst our reign lasts, let us stretch our power
To give our servants one contented hour,
With such unwonted solemn grace and state
As may for ever after force them hate
Our brother's glorious beams, and wish the Night,   150
Crowned with a thousand stars and our cold light;

128. I could] *Q2;* can I *Q1.*   129. I am] *Q2;* am I *Q1.*   138. these mortals, that] *Q2;* those, that *Q1.*   141. hold] *Q1;* keepe *Q2.*   146-55.] *Q2; not in Q1.*   150. wish] *Q3;* with *Q2; not in Q1.*

---

131. *this beauty*] the beauty of the stage audience of court ladies.

132. *these eyes*] the eyes of the court ladies.

135. *One ... moons*] Cf. Jonson, *Cynthia's Revels,* I.i.92-7: '*Diana ...* hath here ... proclaim'd a solemne reuells, which (her god-head put off) shee will descend to grace, with the full and royall expence of one of her cleerest moones.'

137. *reins*] Night and Cynthia are supposed to have arrived in 'chariots' (l. 140).

142. *shadows*] darkness (*OED,* 2.a).

145. *room*] space.

147. *our servants*] i.e. (with playful social indecorum), the noble stage audience.

150. *Our*] my (the royal plural). Elsewhere the plural pronouns refer to both Night and Cynthia, except perhaps at l. 280.
wish] desire.

For almost all the world their service bend
To Phoebus, and in vain my light I lend,
Gazed on unto my setting from my rise
Almost of none but of unquiet eyes.   155

Night. Then shine at full, fair queen, and by thy power
Produce a birth, to crown this happy hour,
Of nymphs and shepherds; let their songs discover,
Easy and sweet, who is a happy lover;
Or, if thou woot, then call Endymion   160
From the sweet flowery bed he lies upon
On Latmus' top, thy pale beams drawn away,
And of this long night let him make his day.

---

156. fair] *Q2;* pale *Q1.*   thy] *Q2;* that *Q1.*   157. crown] *Q2;* fill *Q1.*
158. let] *Q2;* and let *Q1.*   160. then call] *Gurr;* thine owne *Q1;* then call
thine owne *Q2.*   161. bed] *Q2;* banck *Q1.*   162. top] *Q2;* brow *Q1.*
163.] *This ed.;* And of his long night let him make thy day *Q1;* And of this long
night let him make this day *Q2;* And of this long night let him make a day *Q3;*
And of his long night let him make a day *Dyce;* And of his long night let him
make this day *Daniel.*

---

155. *unquiet eyes*] the eyes of restless, uneasy persons.
157. *Produce a birth*] i.e., as Lucina (*lucina dea,* the light-bringing goddess),
a Latin title given to Diana (Cynthia) as presiding over childbirth and bringing
children into the light of the world. Here used figuratively for 'provide a
show'.
158. *nymphs and shepherds*] The chief themes of the pastoral convention in
literature were carefree innocence and a preoccupation with love.
discover] show (*OED,* 4).
159. *Easy and sweet*] (epithets qualifying 'songs').
160. *woot*] wilt.
then call Endymion] Gurr explains Q2's reading as 'a botched correction, the
Q2 compositor printing both cancellation and correction'. If, as is probable,
Beaumont made this revision, he failed to notice that Cynthia's rejoinder
('Thou dreamst ... not mine') no longer related closely to Night's speech
('thine own Endymion').
162. *Thy pale ... away*] when thy pale beams are drawn away. Endymion
was beloved of Cynthia, who cast him into a deep sleep on Mount Latmus in
Caria (in the south part of Turkey, about 100 miles north of Rhodes) so that
she could visit him undisturbed.
163. *And ... day*] And let him make this long night (which we have agreed
shall be as long, or at least as full, as we can make it) his day, i.e., as a happy
lover (cf. Marlowe, *Hero and Leander,* I, 191, cited in l. 117.2 n.). I think that
Q1's 'his' and 'thy' were marked for correction to 'this' and 'his' respectively,
and that Q2's compositor took both corrections to be 'this'. Turner, following
Daniel's reading, explains it as follows: '"Thy pale beames drawne away"
probably signifies that Endymion is sleeping in darkness, as Cynthia's beams
are now shining here rather than there. His eternal slumber, of course, makes a
"long night".'

Cynthia. Thou dreamst, dark queen, that fair boy was not
    mine,
  Nor went I down to kiss him. Ease and wine   165
  Have bred these bold tales; poets when they rage
  Turn gods to men, and make an hour an age.
  But I will give a greater state and glory,
  And raise to time a nobler memory
  Of what these lovers are. Rise, rise, I say,   170
  Thou power of deeps, thy surges laid away,
  Neptune, great king of waters, and by me
  Be proud to be commanded.

                    NEPTUNE *rises.*

Neptune.   Cynthia, see,
  Thy word hath fetched me hither; let me know
  Why I ascend.
Cynthia.   Doth this majestic show   175
  Give thee no knowledge yet?
Neptune.   Yes, now I see
  Something intended, Cynthia, worthy thee.
  Go on, I'll be a helper.
Cynthia.   Hie thee, then,

---

164. queen] *Q2;* power *Q1.*   165. wine] *Q2;* winde *Q1.*   167. Turn] *Q2;*
Turnes *Q1.*   169. nobler] *Q1;* noble *Q2.*   174. fetched] *Q2* (fetcht); force
Q1.

---

165. *Ease and wine*] Cf. *Cupid's Revenge,* I.i.55–6, where the religion of
Cupid is said to have been invented by 'Some one that gave himself to wine and
sloth, / Which breed lascivious thoughts'.
  166. *rage*] are inspired (*OED,* 2.c).
  169. *to time*] for all time, for ever (*OED,* time, 45.a).
  a nobler memory] Metre requires 'nobler' to be trisyllabic and 'memory' to be
stressed on the second syllable, as in Latin *memoria* and in Chaucer's *Miller's
Prologue,* where it rhymes with 'storie' (*Canterbury Tales,* in *Works,* ed. F. N.
Robinson (Cambridge, Mass., 1933), I, 3111–2. This pronunciation is not
recorded in *OED.* 'Memory' has here the meaning 'memorial'.
  170. *these lovers*] lovers considered as a species (*OED,* these, 1.c).
  173.1 *NEPTUNE*] He may have resembled Oceanus in Jonson's *Masque of
Blackness* (opening directions): '*the colour of his flesh, blue; and shaddowed with
a robe of sea-greene; his head grey; and horned; as he is described by the* Ancients:
his beard of the like mixt colour: he was gyrlonded with Alga, *or sea-grasse; and in
his hand a* Trident'.
  175. *this majestic show*] this noble sight (i.e., the stage audience).

And charge the wind-god from his rocky den
Let loose his subjects; only Boreas,   180
Too foul for our intentions as he was,
Still keep him fast chained. We must have none here
But vernal blasts and gentle winds appear,
Such as blow flowers, and through the glad boughs sing
Many soft welcomes to the lusty spring;   185
These are our music. Next, thy watery race
Bring on in couples—we are pleased to grace
This noble night—each in their richest things
Your own deeps or the broken vessel brings.
Be prodigal, and I shall be as kind,   190
And shine at full upon you.
Neptune.   O the wind-
    Commanding Aeolus!

                Enter AEOLUS *out of a rock.*

Aeolus.   Great Neptune?
Neptune.   He.

---

179. wind-god] *This ed.*; winde goe *Q1, Q2*; winde flie *Q3*.   180. his] *Q1;*
thy *Q2*.   185. welcomes] *Q2;* welcome *Q1*.   186. These are our music.
Next] *Q2;* Bid them draw neere to haue *Q1*.   187. Bring] *Q2;* Led *Q1*.
187–8. couples—we ... grace / This ... night—each] *Theobald (subst.);*
couples, we ... grace / This ... night each *Q1, Q2;* couples we ... grace /
This ... night, each *Spencer*.   189. vessel] *Q2;* vessels *Q1*.   191. O] *Q2*
(Oh,); See *Q1*.   191–2. wind-/Commanding] *Theobald;* wind / Commanding
Q1, Q2; Wind! / Commanding *Langbaine*.

---

   179. *the wind-god*] Aeolus, who kept his sons the winds in a cave on Aeolia,
an island to the north of Sicily (Virgil, *Aeneid*, I, 52). He is called 'the Wind-
god' in Marlowe's *Dido, Queen of Carthage*, I.i.115. Qq 'goe' is a misreading
error (d/e), easily made in the secretary hand.
   180. *Boreas*] the north wind.
   181. *foul*] rough, stormy (*OED*, 15).
   183. *vernal*] of the spring.
   184. *blow flowers*] make flowers bloom.
   187–8. *couples ... night*] The sense is not self-evident, and depends on the
punctuation, which in Qq is not helpful. Theobald (followed in this edition
because of the support given by the Jonson quotation at l. 135 n.) treats 'we
... night' as a parenthesis. Spencer's punctuation gives the sense 'couples
whom, on this noble night, we are pleased to favour'.
   189. *Your own deeps*] Cf. ll. 205–6.
   the broken vessel] the sunken ship (considered as a carrier of treasure); cf.
Marlowe, *Hero and Leander*, II, 160–4.

72 THE MAID'S TRAGEDY [ACT I

Aeolus. What is thy will?

Neptune.   We do command thee free
Favonius and thy milder winds to wait
Upon our Cynthia, but tie Boreas strait;   195
He's too rebellious.

Aeolus.   I shall do it.

Neptune.   Do.

> [*Exit* AEOLUS *into the rock.*]

[*To Cynthia*] Great mistress of the flood and all below,
Thy full command has taken.

> [*Enter* AEOLUS, *followed by* FAVONIUS *and other* Winds.]

Aeolus.   O, the Main!
  Neptune!

Neptune.   Here.

Aeolus.   Boreas has broke his chain,

---

194. Favonius] *Q3; Fanonius Q1, Q2.*   195. strait] *Q1, Q2* (straight).
196. too rebellious] *Q2;* rebellious *Q1.*   196–9.] *This ed.; Nep.* Doe great
master of the floud, and all below / Thy full command has taken. / *Eol.* O! the
Maine / *Neptune.* / *Nep.* Heere. *Q1 (subst.), Q2; Nept.* Do (*Exit Aeolus.*)/*Aeol.*
(*within*). Great Master of the Flood, and all below, / Thy full Command has
taken—Ho! The Main! / Neptune! *Nept.* Here. *Theobald.*   197. Great
mistress] *This ed.;* great master *Q2;* maister *Q1.*   198.1. followed ... Winds]
Dyce; not in Q1, Q2.

---

194. *Favonius*] the west wind.
195. *strait* tightly (*OED*, strait, adv., 1).
197–8.] The text of both Qq is corrupt here, and Theobald's revision
(accepted by all editors) is unsatisfactory because (1) it allows Aeolus no time
to do his business with the winds, (2) it requires him to speak off-stage, (3) it
makes him begin addressing Neptune twice in immediate succession. Heath's
manuscript notes (cited by Dyce) remedy the last two defects by giving
Cynthia the words 'Great master ... taken', but leave the first unremedied
('she perceiving the approach of the milder winds set at liberty by Aeolus'
shows that there has to be a break in the action). By emending 'master' to
'mistress' (postulating a misreading error, perhaps caused by the abbreviation
'M^ris') I retain the Qq speech prefixes and the dramatic continuity. Neptune
and his subjects are considered as the tributaries of Cynthia (cf. l. 195, 'our
Cynthia', and l. 241, 'Great queen of us and heaven', who in Marlowe's *Hero
and Leander*, I, 111, 'over-rules the flood'), and his command to Aeolus is in
obedience to her command to him. When Aeolus departs to fulfil it Neptune
goes to report the fact to Cynthia; as he is doing so he is interrupted by Aeolus'
return.
198. *has taken*] has been effected (OED, take, 11).
the Main] the Sea (i.e., Neptune, its god).

And struggling with the rest has got away.   200
Neptune. Let him alone, I'll take him up at sea;
    He will not long be thence. Go once again,
    And call out of the bottoms of the main
    Blue Proteus and the rest; charge them put on
    Their greatest pearls and the most sparkling stone   205
    The beaten rock breeds, till this night is done
    By me a solemn honour to the Moon.
    Fly like a full sail!
Aeolus.   I am gone.   [*Exit.*]
Cynthia.   Dark Night,
    Strike a full silence, do a thorough right
    To this great chorus, that our music may   210
    Touch high as heaven, and make the east break day
    At midnight.
                                         Music.

[*Enter* PROTEUS *and other* Sea-Gods.]

[*First*] *Song.*
Cynthia, to thy power and thee
  We obey.

---

202. He] *Q2*; I *Q1*.   long be] *Q2*; be long *Q1*.   once] *Q2*; hence *Q1*.
203. call out of the bottoms] *Q2*; bid the other call out *Q1*.   206. till] *Q1*,
Q2; tell *Dyce, conj. Mason.*   208. Exit.] *Dyce; not in Q1, Q2.*   212.2. Enter
... Sea-Gods.] *Dyce (subst.); not in Q1, Q2.*

---

  201. *take him up*] arrest him.
  202. *thence*] away from your cave. This is the sense after Q2's pronoun 'He'
(a reading which must have resulted from an annotation). In Q1, after the
pronoun 'I' (i.e., Neptune), the sense is 'away from the sea'.
  203. *bottoms*] depths.
  204. *Blue Proteus*] Cf. Jonson, *Volpone*, III.vii.153: 'the blue Proteus'. In
Marlowe's *Hero and Leander*, II, 155, Neptune is 'the sapphire-visag'd god'.
  206. *beaten*] '(1) beaten by the waves, (2) inlaid with gold or precious
minerals' (Norland): *OED*, beaten, 5.c, noted by Bullen in Daniel's edition.
  till] while (*OED*, 2). Mason's conjecture 'tell', though attractive, is not
necessary, and creates an elliptical sentence ('tell [them that]') which would be
less easy to grasp.
  207. *solemn honour*] ceremonious act of respect.
  209. *do a thorough right*] perform what is thoroughly due (i.e., create a
perfect silence in which the music can be heard as high as heaven).
  211–12. *and make ... midnight*] not literally (both songs wish for a
long night) but figuratively (of the occasion's splendour).

Joy to this great company,   215
   And no day
Come to steal this night away
   Till the rites of love are ended,
And the lusty bridegroom say,
   'Welcome, light, of all befriended!'   220

Pace out, you watery powers below;
   Let your feet,
Like the galleys' when they row,
   Even beat;
Let your unknown measures, set   225
   To the still winds, tell to all
That gods are come, immortal, great,
   To honour this great nuptial.

                           The Measure.

               Second Song.

Hold back thy hours, dark Night, till we have done;
   The day will come too soon.   230
Young maids will curse thee if thou stealst away,
And leav'st their blushes open to the day.
   Stay, stay, and hide
   The blushes of the bride.

Stay, gentle Night, and with thy darkness cover   235
   The kisses of her lover;
Stay, and confound her tears and her shrill cryings,

---

218. rites] *Q1* (rights), *Q2* (rites).   223. galleys'] This ed.; gallies *Q1*, *Q2*.
229. dark] *Q2*; old *Q1*.   232. blushes] *Q2*; losses *Q1*.   237. shrill] *Q2*; loud
Q1.

---

  219. lusty] vigorous.
  220. befriended] greeted as a friend: a nonce-use (not in *OED*).
  223. galleys'] For the image of the galleys' oars as feet cf. Donne, 'The
Calm', ll. 35–8, where 'The crawling Gallies' are likened to ants.
  225. unknown measures] strange dances.
  225–6. set ... winds] in time with the gentle winds (who are singing the
song).
  237. confound] defeat (*OED*, 1). Carew, also in an epithalamion, uses the
word more appropriately of a storm 'Which shall confound with its loude
whistling noyse / Her pleasing shriekes ...' ('On the Mariage of T[homas]
K[illigrew] and C[ecilia] C[rofts] / the Morning stormie', in *Poems*, ed. Rhodes
Dunlap (Oxford, 1949), pp. 79–80, ll. 35–6).

Her weak denials, vows, and often-dyings;
  Stay, and hide all,
  But help not though she call.   240

                         Another Measure.

Neptune. Great queen of us and heaven, hear what I bring
  To make this hour a full one.
Cynthia.   Speak, sea's king.
Neptune. The tunes my Amphitrite joys to have,
  When she will dance upon the rising wave,
  And court me as she sails. My tritons, play   245
  Music to lay a storm. I'll lead the way.

                    [Third] Song.

To bed, to bed! Come, Hymen, lead the bride,
  And lay her by her husband's side;
  Bring in the virgins every one,
    That grieve to lie alone,   250
  That they may kiss while they may say a maid;
  Tomorrow 'twill be other kissed and said.

---

238. often-dyings] *Dyce; often dyings Q1, Q2.*   240. though] *Q2; if Q1.*
240.1. *Another Measure.*] *Daniel, conj. Fleay;* If not her measure. *Q2 (as verse, after l. 242,* a full one,*); Maskers daunce, Neptune leads it Q1.*   241–54.] *Q2; not in Q1.*   241–2. Great . . . one.] *so Theobald;* Great . . . heauen, / Heare . . . one, / If not her measure. *Q2; not in Q1.*   243. The] *Theobald;* Thy *Q2; not in Q1.*   Amphitrite] *Q3;* Amphitrites *Q2; not in Q1.*   244. she] *Theobald;* they *Q2; not in Q1.*   245. she] *Theobald;* the *Q2; not in Q1.*   246. lay] *Dyce, conj. Heath;* lead *Q2; not in Q1.*

---

238. often-dyings] frequent swoonings (i.e., orgasms; see glossary of E. A. M. Colman, *The Dramatic Use of Bawdry in Shakespeare* (1974), p. 191, under 'die', for references).

240.1. *Another Measure.*] Fleay's emendation (I, 193) is right. The words 'If not her measure' ruin the couplet, ll. 241–2 (a decisive argument, since the masque's whole dialogue is in couplets). Norland and Gurr nevertheless retain them and accept Dyce's (pre-Fleay) paraphrase 'endeavouring to make this hour a full one, though perhaps what I bring may not completely fill up the measure'.

243. *Amphitrite*] (four syllables) Neptune's queen.

245. *tritons*] sons of Neptune and Amphitrite. They are often depicted blowing conchs as trumpets, so it is possible that brass instruments were here played by musicians, either 'above' or, more appropriately, under the stage.

251. say] call her; cf. Jonson, *The Haddington masque* (acted 1608), ll. 417–20: 'Good-night, whilst yet we may / Good-night to you a virgin say. / Tomorrow rise the same / Your mother is, and use a nobler name.'

Hesperus, be long a-shining,
Whilst these lovers are a-twining.

                              Measure.

                [Enter AEOLUS.]

Aeolus. Ho, Neptune!
Neptune.   Aeolus?
Aeolus.   The sea goes high;   255
    Boreas hath raised a storm. Go and apply
    Thy trident, else, I prophesy, ere day
    Many a tall ship will be cast away.
    Descend, with all the gods and all their power,
    To strike a calm.
Cynthia.   We thank you for this hour,   260
. . . .
    My favour to you all; to gratulate
    So great a service done at my desire
    Ye shall have many floods, fuller and higher
    Than you have wished for, and no ebb shall dare
    To let the Day see where your dwellings are.   265
    Now back unto your government in haste,
    Lest your proud charge should swell above the waste,
    And win upon the island.

254.1 *Measure.*] *placed here, this ed.; placed after* Song (*l. 246.1*), *Q2; not in*
Q1.   256. hath] *Q2;* has *Q1.*   260–1.] *This ed.;* We thanke you for this
houre, / My fauour to you all to gratulate *Q1;* A thanks to euery one, and to
gratulate *Q2.*   264. and no] *Q1;* no *Q2.*   265. dwellings] *Q1;* dwelling *Q2.*
266. government] *Q2;* gouernments *Q1.*   267. charge] *Q2;* waters *Q1.*

---

253. Hesperus] the evening star.
260–1.] The defective rhyme-scheme suggests that the first line of a couplet
is missing from Q1. In Q2 the sense is merely botched, and the verse is
unmetrical. As Turner says, 'it seems most unlikely that the Q2 reading could
have come into being except in response to an annotation'; but since Q2's
reading cannot possibly be Beaumont's intended wording I follow Q1's
reading. The missing line is irrecoverable. The expression "My favour to you
all' is complete in itself: cf. (Anon., attributed Tourneur) *The Revenger's
Tragedy,* V.i.168: 'Come then, my lords, my favours to you all.'
261. *gratulate*] reward, recompense (*OED*, 5).
267. *Your proud charge*] i.e., the swelling ocean.
   waste] 'ocean: i.e., its bed' (Spencer). *OED*, 1.b.

Neptune.   We obey.

> NEPTUNE *descends, and the* Sea-Gods.
> [*Exeunt* AEOLUS *and the* Winds *into the rock.*]

Cynthia. Hold up thy head, dead Night; seest thou not Day?
    The east begins to lighten; I must down   270
    And give my brother place.
Night.   O, I could frown
    To see the Day, the Day that flings his light
    Upon my kingdoms, and contemns old Night!
    Let him go on and flame, I hope to see
    Another wild-fire in his axle-tree,   275
    And all fall drenched—but I forget. Speak, queen.
    The day grows on; I must no more be seen.
Cynthia. Heave up thy drowsy head again and see
    A greater light, a greater majesty,
    Between our set and us. W̧hip up thy team: 280

268.1. NEPTUNE ... Sea-Gods.] *Q2; Exeunt Maskers (after* island.*); Descend
(after* We obey.*) Q1.*   268.2. *Exeunt ... rock.*] *Turner; not in Q1, Q2.*
273. kingdoms] *Q2;* kingdome *Q1.*   277. must] *Q2;* dare *Q1.*   278. Heave
up] *Q2;* Once heaue *Q1.*   280. set] *Theobald, conj. Seward;* sect *Q1, Q2.*
Whip] *Q2;* lash *Q1.*

---

268. *win upon*] get the better of (here with the sense 'overflow'); cf. *Cor.*,
I.i.217–58: 'it [the rabble] will in time / Win upon power.' The thought and
expression probably derive from Shakespeare's Sonnet lxiv, 5–8.
    the island] Rhodes.
    269. *dead*] fast asleep; cf. l. 278.
    271–6. *O ... drenched*] Cf. Marlowe, *Hero and Leander*, II, 332–4: 'And
with his [i.e., Hesperus', the morning-star's] flaring beams mock'd ugly
Night, / Till she, o'ercome with anguish, shame, and rage, / Dang'd down to
hell her loathsome carriage.'
    273. *kingdoms*] all the lands that Night has been covering.
    contemns] scorns.
    274–6. *I hope ... drenched*] alluding to Phaeton's disastrous attempt to
drive the sun-chariot of his father Phoebus. He lost control of the horses and
driving too near the earth scorched it. Killed by Jove's thunderbolt, he fell to
earth at the mouth of the river Eridanus (the Po).
    275. *wild-fire*] conflagration (*OED*, 1).
    axletree] axle-beam, here used for the whole chariot.
    278. *Heave ... head*] Cf. Marlowe, *Hero and Leander*, I, 190, quoted at l.
117.2 n.
    279. *A ... majesty*] i.e., displayed by the King.
    280. *set*] place of setting (*OED*, 1), relating to 'I must down, l. 270, and
to the emphatic 'here' of l. 281. Qq's 'sect' can be defended as meaning 'the
courtly audience, servants of Night and Cynthia (l. 147), before whom the
King is placed' (Turner): *OED*, sect, 3: 'Body of followers or adherents'. But

78   THE MAID'S TRAGEDY   [ACT I

The day breaks here, and yon same flashing stream
Shot from the south. Say, wilt thou go? Which way?
Night. I'll vanish into mists.
Cynthia.   I into day.
            Exeunt [NIGHT *and* CYNTHIA].

281. same flashing] *Q2;* sun flaring *Q1.*   282. Say, wilt thou go? Which
way?] *Theobald;* say which way wilt thou goe. *Q1;* say, which way wilt thou
goe? *Q2;* Which way wilt thou go? say. *Dyce.*

since the stage audience has not been mentioned for some time, and the
immediate context (ll. 269–83) treats daybreak as affecting the whole globe
(cf. 'my kingdoms', l. 273), I accept—with some hesitation—the emendation
treating 'sect' as a misreading error for 'sett'.
    281. *here*] i.e., in the king's countenance.
    stream] ray.
    282. *the south*] both (1) the south as the source of warmth (figuratively, royal
bounty) and (2) the south as the traditional location of the monarch at royal
entertainments indoors. 'The Great Hall at Whitehall ... was aligned due
north and south, as was the Banqueting House, where in Jonson's day the
monarch sat at the south end and was frequently addressed as a figure of the
sun' (John Orrell, *The Quest for Shakespeare's Globe* (Cambridge, 1983),
p. 152, quoting Jonson's *Oberon*, ll. 350–3). Spencer suggests that 'though the
ostensible object of the flattery is the King of the play' the compliment is to
'the brilliance of the audience'; but since the King and stage audience must be
placed up stage (so as not to block the theatre audience's view) Cynthia's
compliment cannot be delivered in both directions. Ll. 281–2 do not have to
relate to the actual orientation of the theatre. The second Globe (and
presumably the first, on the foundations of which it stood) had its main axis
facing east (Orrell, p. 153). This would put the up-stage area in the west. But
at the Blackfriars 'the stage was at one end, presumably the south, since the
entrance up the great staircase was at the north end' (Gurr, *The Shakespearean
Stage*, p. 104), so the King's position there would be strictly correct.
    282–3. *Say, wilt ... into day*] The readings of both Q1 and Q2 must be
wrong. It is incredible that the masque (in pentameter couplets throughout)
should end without rhyme (and in Q1 without metre), though it might be
implausibly argued that this shows in what disarray Cynthia and Night are
leaving. Gurr maintains that Q1's 'Adew' was 'probably intended as the rhyme
word to match *goe* ... and was omitted as a consequence of a clumsy
correction in Q2' (he therefore prints a final alexandrine). But I can find no
instance of this rhyme (Shakespeare rhymes 'adieu' with 'you' in *Rom.*,
III.v.58–9, and with 'true' in *AYL.*, V.iv.114–5), and think that 'Adew' is
Q1's desperate piecing-out of defective copy in order to give Cynthia some
reply to Night. The masque's final line, 'I'll vanish into mists. I into day',
seems to leave no room for improvement, so if emendation is agreed to be
necessary it must be in the penultimate line. Theobald and Dyce postulate a
transposition error. I prefer Theobald's emendation as being the more
idiomatic ('Wilt thou go?' is frequently used when inviting a companion to
depart: cf. II.i.125) and the easier to deliver.

Finis Masque.

King. Take lights there; ladies, get the bride to bed.
    [*To Evadne*] We will not see you laid. [*To Amintor*] Good
       night, Amintor;   285
    We'll ease you of that tedious ceremony;
    Were it my case I should think time run slow.
    If thou be'st noble, youth, get me a boy
    That may defend my kingdoms from my foes.
Amintor. All happiness to you.
King.   Good night, Melantius.   290
                                     Exeunt.

283.] *Q2;* NIGHT. Ile vanish into mists. CINTH. Adew. *Q1;* NIGHT. Ile vanish
into mists. CYNTHIA. I into day. Adew. *Gurr.*   283.2. *Finis Masque.*] *Q2*
(*Finis Maske.*)*; not in Q1.*   284. Take lights there; ladies,] *Theobald;* Take
light their Ladyes, *Q1;* Take lights there Ladies, *Q2.*   289. kingdoms] *Q1,*
Q2; kingdom *Q3.*

---

283. *I into day*] Since Night vanishes as she appeared, Cynthia requires to
vanish equally positively. In view of ll. 279–83 she may make a deep obeisance
at the foot of the King's chair, thus figuratively losing herself in his light; she
can then make her actual exit under cover of the applause greeting the masque
and of the King's rising, or she can remain in position until the general exeunt
half a dozen lines later. Alternatively, if she descended (cf. l. 127.1 n.) she may
now ascend, when the image in 'I into day' would be that of the moon's fading
in the brightening sky.
    284. *Take lights there*] a command to servants to take the torches from the
walls and light him and the stage audience to their chambers.
    285. *We*] I (the royal plural).
    see you laid] pay you the customary complimentary visit when you are in
bed.
    287. *run*] ran.
    289. *kingdoms*] 'Because Melantius's conquests have been so extensive
(IV.ii.169–70), the King probably holds sway over more than one kingdom'
(Turner); cf. SPEAKERS, l. 27 n. (*RHODES*).

Act II

Enter EVADNE, ASPATIA [*with a willow garland*], *and other* Ladies.

Dula. Madam, shall we undress you for this fight?
> The wars are nak'd that you must make tonight.

Evadne. You are very merry, Dula.

Dula.   I should be
> Far merrier, madam, if it were with me
> As it is with you.

Evadne.   How's that?

Dula.   That I might go   5
> To bed with him wi'th' credit that you do.

Evadne. Why, how now, wench?

Dula.   Come, ladies, will you help?

Evadne. I am soon undone.

Dula.   And as soon done.
> Good store of clothes will trouble you at both.

Evadne. Art thou drunk, Dula?

Dula.   Why, here's none but we.   10

Evadne. Thou thinkst belike there is no modesty
> When we're alone.

Dula. Ay, by my troth, you hit my thoughts aright.

Evadne. You prick me, lady.

Act II] *Q1, Q2 (Actus Secundus.)*   o.1. *with a willow garland*] *This ed.; not in Q1, Q2.*   2. nak'd] *Q1, Q2* (nak't).   3. very merry] *Q2;* merry *Q1.* 3–5. I ... you] *so Dyce;* I ... me / As ... you *Q1, Q2.*   5–6. How's ... do] *so Dyce;* Howes that? / DVL. That ... doe *Q1; not in Q2.*   6. wi'th'] *Theobald;* with *Q1; not in Q2.*   12. we're] *Q1* (we'are); we are *Q2.* 13. aright] *Q2;* right *Q1.*

   The act-interval appears to be observed, with the stage cleared at the end of the masque, and Evadne and the other ladies now re-entering.

   o.1. with a willow garland] Cf. ll. 119–20, which require the garland to be actual. Until then Aspatia can carry the garland in her hand.

   6. *credit*] good name (i.e., being entitled by marriage).

   8. *undone*] helped out of my clothes.

   done] sexually enjoyed.

1 Lady.   'Tis against my will.

Dula. Anon you must endure more and lie still;   15
    You're best to practise.

Evadne.   Sure, this wench is mad.

Dula. No, 'faith, this is a trick that I have had
    Since I was fourteen.

Evadne.   'Tis high time to leave it.

Dula. Nay, now I'll keep it till the trick leave me.
    A dozen wanton words put in your head   20
    Will make you livelier in your husband's bed.

Evadne. Nay, 'faith, then take it.

Dula.   Take it, madam? Where?
    We all, I hope, will take it that are here.

Evadne. Nay, then, I'll give you o'er.

Dula.   So will I make
    The ablest man in Rhodes, or his heart ache.   25

Evadne. Wilt take my place tonight?

---

14. lady] *Q2;* Madame *Q1.*   14–15. *1 Lady.* 'Tis ... will. / *Dula.* Anon] *Q1;*
Dul. Tis ... will, / Anon *Q2.*   16. You're] *Q2;* Tis *Q1.*   18. high time]
Q2; time *Q1.*   23. We ... it] *Q2;* We all will take it I hope *Q1.*   26. take]
Q2; lie in *Q1.*   26–7. I'll ... cards / Against ... know] *so Theobald*
('Gainst); *as one line, Q1, Q2.*

---

14. *You ... will*] Evadne and the Lady speak without innuendo, but the
bawdy sense of 'prick' and 'will' (i.e., the genital organs: see glossary of
E. A. M. Colman, *The Dramatic Use of Bawdry in Shakespeare,* for references)
prepares for Dula's rejoinder; cf. *The Scornful Lady,* V.iv.122–6: '"A will
make the better husband: you have tride him?" "Against my will Sir." "Hee'le
make your will amends soone, doe not doubt it."'
16. *You're*] You were.
17. *trick*] habit (*OED,* 7).
19. *till ... me*] (with the innuendo 'Till I am too old to feel sexual
pleasure').
22. *take it*] in contrast to 'leave it' (l. 18), as in the phrase 'take it or leave it'.
In Dula's suggestive reply 'all ... that are here' may extend to the audience
(cf. I.ii.14).
24. *give you o'er*] i.e., as hopelessly frivolous. Dula's reply gives the words a
sexual implication.
26. *take my place*] i.e., in the marriage bed.
26–7. *I'll ... know*] I'll play the cards that you have been dealt against any
two opponents I know. This reply is consistent with Evadne's question. Dula's
next speech (l. 28) implies either that she and Evadne will take on separate
opponents or that they will be partners against an opposing pair, an idea which
is continued in her rejection of Aspatia as a partner (ll. 29–30).

Dula.   I'll hold your cards
   Against any two I know.
Evadne.   What wilt thou do?
Dula. Madam, we'll do't, and make 'em leave play too.
Evadne. Aspatia, take her part.
Dula.   I will refuse it:
   She will pluck down a side, she does not use it.   30
Evadne [To Aspatia]. Why, do, I prithee.
Dula [To Evadne].   You will find the play
   Quickly, because your head lies well that way.
Evadne. I thank thee, Dula. Would thou couldst instill
   Some of thy mirth into Aspatia!
   Nothing but sad thoughts in her breast do dwell;   35
   Methinks a mean betwixt you would do well.
Dula. She is in love; hang me if I were so,
   But I could run my country. I love too
   To do those things that people in love do.
Aspatia. It were a timeless smile should prove my cheek: 40
   It were a fitter hour for me to laugh

---

30. a side] *Q2;* aside *Q1.*   31. Why, do] *Q2;* Doe *Q1.*   I prithee] *Q1; not in Q2.*   40. cheek] *Q1* (cheeke); checke *Q2.*

---

28. *make ... play*] with the innuendo 'exhaust them sexually'.

29. *take her part*] back her up (*OED*, part, 23.c), i.e., in her cheerfulness.

30. *pluck ... side*] weaken a partnership or a team in which one plays (*OED*, pluck, 3.b, 'pluck down a side').

use it] do it, i.e., play cards (with sexual innuendo, carried on in Dula's next speech).

31. *You*] (emphatic).

find the play] learn the game.

32. *your head lies well*] equivocal; (1) you have a mental aptitude, (2) your maidenhead is well placed.

36. *mean*] middle course.

37. *hang me*] a mild imprecation.

38. *run my country*] flee my domicile: *OED*, run, 38 (Cotgrave, 1611: '*Faire le saut*, to breake, fall bankrupt, runne his countrey for debt'); not to be confused with *OED*, run, 34.b (Cotgrave, 1611: '*Fendre le vent*, to runne his countrey'; '*Tirer paiz* (in hunting), to runne his countrey; or, to flye directly forward'). Dula's jest lies in taking 'in love' as though Love were a place, like Rhodes: i.e., 'If I were in Love, I should require to be able to escape from it at will.'

40. *It were ... cheek*] This is no time for me to be smiling. (Literally: a smile that might try my cheek would be untimely.)

When at the altar the religious priest
Were pacifying the offended powers
With sacrifice, than now. This should have been
My night, and all your hands have been employed   45
In giving me a spotless offering
To young Amintor's bed, as we are now
For you. Pardon, Evadne; would my worth
Were great as yours, or that the King, or he,
Or both, thought so! Perhaps he found me worthless,   50
But, till he did so, in these ears of mine,
These credulous ears, he poured the sweetest words
That art or love could frame. If he were false,
Pardon it, heaven; and if I did want
Virtue, you safely may forgive that too,   55
For I have lost none that I had from you.

Evadne. Nay, leave this sad talk, madam.

Aspatia.   Would I could,
Then I should leave the cause.

Evadne. See, if you have not spoiled all Dula's mirth.

Aspatia. [*To Dula*] Thou thinkst thy heart hard, but if thou
be'st caught   60
Remember me; thou shalt perceive a fire
Shot suddenly into thee.

Dula.   That's not so good;
Let 'em shoot anything but fire, and
I fear 'em not.

Aspatia.   Well, wench, thou mayst be taken.

---

45. night] *Q2*; right *Q1*.   57–8. Would I could / Then ... cause] *so
Theobald; as one line, Q1, Q2.*   59. See] *Q2*; Loe *Q1*.   60–2. Thou ...
thee] *so Q1* (... / remember ... / shot ...); Thou ... beest / caught ... fire /
shot ... thee *Q2.*   62. into *Q2*; vnto *Q1*.   62–4.] *so this ed.*; Thats ...
thing / but ... not *Q1, Q2.*   64. fire, and I] *Q1*; fire, I *Q2.*   fear 'em] *Q1*
(feare'm), *Q2.*   mayst] *Q2* (maist); must *Q1.*

---

45. *night*] i.e., wedding-night. Dyce and most modern editors defend Q1's
'right' as a variant spelling of 'rite'. At I.ii.218 and II.i.144 Q1 has 'rights' and
Q2 changes the spelling to 'rites'. Q2's reading here suggests that Q1's 'right'
was recognised as an error.

53–6. *If he ... from you*] These lines are all addressed to 'heaven', i.e., the
gods, who are the 'you' of ll. 55 and 56.

60. *caught*] i.e., by love; so also 'taken', l. 64.

Evadne. Ladies, good night, I'll do the rest myself.   65
Dula. Nay, let your lord do some.
Aspatia [Sings] Lay a garland on my hearse
     Of the dismal yew—
Evadne. That's one of your sad songs, madam.
Aspatia. Believe me, 'tis a very pretty one.   70
Evadne. How is it, madam?
Aspatia [Sings] Lay a garland on my hearse
     Of the dismal yew;
     Maidens, willow branches bear;
     Say I dièd true.   75
     My love was false, but I was firm
     From my hour of birth;
     Upon my buried body lay
     Lightly, gentle earth!

Evadne. Fie on't, madam! The words are so strange, they are   80
     able to make one dream of hobgoblins. 'I could never have
     the power', sing that, Dula.
Dula [Sings]. *I could never have the power*
     To love one above an hour,

67–89.] *Q2; not in Q1.*   67–8.] *so Weber; as one line, Q2; not in Q1.*
72. *Sings*] *Dyce; Song. Q2 (centred between ll. 71 and 72); not in Q1.*
72–9.] *so Weber;* Lay . . . Yew, / Maidens . . . true, / My . . . birth, / Vpon . . .
earth. *Q2; not in Q1.*   75. dièd] *This ed.; died Q2; not in Q1.*   78. lay] *Q2;*
lie *Theobald (lye); not in Q1.*   79. gentle] *Q4; gently Q2; not in Q1.*

   63, 64. *'em*] i.e., men (during the sexual act).
   65. *the rest*] i.e., of my undressing. Dula's reply extends 'the rest' to mean
'what follows on the wedding night'.
   67. *hearse*] coffin on a bier.
   74. *willow*] i.e., signifying her forsaken condition. 'To wear the willow' was
proverbial (Tilley, W 403). See ll. 119–20, and cf. *Oth.*, IV.iii.49.
   75. dièd] two syllables, for the metre. This is probably the intention in Q2's
reading 'died'; at II.ii.9 the monosyllable is given as 'di'd'.
   78–9. Upon . . . earth!] borrowed from Jonson's Epigram 22, 'On My First
Daughter', l. 12: 'Which [i.e., the child's body] cover lightly, gentle earth.'
The poem 'probably belongs to Jonson's Catholic period, i.e., between 1598
and 1610' (Ian Donaldson, ed., Ben Jonson: *Poems* (1975), p. 16). The
borrowing was noticed independently by Charles R. Forker in *Notes and
Queries*, CCVIII (1983), 150–1, and by John Kerrigan, 'Revision, Adaptation,
and the Fool in *King Lear*' in *The Division of the Kingdoms: Shakespeare's
Two Versions of 'King Lear'*, ed. G. Taylor and M. Warren (Oxford, 1983),
pp. 235–6.
   78. lay] lie (*OED*, 43).

  But my heart would prompt mine eye   85
  On some other man to fly.
  Venus, fix mine eyes fast,
  Or, if not, give me all that I shall see at last.
Evadne. So, leave me now.
Dula.   Nay, we must see you laid.
Aspatia. Madam, good night. May all the marriage joys 90
  That longing maids imagine in their beds
  Prove so unto you! May no discontent
  Grow 'twixt your love and you! But if there do,
  Inquire of me and I will guide your moan,
  And teach you an artificial way to grieve,   95
  To keep your sorrow waking. Love your lord
  No worse than I, but if you love so well,
  Alas, you may displease him: so did I.
  This is the last time you shall look on me:
  Ladies, farewell. As soon as I am dead,   100
  Come all and watch one night about my hearse;
  Bring each a mournful story and a tear
  To offer at it when I go to earth;
  With flattering ivy clasp my coffin round;
  Write on my brow my fortune; let my bier   105
  Be borne by virgins that shall sing by course
  The truth of maids and perjuries of men.
Evadne. Alas, I pity thee.
Ladies.   Madam, good night.
           Exit EVADNE.
1 Lady. Come, we'll let in the bridegroom.
Dula.   Where's my lord?

92. no] *Q2;* not *Q1.* 108. *Ladies.*] *Q1, Q2 (subst.: Omnes).*

---

 87. *Venus . . . last*] Venus, give me constancy, or, if not, give me, sooner or later, every man my inconstancy makes me desire. Cf. *Arcadia,* bk II, chap. 14, p. 240: 'all those fooles [i.e., lovers] that will have all they see'.
 89. *laid*] Cf. I.ii.285.
 95. *artificial*] according to the rules of art.
 96. *waking*] awake.
 101. *watch*] keep a vigil.
 104. *flattering*] because it clings. Beaumont gives it the same epithet in the poem *Salmacis and Hermaphroditus,* l. 867.
 105. *Write . . . fortune*] Place on my brow an inscribed paper telling my story.
 106. *by course*] in turn.

Enter AMINTOR.

1 Lady. Here, take this light.

Dula.   You'll find her in the dark.   110

1 Lady. Your lady's scarce abed yet; you must help her.

Aspatia. Go, and be happy in your lady's love.

    May all the wrongs that you have done to me

    Be utterly forgotten in my death!

    I'll trouble you no more, yet I will take   115

    A parting kiss, and will not be denied.   [*Kisses him.*]

    You'll come, my lord, and see the virgins weep

    When I am laid in earth, though you yourself

    Can know no pity? Thus I wind myself

    Into this willow garland, and am prouder   120

    That I was once your love, though now refused,

    Than to have had another true to me.

    So with my prayers I leave you, and must try

    Some yet unpractised way to grieve and die. *Exit* ASPATIA.

Dula. Come, ladies, will you go?

Ladies.   Good night, my lord.   125

Amintor. Much happiness unto you all!

                   Exeunt Ladies.

    I did that lady wrong. Methinks I feel

    Her grief shoot suddenly through all my veins;

    Mine eyes run; this is strange at such a time.

    It was the King first moved me to't, but he   130

    Has not my will in keeping. Why do I

    Perplex myself thus? Something whispers me,

    Go not to bed. My guilt is not so great

---

110. You'll] *Q2* (You'le); Heele *Q1*.   111. abed yet] *Q2* (a bed yet); abed *Q1*
(a bed).   116. *Kisses him.*] *Dyce (subst.); not in Q1, Q2.*   123. with my
prayers] *Q3;* with praiers *Q1, Q2.*   125. *Ladies.*] *Q2 (subst.: Om[nes].);*
1. LAD. *Q1.*   128. Her *Q2;* A *Q1.*   129. run] *Q2* (runne); raine *Q1.*
131. do *Q2;* did *Q1.*

   119-20. *Thus ... garland*] Cf. *Ado,* II.i.166-70, where Benedick, proposing to take Claudio to 'the next willow', asks him 'What fashion will you
wear the garland of? About your neck, like an usurer's chain, or under your
arm, like a lieutenant's scarf?' Aspatia's words suggest the latter manner.

   123. *So ... try*] There is no point in the metrical irregularity of Qq 1 and 2,
so Q3's emendation (restoring the metre by supplying the natural word) is
adopted here.

As mine own conscience, too sensible,
Would make me think: I only brake a promise,   135
And 'twas the King that forced me. Timorous flesh,
Why shak'st thou so? Away, my idle fears!

Enter EVADNE.

Yonder she is, the lustre of whose eye
Can blot away the sad remembrance
Of all these things. [*To her*] O, my Evadne, spare   140
That tender body; let it not take cold!
The vapours of the night shall not fall here:
To bed, my love; Hymen will punish us
For being slack performers of his rites.
Cam'st thou to call me?
Evadne.   No.
Amintor.   Come, come, my love,   145
And let us lose ourselves to one another.
Why art thou up so long?
Evadne.   I am not well.
Amintor. To bed, then, let me wind thee in these arms
Till I have banished sickness.
Evadne.   Good my lord,
I cannot sleep.
Amintor.   Evadne, we'll watch.   150
I mean no sleeping.
Evadne.   I'll not go to bed.
Amintor. I prithee, do.
Evadne.   I will not for the world.

135. brake] *Q2;* breake *Q1.*   136. that forced] *Q2* (that forst)*; inforst *Q1.*
138. she is] *Q2;* is she *Q1.*   142. shall] *Q1;* will *Q2.*   146. lose] *Q1, Q2*
(loose).   148. To bed, then, let] *Theobald (subst.);* To bed, then let *Q1, Q2.*
149–51. Good ... sleeping] *so Theobald;* Good ... sleep. / AMIN. ...
sleeping *Q1, Q2.*

___

134. *conscience*] (three syllables)
sensible] sensitive.
139. *remembrance*] (four syllables)
142. *vapours*] cold dews.
146. *lose*] 'loose' (Qq) is a spelling of both the verbs 'loose' and 'lose'; 'loose'
might mean, in the context, 'let fly' (like arrows), but 'lose' (i.e., give away)
seems more appropriate to Amintor's idealistic mood.
148. *wind*] entwine.
150. *we'll*] (two syllables: 'we 'ill')

Amintor. Why, my dear love?
Evadne.   Why? I have sworn I will not.
Amintor. Sworn!
Evadne.   Ay.
Amintor.   How! sworn, Evadne?
Evadne. Yes, sworn, Amintor, and will swear again   155
    If you will wish to hear me.
Amintor. To whom have you sworn this?
Evadne. If I should name him the matter were not great.
Amintor. Come, this is but the coyness of a bride.
Evadne. The coyness of a bride!
Amintor.   How prettily   160
    That frown becomes thee!
Evadne.   Do you like it so?
Amintor. Thou canst not dress thy face in such a look
    But I shall like it.
Evadne.   What look likes you best?
Amintor. Why do you ask?
Evadne. That I may show you one less pleasing to you.   165
Amintor. How's that?
Evadne. That I may show you one less pleasing to you.
Amintor. I prithee, put thy jests in milder looks;
    It shows as thou wert angry.
Evadne.   So perhaps
    I am indeed.
Amintor.   Why, who has done thee wrong?   170
    Name me the man, and by thyself I swear,

160–1. How ... thee] *so Theobald; as one line, Q1, Q2.*   163. likes] *Q2;* will like *Q1.*   169–70. So ... indeed] *so Theobald; as one line, Q1, Q2.*   171. I swear] *Q2;* sweete loue *Q1.*

154. *Why? I ... will not.*] This is the punctuation of both Qq; I retain it, giving the sense that Evadne repeats Amintor's 'Why?' and then answers his question. This seems dramatically preferable to the possibility that Evadne is simply using 'Why' in an exclamatory manner, though the variable punctuation of both Q1 and Q2 leaves both possibilities open. At l. 170 both Qq have 'Why, who'; at l. 154 Q1 has 'How? sworne *Euadne.*' and Q2 has 'How sworne, *Euadne?*'. In this scene the punctuation of Q1 has been extensively revised in Q2. At III.i.109 both Qq have 'Why? this is strange.'
158. *If ... great*] Never mind who. (Literally: It would not be an important matter to me if I did name him.)
169. *shows as*] looks as though.

> Thy yet unconquered self, I will revenge thee.
> *Evadne*. Now I shall try thy truth. If thou dost love me,
>   Thou weighst not anything compared with me;
>   Life, honour, joys eternal, all delights   175
>   This world can yield, or hopeful people feign
>   Are in the life to come, are light as air
>   To a true lover when his lady frowns
>   And bids him 'Do this'. Wilt thou kill this man?
>   Swear, my Amintor, and I'll kiss the sin   180
>   Off from thy lips.
> *Amintor*.   I wo' not swear, sweet love,
>   Till I do know the cause.
> *Evadne*.   I would thou wouldst.
>   Why, it is thou that wrongst me, I hate thee,
>   Thou shouldst have killed thyself.
> *Amintor*. If I should know that, I should quickly kill   185
>   The man you hated.
> *Evadne*.   Know it, then, and do't.

---

172. thee] *Q2;* it *Q1.* 174. with] *Q2;* to *Q1.* 176. This] *Q2;* The *Q1.*
176–7. or ... feign / Are ... come] *Langbaine;* or hopefull people faine / Or in
the life to come *Q2; not in Q1.* 180–1. sin / Off from] *Q2;* sun / Of *Q1.*
181–2. I wo' not ... cause] *so Q2; as one line, Q1.* 181. wo' not] *Q1, Q2*
(wonnot). 182. do know] *Q2;* know *Q1.* 186. Know it, then] *Q2;* Know
it *Q1.*

---

172. *yet unconquered*] virgin.

176–7. *or hopeful ... come*] Langbaine's emendation, though accepted only
by Theobald, is necessary because 'or in the life to come' is otherwise left in
syntactical limbo (an implied 'that' governs the two previous phrases, each of
which has a verb). 'Or' for 'Are' could result from Q2's compositor's carrying
the phrase phonetically in his head (especially after setting 'or' in the preceding
line). For the thought and expression cf. *Cupid's Revenge*, III.ii.163–5: 'I'me
carelesse, and doe weigh / The world, my life, and all my after hopes / Nothing
without thy Love.' Q1's omission treats the ten words as a complete unit and
may be an expurgation of profanity. Evadne's blasphemous implication about
a future life is in keeping with her cynical attitude in this dialogue (contrast her
piety at IV.i.277–8). The metrical irregularity of Q1 shows that the words
(restored in Q2) were always part of the speech.

180–1. *kiss ... lips*] The sin Evadne means Amintor to understand is that of
swearing to kill (thus to break the sixth commandment), and the kiss is to
follow directly on the oath-taking. Danby's interpretation, 'it is Amintor's
suicide she is demanding, and Amintor's dead lips she would kiss .... The
blasphemous and the necrophilic combine' (*Poets on Fortune's Hill* (1952), 191)
inappropriately looks beyond the dramatic present.

185. *that*] the fact that I have wronged thee.

Amintor. O no, what look soe'er thou shalt put on
    To try my faith, I shall not think thee false;
    I cannot find one blemish in thy face
    Where falsehood should abide. Leave, and to bed.   190
    If you have sworn to any of the virgins
    That were your old companions to preserve
    Your maidenhead a night, it may be done
    Without this means.
Evadne.   A maidenhead, Amintor,
    At my years?
Amintor. [*Aside*] Sure, she raves. [*To her*] This cannot be   195
    Thy natural temper. Shall I call thy maids?
    Either thy healthful sleep hath left thee long,
    Or else some fever rages in thy blood.
Evadne. Neither, Amintor. Think you I am mad,
    Because I speak the truth?
Amintor.   Is this the truth?   200
    Will you not lie with me tonight?
Evadne.   Tonight!
    You talk as if you thought I would hereafter.
Amintor. Hereafter! Yes, I do.
Evadne.   You are deceived.
    Put off amazement, and with patience mark
    What I shall utter, for the oracle   205
    Knows nothing truer. 'Tis not for a night
    Or two that I forbear thy bed, but ever.

---

187. shalt] *Q2;* should'st *Q1.*   188. shall not] *Q2;* cannot *Q1.*   194–5. A
maidenhead ... years] *so Theobald; as one line, Q1, Q2.*   196. Thy] *Q2;* Her
Q1.   199. Neither, Amintor. Think you] *Q2* (Neither *Amintor* thinke you*);*
Neither of these, what thinke you *Q1.*   200. Is this the truth?] *Q1; not in
Q2.*   201–2. Tonight! ... hereafter] *so Theobald;* To night? you talke as if
I would hereafter *Q2;* You talke as if you thought I would hereafter *Q1.*
203–4. You ... mark] *so Langbaine; as one line, Q1, Q2.*   207. thy] *Q2;*
your *Q1.*

---

    188. *false*] morally wrong, wicked.
    190. *Leave*] Leave off this talk.
    195. *At my years?*] The stress falls on 'my'. Such metrical control of
emphasis is notable throughout the dialogue (e.g., ll. 183–4, 201, 301–5).
    196. *temper*] disposition (*OED*, 9).
    205–6. *the oracle ... truer*] i.e., my words are as true as a response by or on
behalf of a god.

Amintor. I dream—awake, Amintor!

Evadne.   You hear right.

    I sooner will find out the beds of snakes,

    And with my youthful blood warm their cold flesh,   210

    Letting them curl themselves about my limbs,

    Than sleep one night with thee. This is not feigned,

    Nor sounds it like the coyness of a bride.

Amintor. Is flesh so earthly to endure all this?

    Are these the joys of marriage? Hymen, keep   215

    This story, that will make succeeding youth

    Neglect thy ceremonies, from all ears;

    Let it not rise up for thy shame and mine

    To after ages: we will scorn thy laws

    If thou no better bless them. Touch the heart   220

    Of her that thou hast sent me, or the world

    Shall know: there's not an altar that will smoke

    In praise of thee; we will adopt us sons;

    Then virtue shall inherit, and not blood.

    If we do lust, we'll take the next we meet,   225

    Serving ourselves as other creatures do,

    And never take note of the female more,

    Nor of her issue. [*Aside*] I do rage in vain;

    She can but jest. [*To her*] O, pardon me, my love,

    So dear the thoughts are that I hold of thee   230

    That I must break forth. Satisfy my fear;

    It is a pain beyond the hand of death

    To be in doubt; confirm it with an oath

    If this be true.

---

209. will] *Q2;* would *Q1.*   213. coyness] *Q2;* kisses *Q1.*   221. that] *Q2;* whom *Q1.*   222. Shall know: there's not an altar that will smoke] *Q2* (Shall know ther'es not an altar that will smoke)*;* Shall know this, not an altar then will smoake *Q1.*   229. can but] *Q2;* cannot *Q1.*   230. that] *Q2;* which *Q1.*   232. hand] *Q2;* paine *Q1.*

---

    214. *earthly*] earth-like, i.e., stolid, dull (*OED*, earthly, 3.c). Earth, in the old physiology, was the heaviest of the four elements, uniting the properties of dryness and coldness, and therefore typified grossness and dullness of nature.

    226. *we'll take ... issue*] It was a common belief that mating among the animals was random and impermanent, though there were exceptions, e.g. turtle-doves.

    228. *issue*] offspring.

    231. *Satisfy*] free from doubt.

    232. *hand of death*] blow delivered by death.

Evadne.   Do you invent the form,
          Let there be in it all the binding words   235
          Devils and conjurers can put together,
          And I will take it. I have sworn before,
          And here by all things holy do again,
          Never to be acquainted with thy bed.
          Is your doubt over now?   240
Amintor. I know too much: would I had doubted still!
          Was ever such a marriage night as this?
          You powers above, if you did ever mean
          Man should be used thus, you have thought a way
          How he may bear himself, and save his honour: 245
          Instruct me in it, for to my dull eyes
          There is no mean, no moderate course to run.
          I must live scorned or be a murderer.
          Is there a third? Why is this night so calm?
          Why does not heaven speak in thunder to us,   250
          And drown her voice?
Evadne.   This rage will do no good.
Amintor. Evadne, hear me. Thou hast ta'en an oath,
          But such a rash one that to keep it were
          Worse than to swear it. Call it back to thee.
          Such vows as those never ascend the heaven;   255
          A tear or two will wash it quite away.
          Have mercy on my youth, my hopeful youth,
          If thou be pitiful, for (without boast)
          This land was proud of me. What lady was there
          That men called fair and virtuous in this isle   260
          That would have shunned my love? It is in thee
          To make me hold this worth. O, we vain men,

246. Instruct me in] *Q2;* Instant me with *Q1.*   251. her] *Q2;* their *Q1.*
255. those] *Q2;* that *Q1.*

236. *conjurers*] magicians in league with the devil.
245. *bear*] behave.
248. *a murderer*] i.e., of Evadne's lover (cf. ll. 157–8, III.i. 244: Amintor is already beginning to guess at the truth, though he resists accepting it as long as he can), or, alternatively, of Evadne herself (cf. ll. 278–9).
252–4. *Thou hast ... swear it*] Cf. *2H6*, V.i.182–3: 'It is great sin to swear unto a sin; / But greater sin to keep a sinful oath.'
255. *ascend*] go up into (*OED*, 5).
262. *vain*] foolish.

That trust all our reputation
To rest upon the weak and yielding hand
Of feeble woman! But thou art not stone;   265
Thy flesh is soft, and in thine eyes does dwell
The spirit of love; thy heart cannot be hard.
Come, lead me from the bottom of despair
To all the joys thou hast, I know thou wilt,
And make me careful lest the sudden change   270
O'ercome my spirits.

Evadne.   When I call back this oath,
The pains of hell environ me!

Amintor. I sleep and am too temperate. Come to bed,
Or by those hairs which, if thou hadst a soul
Like to thy locks, were threads for kings to wear   275
About their arms—

Evadne.   Why, so perhaps they are.

Amintor. I'll drag thee to my bed, and make thy tongue
Undo this wicked oath, or on thy flesh
I'll print a thousand wounds to let out life.

Evadne. I fear thee not, do what thou dar'st to me;   280
Every ill-sounding word or threatening look
Thou showest to me will be revenged at full.

Amintor. It will not, sure, Evadne.

Evadne. Do not you hazard that.

Amintor.   Ha' ye your champions?

Evadne. Alas, Amintor, thinkst thou I forbear   285
To sleep with thee because I have put on
A maiden's strictness? Look upon these cheeks,

---

263. trust] *Q1, Q2*; trust out *Q3*.   266. does] *This ed.*; doe *Q1, Q2*; doth
Q3.   271-2. When ... me] *so Theobald;* When ... hell / inviron me *Q1,
Q2*.   274-5. Or ... soul / Like ... wear] *so Theobald;* Or ... locks, / Were
... weare *Q1, Q2*.   274. hadst] *Theobald;* hast *Q1, Q2*.

---

263. *That ... reputation*] a defective line. *Q3*'s emendation 'trust out' may
be right.

266. *does*] The 'doe' of *Q1* and *Q2* may be an authorial slip caused by the
proximity of the plural 'eyes', but it is perhaps more probably a printer's error
in *Q1*, uncorrected in *Q2*, and guessingly corrected in *Q3*.

268. *bottom*] lowest depth.

270. *make me careful*] give me cause to take care.

271. *spirits*] vital spirits. Amintor means that he may be killed by sudden
joy.

And thou shalt find the hot and rising blood
Unapt for such a vow. No, in this heart
There dwells as much desire, and as much will   290
To put that wished act in practice as ever yet
Was known to woman, and they have been shown
Both; but it was the folly of thy youth
To think this beauty, to what hand soe'er
It shall be called, shall stoop to any second.   295
I do enjoy the best, and in that height
Have sworn to stand, or die; you guess the man.
Amintor. No: let me know the man that wrongs me so,
    That I may cut his body into motes
    And scatter it before the northern wind.   300
Evadne. You dare not strike him.
Amintor.   Do not wrong me so.
    Yes, if his body were a poisonous plant
    That it were death to touch, I have a soul
    Will throw me on him.
Evadne.   Why, 'tis the King.
Amintor.   The King!
Evadne. What will you do now?

---

291. put that wished act in practice as] *Q2* (put that wisht act in practise, as)*;*
put that wished act, as *Q1*.   294. hand] *Daniel, conj. Bullen;* land *Q1, Q2.*

289–93. *No, in ... Both*] Evadne's distinction is between involuntary
sexual desire and the voluntary conversion of that desire into action. Q1's
spelling 'wished' (i.e., 'wishèd') suggests that l. 291 may have been worked
over in the copy, the original reading perhaps being 'To do that wishèd act as
ever yet'.

294. *to what ... second*] The imagery is from hawking, where the hawk is
trained to descend ('stoop') to the falconer's gloved fist ('hand'), which is
equipped with a lure of feathers; cf. Kyd, *The Spanish Tragedy*, II.i.4: 'In time
all haggard hawks will stoop to lure.' Spencer thinks the figure is continued in
'height' (l. 296), but since 'stand' is not a hawking term this is unlikely; cf.
'height' at III.i.172.

296. *the best*] the man of highest rank; cf. I.ii.32, 'the best of Rhodes'.

297. *stand*] continue.

299. *motes*] atoms.

300. *And ... wind*] because the north wind is particularly violent; cf.
Boreas in I.ii.

302. *Yes*] the emphatic form of the affirmative, used with contradictory
intent (cf. French 'si').

Amintor.   'Tis not the King!   305
Evadne. What did he make this match for, dull Amintor?
Amintor. O, thou hast named a word that wipes away
 All thoughts revengeful; in that sacred name
 'The King' there lies a terror. What frail man
 Dares lift his hand against it? Let the gods   310
 Speak to him when they please; till when, let us
 Suffer and wait.
Evadne. Why should you fill yourself so full of heat,
 And haste so to my bed? I am no virgin.
Amintor. What devil hath put it in thy fancy, then,   315
 To marry me?
Evadne.   Alas, I must have one
 To father children, and to bear the name
 Of husband to me, that my sin may be
 More honourable.
Amintor.   What a strange thing am I!
Evadne. A miserable one, one that myself   320
 Am sorry for.
Amintor.   Why, show it then in this:
 If thou hast pity, though thy love be none,
 Kill me, and all true lovers that shall live
 In after ages crossed in their desires
 Shall bless thy memory, and call thee good,   325
 Because such mercy in thy heart was found
 To rid a lingering wretch.
Evadne.   I must have one
 To fill thy room again if thou wert dead,
 Else, by this night, I would: I pity thee.

305. 'Tis] *Q2;* It is *Q1.*   308. name] *Q2;* word *Q1.*   319. a strange] *Q2;*
strange *Q1.*   320. *Evadne.*] *Q2; not in Q1.*   323. live] *Q2;* loue *Q1.*
326. heart] *Q2;* breast *Q1.*   329. would] *Q2;* could *Q1.*

---

 305. *'Tis*] Q2's contracted form improves the metre, the stresses falling on
'What', 'you', 'now', 'not', and 'King'.
 311. *Speak to him*] rebuke him (i.e., the King).
 319. *strange thing*] monster.
 327. *rid*] destroy.
 328. *room*] place.
 329. *by this night*] an appropriate asseveration; the usual one is 'by this light'
(cf. I.ii.7). In Jonson, *The Alchemist*, III.v.40–3, the blindfolded Dapper first
swears 'by this good light', and then, being rebuked for equivocation, 'by this
good dark'.

Amintor. These strange and sudden injuries have fall'n   330
    So thick upon me that I lose all sense
    Of what they are. Methinks I am not wronged
    Nor is it aught, if from the censuring world
    I can but hide it: reputation,
    Thou art a word, no more. [*To her*] But thou hast shown   335
    An impudence so high that to the world
    I fear thou wilt betray or shame thyself.
Evadne. To cover shame I took thee; never fear
    That I would blaze myself.
Amintor.   Nor let the King
    Know I conceive he wrongs me; then mine honour   340
    Will thrust me into action; that my flesh
    Could bear with patience; and it is some ease
    To me in these extremes that I know this
    Before I touched thee; else, had all the sins
    Of mankind stood betwixt me and the King,   345
    I had gone through 'em to his heart and thine.
    I have left one desire. 'Tis not his crown
    Shall buy me to thy bed, now I resolve
    He has dishonoured thee. Give me thy hand,
    Be careful of thy credit, and sin close: 350
    'Tis all I wish. Upon thy chamber floor
    I'll rest tonight, that morning visitors
    May think we did as married people use:

346. through 'em] *Q2;* through, e'ne *Q1.*   347. left] *Q1;* lost *Q2.*

---

334. *reputation*] (five syllables).
339. *blaze*] blazon, proclaim.
340. *conceive*] understand.
    then] if you do.
341. *that*] 'The situation, given that concealment (expressed in ll. 339–40)' (Spencer).
347. *I ... desire*] I have one remaining desire (i.e., that you 'sin close', l. 350); cf. l. 351, ''Tis all I wish'. Editors who follow Q2's reading (a mistaken correction by the annotator?) understand it to refer to Amintor's no longer wishing to share Evadne's bed; but if that is *one* desire he has lost, what are the others he has retained? He would not consider his desire for Evadne on his wedding day as merely *one* of his desires.
348. *resolve*] 'am convinced' (Weber), a usage not recorded in *OED* (the nearest being 19.d: 'To assure, satisfy, or convince (oneself) on some point').
349. *Give ... hand*] i.e., in agreement to the following plan.
350. *close*] secretly.
353. *use*] are accustomed to do.

> And prithee, smile upon me when they come,
> And seem to toy, as if thou hadst been pleased   355
> With what we did.

Evadne.   Fear not, I will do this.

Amintor. Come, let us practise, and as wantonly
> As ever loving bride and bridegroom met
> Let's laugh and enter here.

Evadne.   I am content.

Amintor. Down, all the swellings of my troubled heart!   360
> When we walk thus entwined, let all eyes see
> If ever lovers better did agree.   [*Exeunt.*]

[ACT II SCENE ii]

Enter ASPATIA, ANTIPHILA, [*and*] OLYMPIAS.

Aspatia. Away, you are not sad! Force it no further.
> Good gods, how well you look! Such a full colour
> Young bashful brides put on; sure, you are new married.

Antiphila. Yes, madam, to your grief.

Aspatia.   Alas, poor wenches,
> Go learn to love first, learn to lose yourselves,   5
> Learn to be flattered, and believe and bless
> The double tongue that did it; make a faith
> Out of the miracles of ancient lovers,

---

356. we] *Q2;* I *Q1.*   358. loving] *Q2;* longing *Q1.*   360. *Amintor.*] *Q2; not in Q1.*   362. *Exeunt.*] *Theobald; Exit. Q1, Q2.*

1. not sad] *Q2;* not *Q1.*   2. Good gods] *Q2;* Good, good *Q1.*   7–12.] *so Theobald;* The double tongue that did it, / Did you ere loue yet wenches, speake *Olimpas* [*sic*], / Thou hast a metled temper, fit for stamp. *Q1;* The double tongue that did it, / Make a faith out of the miracles of ancient louers, / Did you nere loue yet wenches? Speake *Olimpias,* / Such as speake truth and di'd in't, / And like me beleeue all faithfull, and be miserable, / Thou hast an easie temper, fit for stampe. *Q2.*

---

355. *toy*] dally affectionately.
357. *wantonly*] voluptuously.
361. *entwined*] arm in arm, or with the arm of each about the other.
361. *all eyes*] i.e., (at the present moment) those of the audience (cf. I.ii.14, 'all the company'); (in the future) those of 'morning visitors' (l. 352).

1. *force it*] strain (*OED*, 5) the sadness you cannot feel.
5. *lose*] destroy, ruin.
7. *double*] deceitful (*OED*, 5).

Such as spake truth and died in't; and, like me,
Believe all faithful, and be miserable.   10
Did you ne'er love yet, wenches? Speak, Olympias;
Thou hast an easy temper, fit for stamp.
Olympias. Never.
Aspatia.   Nor you, Antiphila?
Antiphila.   Nor I.
Aspatia. Then, my good girls, be more than women, wise;
At least be more than I was, and be sure   15
You credit anything the light gives life to
Before a man. Rather believe the sea
Weeps for the ruined merchant when he roars;
Rather the wind but courts the pregnant sails,
When the strong cordage cracks; rather the sun   20
Comes but to kiss the fruit in wealthy autumn,
When all falls blasted. If you needs must love,
Forced by ill fate, take to your maiden bosoms
Two dead-cold aspics, and of them make lovers;
They cannot flatter nor forswear: one kiss   25
Makes a long peace for all. But man —

9. spake] *Theobald;* speake *Q2; not in QI.*   11. ne'er] *Q2* (nere); ere *QI.*
12. an easy] *Q2;* a metled *QI.*   13. Nor I] *QI (corrected), Q2;* Nere I *QI*
(uncorrected).   15–27. and ... beast, man] *so Langbaine; as prose, Q2; not in*
QI.   19. but courts] *Turner;* courts but *Q2; not in QI.*   24. dead-cold]
Theobald; dead cold *Q2; not in QI.*   26. man—] *Q2* (man,); Man, base
Man—*Theobald; not in QI.*

7–9. *make ... died in't*] Cf. Donne, 'The Relique', ll. 22–3: 'What miracles
wee harmlesse lovers wrought. / First, we lov'd well and faithfully.'
12. *easy temper*] yielding disposition. QI's 'metled' (i.e., mettled, spirited) is
more poetically consistent with 'fit for stamp', where the image is of stamping a
design or inscription on metal. Gurr concludes that Beaumont modified
Fletcher's original expression to suit Olympias' character as he saw it. Perhaps
Beaumont thought the word-play in 'mettled' distracting.
fit for stamp] ready to take an impression.
18. *ruined merchant*] merchant ship (*OED*, 4) beaten to pieces.
19. *pregnant*] swelling; cf. *MND.*, II.i.128–9: 'To see the sails conceive, /
And grow big-bellied with the wanton wind.'
20. *cordage*] rigging.
22. *blasted*] blighted (through excessively hot dry weather).
24. *aspics*] asps; probably with a recollection of the death of Cleopatra
(*Ant.*, V.ii.301–11).
26. *for all*] for ever; cf. *R2*, II.ii.148: 'Farewell at once—for once, for all,
and ever.'

O, that beast, man! Come, let's be sad, my girls.
That downcast of thine eye, Olympias,
Shows a fine sorrow; mark, Antiphila;
Just such another was the nymph Oenone's   30
When Paris brought home Helen. Now a tear,
And then thou art a piece expressing fully
The Carthage queen when from a cold sea rock,
Full with her sorrow, she tied fast her eyes
To the fair Troyan ships, and having lost them,   35
Just as thine does, down stole a tear. Antiphila,
What would this wench do if she were Aspatia?
Here she would stand, till some more pitying god
Turned her to marble. 'Tis enough, my wench.
[*To Antiphila*] Show me the piece of needlework you
          wrought.   40

Antiphila. Of Ariadne, madam?

Aspatia.   Yes, that piece.

                              [*Antiphila shows it.*]

---

29. fine] *Q2*; faind *Q1*.   30. Oenone's] *Q2* (*Ænones*); Oenes *Q1*.   32. fully]
Q2; furie, *Q1*.   35. Troyan] *This ed.*; Troian *Q1, Q2*.   and having] *Q2*;
hauing *Q1*.   41.1. *Antiphila shows it.*] *This ed.; not in Q1, Q2*.   42. 'has]
Q1, Q2 (has).

---

28. *downcast*] downward cast (*OED*, sb. 1).

30. *Oenone*] a nymph of Mount Ida, loved by Paris but deserted by him in
favour of Helen whom he carried off from Sparta to Troy.

32. *piece expressing*] picture representing.

33. *the Carthage queen*] Dido, lamenting Aeneas' departure. She is called 'the
Carthage queen' in *MND.*, I.i.173. With the picture of her in these lines (and
that of Ariadne in ll. 66–77 below) cf. *Mer.*, V.i.9–12: 'in such a night / Stood
Dido with a willow in her hand / Upon the wild sea-banks, and waft her love /
To come again to Carthage.'

35. *Troyan*] representing the probable pronunciation of Qq's Troian; the
two spellings 'Troian' and 'Troyan' were both used in the early 17th century
for modern 'Trojan'.

36. *thine*] thy tear.

38–9. *Here . . . marble*] 'Like Niobe, who was turned into a weeping statue
by the gods' (Gurr). Cf. Chapman, *Bussy D'Ambois*, V.iii.144–5: 'Here like a
Roman statue I will stand / Till death hath made me marble.'

38. *more pitying*] i.e., more pitying than man.

40. *piece of needlework*] picture made of needlework.

41. *Ariadne*] the daughter of Minos, king of Crete. She enabled Theseus to
find his way out of the labyrinth (after killing the Minotaur) by means of a
thread. He escaped with her, but deserted her on the island of Naxos.

42. *cozening*] deceiving, untrustworthy.

This should be Theseus; 'has a cozening face.
You meant him for a man?
Antiphila.   He was so, madam.
Aspatia. Why then, 'tis well enough. —Never look back;
    You have a full wind and a false heart, Theseus. —   45
    Does not the story say his keel was split,
    Or his masts spent, or some kind rock or other
    Met with his vessel?
Antiphila.   Not as I remember.
Aspatia. It should ha' been so. Could the gods know this,
    And not, of all their number, raise a storm?   50
    But they are all as ill. This false smile
    Was well expressed; just such another caught me. —
    You shall not go so. —
    Antiphila, in this place work a quicksand,
    And over it a shallow smiling water   55
    And his ship ploughing it, and then a Fear:

---

44. back] *Q2;* black *Q1.*   50. not] *Q2;* none *Q1.*   51–3.] *so Dyce;* But they
are all as ill, this false smile was exprest well, / Iust such another caught me,
you shall not goe so *Q1;* But they are all as ill. This false smile was well exprest,
/ Iust such another caught me, you shall not goe so *Antiphila, Q2.*   51. ill]
Q1, Q2; evil *Dyce.*   52. well expressed] *Q2;* exprest well *Q1.*   54.] *Q1;*
In this place worke a quicke-sand *Q2.*   55.] *This line repeated in Q1.*
56. Fear] *Colman;* feare *Q1, Q2.*

---

43. *You ... man?*] Aspatia's question, to which Antiphila (who takes it
literally) replies with what sounds like a puzzled affirmative, probably means
'You meant him for a typical man?' (i.e., a deceiver).

47. *spent*] worn out, i.e., ready to break.

kind] either (1) friendly to Ariadne in avenging her wrong, or (2) friendly
(with an ironical tone) to Theseus and his vessel.

50. *And not ... storm?*] and not raise a storm, not one of them all?

51. *But ... smile*] The absence of a syllable from the metre may reflect the
natural pause as Aspatia turns back to the picture. If emendation is thought
desirable, 'this his false smile' would be as plausible as Dyce's 'all as evil' or
Theobald's 'Ay, this false smile'.

53. *You ... so*] You (i.e., Theseus) shall not escape so.

55. *smiling*] dimpled with ripples.

56. *a Fear*] Not 'on the face of Theseus' (Gurr) but a personification.
Norland interprets 'a personification apprehending danger', and Fear in
Spenser, *Faerie Queene*, III, xii, 12, fits that description. But I think Aspatia's
sense is 'a personification embodying frightfulness' ('some fear' is used in the
sense 'something to be afraid of' in *MND.*, V.i.21–2).

Do that Fear to the life, wench.
Antiphila.   'Twill wrong the story.
Aspatia. 'Twill make the story, wronged by wanton poets,
    Live long and be believed. But where's the lady?
Antiphila. There, madam.   60
Aspatia. Fie, you have missed it here, Antiphila;
    You are much mistaken, wench.
    These colours are not dull and pale enough
    To show a soul so full of misery
    As this sad lady's was. Do it by me;   65
    Do it again by me, the lost Aspatia,
    And you shall find all true but the wild island.
    And think I stand upon the sea-beach now,
    Mine arms thus, and mine hair blown with the wind,
    Wild as that desert, and let all about me   70
    Tell that I am forsaken. Do my face

---

57. to the life] *Q2;* brauely *Q1.*   *Antiphila.*] *Q2;* OLIM. *Q1.*   61. here] *Q2*
(heere)*;* there *Q1.*   65. sad] *Q2;* poore *Q1.*   67. shall] *Q2;* will *Q1.*
68. And ... now,] *Gurr;* Suppose I stand vpon the Sea, breach now *Q1;* I
stand vpon the sea breach now, and thinke *Q2.*   sea-beach] *Langbaine;* Sea,
breach *Q1;* sea breach *Q2.*   70. that desert, and] *Q2;* the place she was in,
Q1.   71. Tell that I am forsaken] *Q2;* Be teares of my story *Q1.*

---

57. *to the life*] in most lifelike form.
58. *wanton*] irresponsible.
65. *by me*] taking me as your model.
66. *lost*] slain (by grief).
67. *the wild island*] the desert island (of Naxos).
68. *And think*] Gurr persuasively argues that these words, substituted in
revision for the synonymous 'Suppose' of Q1, were mistakenly added to the
end of the line in Q2.
    sea-beach] the shore, particularly a pebbled shore (*OED*, beach, 1, the
original sense, is a collective noun meaning the pebbles themselves); cf. the
epithets 'beached', *MND.*, II.i.85, *Tim.*, V.i.214, and 'beachy', *2H4*, III.i.50.
'Breach' can mean only the breaking of the waves (cf. *Philaster*, V.iii.184–5:
'let me stand the shock / Of this mad sea-breach'), and therefore emendation is
necessary.
69. *thus*] either (1) stretched out in appeal to the deserter, or (2) folded in
sign of grief, a gesture characteristic of melancholy lovers of both sexes (cf.
Sidney, *Astrophil and Stella*, 8th Song, l. 19) and portrayed on the original title-
page of Burton's *Anatomy of Melancholy* (1621). A reference to the latter
gesture in *Philaster*, II.iii.54–5 ('if it be love / To sit cross-armed and think
away the day') is not analogous enough to the present passage to imply the
second gesture here, nor to justify the Q2 reading in l. 68 (where 'and think'
appears as an intransitive verb).

(If thou hadst ever feeling of a sorrow)
Thus, thus, Antiphila: strive to make me look
Like sorrow's monument, and the trees about me,
Let them be dry and leafless; let the rocks   75
Groan with continual surges; and behind me
Make all a desolation. Look, look, wenches,
A miserable life of this poor picture!
Olympias. Dear madam—
Aspatia.   I have done. Sit down, and let us
Upon that point fix all our eyes, that point there.   80
Make a dumb silence till you feel our sadness
Give us new souls.   [*They all sit.*]

Enter CALIANAX.

Calianax. The King may do this, and he may not do it;
    My child is wronged, disgraced—
[*To Antiphila and Olympias*] Well, how now, hussies?

---

73. strive to make me look] *Q2;* make me looke good girle *Q1.*
74. monument] *Q2;* mount *Q1.*   77. Look, look] *Q2;* see, see *Q1.*   81. till
you feel our sadness] *This ed.;* till you feele a sudden sadnesse *Q1, Q2;* till you
feel a sullen sadness *conj. Seward;* till you feel a sadness *Theobald;* till a sudden
sadness *conj. Deighton.*   84. hussies] *This ed.;* huswiues *Q1, Q2.*

---

74. *monument*] statue (*OED,* 5.c).
78. *life*] 'living image' (Norland). She is the suffering human reality of what
the picture merely represents.
poor] i.e., merely inanimate.
81. *Make . . . sadness*] Since no elision can reduce Qq's version of this line to
a pentameter it is presumably corrupt, especially as its sense is not apparent:
why should they feel the effect of a *sudden* sadness? They feel sadness (*OED,* 5:
sorrowfulness) already, and the meditative pose that Aspatia enjoins would be
a continuous state of sadness (*OED,* 2: gravity of mind or demeanour). I think
'sudden' came from an imperfectly deleted miswriting of 'sadness' (i.e.,
'sadden[esse]', the first six letters only being written before the deletion) which
the Q1 compositor mistook for 'sudden', and that 'a' came from his
memorising 'our' phonetically while setting the line (cf. 'A griefe' for 'Her
griefe', II.i.128).
83. *The King . . . do it*] The King has a political right, but not a moral right,
to break off my daughter's marriage.
84. *hussies*] worthless women. The word (*OED* first in 1530) is 'a phonetic
reduction of "housewife"' (*OED*), which in this opprobrious sense (*OED,*
housewife, 2) it has replaced in modern use (*OED,* hussy, 3; first example,
1647). If the old form of the word is kept it must be pronounced 'hussifs', not
'housewives'.

What, at your ease? Is this a time to sit still?   85
Up, you young lazy whores, up, or I'll swinge you!
Olympias. Nay, good my lord—
Calianax. You'll lie down shortly. Get you in and work!
What, are you grown so resty? You want heats:
We shall have some of the court boys do that office.   90
Antiphila. My lord, we do no more than we are charged:
It is the lady's pleasure we be thus,
In grief she is forsaken.
Calianax.   There's a rogue too,
A young dissembling slave. Well, get you in!
I'll have a bout with that boy: 'tis high time   95
Now to be valiant; I confess my youth
Was never prone that way. What, made an ass?
A court stale? Well, I will be valiant

85–6.] *so Theobald;* What ... young / Lazie ... you *Q1, Q2.*   88. get
you in and work] *Q2;* in and whine there *Q1.*   89. resty] *Q2* (reasty)*; rustie
Q1.*   90. do that office] *Q2;* heat you shortly *Q1.*   91–3. My lord ...
forsaken] *so Theobald;* My Lord we doe no more then we are charg'd: / It is
the Ladies pleasure we be thus in griefe, / Shee is forsaken *Q2;* Good my Lord
be not angry, we doe nothing / But what my Ladies pleasure is, we are thus in
griefe, / She is forsaken *Q1.*   92–3. thus, / In grief ... forsaken.] *Dyce
(subst.);* thus in griefe, / ... forsaken *Q1, Q2;* thus; / In grief ... forsaken.
Daniel, conj. Mason.   94. young] *Q2;* slie *Q1.*   95. a bout] *Q2;* about *Q1.*
97. What, made an ass?]*Q2; not in Q1.*   98. will] *Q2;* must *Q1.*

---

85. *to sit still*] always to be seated (stress 'sit').
86. *swinge*] thrash.
88. *lie down*] i.e., progress to the final stage of idleness, after the sitting-
down stage (stress 'lie'). The phrase prepares for l. 90, since 'lie down' has
sexual associations.
work] do your needlework.
89. *resty*] disinclined to action or exertion; sluggish, indolent, lazy, inactive
(*OED*, resty, 2).
want] need.
heats] A heat is 'a run given to a racehorse by way of exercise in preparation
for a race' (*OED*, 8.c; first example, 1670).
90. *court boys*] pages, or perhaps (with the derogatory sense of 'boy') young
courtiers. Calianax expects them to exercise Aspatia's women sexually.
93. *In grief ... forsaken*] to show our sorrow that she has been forsaken.
a rogue] i.e., Amintor.
94. *slave*] villain.
97. *prone*] inclined.
98. *court stale*] laughing-stock at court. Cf *3H6*, III.iii.260–1: 'Had he none
else to make a stale but me? / Then none but I shall turn his jest to sorrow.'

And beat some dozen of these whelps; and there's
Another of 'em, a trim cheating soldier: 100
I'll maul that rascal! 'Has out-braved me twice,
But now, I thank the gods, I am valiant.
Go, get you in! I'll take a course with all.   *Exeunt.*

---

99. whelps; and] *Q1*; whelps I will, and *Q2*.   101. 'Has] *Q1, Q2* (has).
103. *Exeunt.*] *Q1, Q2* (*subst.: Exeunt om[nes].*).

99.] Turner persuasively argues that Q2's 'I will' resulted from the
correction of Q1's 'I must' to 'I will' in the previous line.

100. *trim*] fine (ironical): cf. *MND.*, III.ii.157: 'A trim exploit, a manly
enterprise'.

101. *'Has*] He has.

out-braved me] overcome me in mutual defiance.

102. *valiant*] This word, applied with sincerity to Amintor at I.i.47, is
henceforward satirically associated with Calianax.

103. *take* ... *all*] take steps (*OED*, take, 21) [to deal] with [them] all.
Alternatively, if 'with all' has been accidentally printed for 'withal' (spelled
'withall' by both Qq at III.ii.85), the sense is 'take steps [to deal] with [the
matter]'.

Act III

ACT III   [SCENE i]
Enter CLEON, STRATO, [*and*] DIPHILUS.

Cleon. Your sister is not up yet.

Diphilus. O, brides must take their morning's rest,
  The night is troublesome.

Strato.   But not tedious.

Diphilus. What odds he has not my sister's maidenhead
  tonight?   5

Strato. None: it's odds against any bridegroom living, he ne'er
  gets it while he lives.

Diphilus. Y'are merry with my sister: you'll please to allow me
  the same freedom with your mother.

Strato. She's at your service.   10

Diphilus. Then she's merry enough of herself, she needs no
  tickling. Knock at the door.

Strato. We shall interrupt them.

Diphilus. No matter, they have the year before them.

                                        [*Knocks at the door.*]

ACT III] *Q1, Q2 (Actus Tertius.)*   2. O] *Q2* (Oh)*; Our Q1.*   6. None] *Q1*;
No *Q2.*   14.1. *Knocks at the door.*] *Norland; not in Q1, Q2.*

6–7. *None ... lives*] Strato's cynical implication is that the average bride
has lost it before marriage. Gurr argues for 'a double innuendo', the other
being that 'the bridegroom of course "dies" in getting his bride's maidenhead'
(cf. I.ii.238 n.); but this is strained when the obvious jest is so thoroughly in
keeping with Strato's personality.

12. *tickling*] i.e., to make her laugh. In this reply Diphilus jestingly gives a
sexual sense to Strato's permission to use (verbal) 'freedom'.

12–14. *Knock ... before them*] The stage action, and the text, are
ambiguous here. It is not impossible that 'knock at the dore' (attached
to the rest of the speech by a comma in Q1 and so reprinted in Q2) is a
stage direction in the common imperative form; but since Q2's annotator
cannot have found a stage direction set out as such in the manuscript he was
following, it would be rash to emend. Granted that the words belong to
Diphilus' speech, it is debatable whether Strato knocks at the door or hesitates
to do so. I follow Norland in supposing that Diphilus has to do the knocking
himself, as he is certainly at the door when addressing the off-stage Evadne,
and it is he, not Strato, whom Amintor first sees on entering.

Good morrow, sister! Spare yourself today;   15
The night will come again.

Enter AMINTOR.

Amintor. Who's there? My brother? I am no readier yet.
    Your sister is but now up.
Diphilus. You look as you had lost your eyes tonight;
    I think you ha' not slept.
Amintor.   I' faith, I have not.   20
Diphilus. You have done better then.
Amintor. We have ventured for a boy; when he is twelve
    'A shall command against the foes of Rhodes.
    Shall we be merry?
Strato.   You cannot, you want sleep.
Amintor. 'Tis true; (*Aside*) but she,   25
    As if she had drunk Lethe, or had made
    Even with heaven, did fetch so still a sleep,
    So sweet and sound—
Diphilus.   What's that?
Amintor. [*To him*]   Your sister frets
    This morning, and does turn her eyes upon me,

15–16.] *so Langbaine; as prose, Q1, Q2.*   17–18.] *so Weber; as prose, Q1, Q2.*
19–20.] *so Langbaine; as prose, Q1, Q2.*   20. have] *Q2;* did *Q1.*   22. We
have] *Q1;* We *Q2.*   25. Aside] *Q2 (opposite this line), Q1 (opposite l. 27).*
28–32.] *so Colman; as prose, Q1, Q2.*   29. does] *Q2;* doth *Q1.*

15. *Spare yourself*] 'lend yourself' (*OED*, 8), i.e., bestow your presence on us; perhaps with the ironical secondary sense 'do not treat yourself severely' (*OED*, 1), i.e., give yourself a rest from sexual activity.

17. *brother*] brother-in-law.

no readier yet] Amintor enters putting on his doublet; cf. Evadne's 'I am not ready [dressed] yet' (l. 78).

19. *You ... tonight*] i.e., your eyelids are drooping over your eyes this morning.

22. *ventured*] made a merchant-venturers' voyage (here figuratively, for begetting a child).

26. *drunk Lethe*] drunk the waters of oblivion. The waters of the river Lethe in the underworld caused souls to forget the past.

26–7. *made ... heaven*] settled her spiritual account with heaven.

27. *fetch*] take. The relevant sense in *OED* is 7: 'To draw, get, take (breath)'. The phrase here combines the ideas of sleeping quietly and breathing gently (cf. ll. 37–9).

As people on their headsman. She does chafe,   30
And kiss, and chafe again, and clap my cheeks:
She's in another world.
Diphilus. Then I had lost. I was about to lay
    You had not got her maidenhead tonight.
Amintor. [*Aside*] Ha! Does he not mock me? [*To him*] Y'ad
    lost indeed;   35
I do not use to bungle.
Cleon.   You do deserve her.
Amintor. (*Aside*) I laid my lips to hers, and that wild breath,
    That was so rude and rough to me last night,
    Was sweet as April. I'll be guilty too,
    If these be the effects.   40

Enter MELANTIUS.

Melantius. Good day, Amintor, for to me the name
    Of brother is too distant: we are friends,
    And that is nearer.
Amintor.   Dear Melantius,
    Let me behold thee. Is it possible?
Melantius. What sudden gaze is this?

---

30. their] *Q2;* the *Q1.*   31. chafe again] *Q2;* chafe *Q1.*   35. *Aside*] *Weber;*
not in *Q1, Q2.*   Ha! Does he not mock me?] *Q1* (Ha, does hee not mocke
mee,)*;* Ha, he does not mocke me, *Q2.*   36. use to bungle] *Q2;* bungle *Q1.*
37. *Aside*] *Q2* (*opposite l. 38*); not in *Q1.*   breath] *Q2;* breach *Q1.*

---

   30. *headsman*] executioner; with word-play on loss of maidenhead (cf. *Rom.*,
I.i.23–5: 'cut off ... the heads of the maids').
    chafe] fret.
    31. *clap*] pat.
    32. *in another world*] beside herself with happiness. Though not in Tilley,
evidently proverbial (cf. *The Scornful Lady*, II.i.246).
    33. *lay*] wager.
    35. *Ha ... mock me?*] Both Q1's and Q2's readings make sense. In Q1
Amintor's words express a single idea (that Diphilus is perhaps taunting him
with Evadne's guilt), which he then silently rejects and gives a good-humoured
reply. In Q2 Amintor first starts apprehensively ('Ha!') and then (still in an
aside) reassures himself that Diphilus is not taunting him. But the aside has to
be delivered fairly rapidly, and so I follow Q1 and regard Q2's reading as a
compositor's transposition error.
    36. *use to bungle*] make a habit of bungling.
    39–40. *I'll ... effects*] If her evil-doing gives her such untroubled sleep, I
too will do evil.

Amintor.   'Tis wondrous strange.   45
Melantius. Why does thine eye desire so strict a view
    Of that it knows so well? There's nothing here
    That is not thine.
Amintor.   I wonder much, Melantius,
    To see those noble looks that make me think
    How virtuous thou art; and on the sudden   50
    'Tis strange to me thou shouldst have worth and honour,
    Or not be base, and false, and treacherous,
    And every ill. But—
Melantius.   Stay, stay, my friend:
    I fear this sound will not become our loves;
    No more; embrace me.   [*Embraces Amintor.*]
Amintor.   O, mistake me not!   55
    I know thee to be full of all those deeds
    That we frail men call good, but by the course
    Of nature thou shouldst be as quickly changed
    As are the winds, dissembling as the sea,
    That now wears brows as smooth as virgins' be,   60

50. the] *Q2;* this *Q1.*   53. But—] *Q2* (But); *not in Q1;* But yet—*conj. this ed.*   Stay, stay] *Q2;* Say, stay *Q1.*   54–5. I fear ... embrace me] *so Langbaine; as one line, Q1, Q2.*   55. No more; embrace me.] *F2* (no more, embrace me.*);* no more embrace me. *Q1, Q2.*

45. *sudden*] unexpected.
53. *But*—] I conjecture 'But yet—', not merely to fill up the metre but to turn Melantius' 'Stay, stay, my friend' into the interruption which it requires to be: it must not follow a pause. Possibly the annotator for Q2, with 'But yet' before him in the manuscript, mistook the two words for alternatives; or the compositor may simply have forgotten to set 'yet' (there is no punctuation after 'But').
54. *become*] befit.
55. *No more; embrace me.*] The absence of punctuation in Q1 is typical of that text (cf. V.iii.150: 'No more persue me not.'), and, though this passage remains unpunctuated in Q2 (which corrects V.iii.150), the emended punctuation of F2 is right. Unpunctuated, Melantius' words would have to mean either (in the more natural interpretation) 'never embrace me again' or (in the less natural one) 'release me from your present embrace'; in either case he would be repelling Amintor. But this would be inconsistent with his sincere reiteration of 'my friend' (ll. 53, 66) and his bewilderment, not anger, at Amintor's words. The correct stage business (contrast that of Norland, who makes Amintor embrace Melantius at l. 44 and Melantius push Amintor away at l. 55) is as follows: at l. 44 Amintor holds Melantius in an arm's-length embrace ('Let me behold thee') and at l. 55 Melantius enfolds Amintor in his arms ('No more; embrace me.').

Tempting the merchant to invade his face,
And in an hour calls his billows up
And shoots 'em at the sun, destroying all
'A carries on him. (*Aside*) O, how near am I
To utter my sick thoughts!　　　　　　　　　　　65
Melantius. But why, my friend, should I be so by nature?
Amintor. I have wed thy sister, who hath virtuous thoughts
Enow for one whole family, and it is strange
That you should feel no want.
Melantius. Believe me, this is compliment too cunning for me.　　70
Diphilus. What should I be, then, by the course of nature,
They having both robbed me of so much virtue?
Strato. O, call the bride, my lord Amintor,
That we may see her blush and turn her eyes down:
It is the prettiest sport!　　　　　　　　　　　75
Amintor. Evadne!
Evadne. (*Within*) My lord?
Amintor.　　　　　　　　Come forth, my love.
Your brothers do attend to wish you joy.
Evadne. [*Within*] I am not ready yet.
Amintor.　　　　　　　　Enough, enough!
Evadne. [*Within*] They'll mock me.
Amintor.　　　　　　　　'Faith, thou shalt come in.

Enter EVADNE.

Melantius. Good morrow, sister. He that understands　　80
Whom you have wed need not to wish you joy:
You have enough; take heed you be not proud.
Diphilus. O, sister, what have you done?
Evadne. I done! Why, what have I done?
Strato. My lord Amintor swears you are no maid now.　　85
Evadne. Push!
Strato. I' faith he does.

---

62. calls] Q2 (cals); call Q1.　　63. shoots] Q2; shoot Q1.　　66. But why] Q2;
Why Q1.　　73-5.] so Weber; as prose, Q1, Q2.　　78. Within] Dyce; not in Q1,
Q2.　　79. Within] Dyce; not in Q1, Q2.　　84. I done! Why] Q2; Why Q1.

---

61. *merchant*] merchant ship; cf. II.ii.18.
62. *hour*] (two syllables).
70. *cunning*] ingenious.
86. *Push!*] an interjection of mild annoyance.

Evadne.   I knew I should be mocked.

Diphilus. With a truth.

Evadne. If 'twere to do again,
   In faith, I would not marry.

Amintor. (Aside)   Nor I, by heaven!   90

Diphilus. Sister, Dula swears
   She heard you cry two rooms off.

Evadne.   Fie, how you talk!

Diphilus. Let's see you walk. By my troth, y'are spoiled.

Melantius.   Amintor—

Amintor. Ha?

Melantius.   Thou art sad.

Amintor.   Who, I? I thank you for that.
   Shall Diphilus, thou and I sing a catch?   95

Melantius. How!

Amintor. Prithee, let's.

Melantius.   Nay, that's too much the other way.

Amintor. I am so lightened with my happiness!
   [*To Evadne*] How dost thou, love? Kiss me.

Evadne. I cannot love you, you tell tales of me.   100

Amintor. Nothing but what becomes us. Gentlemen,

89–92. If ... off] *so Weber;* If ... mary. / AMIN. Nor ... heauen. / DIPH.
Sister ... off *Q1, Q2.*   90. *Aside] Q2; not in Q1.*   93. Let's ... spoiled]
Turner; Lets see you walke. / EVAD. By my troth y'are spoild *Q1, Q2;* Let's
see you walk, Evadne. By my troth, you're spoil'd *Colman.*   94–5. Who
... catch?] *so Langbaine; as prose, Q1, Q2.*   98–9. I ... me] *so Langbaine;
as prose, Q1, Q2.*   98. lightened] *Q2 (lightned);* heighned [*sic*] *Q1.*

---

93. *Let's ... spoiled*] Q1, followed by Q2, gives 'By my troth, y'are spoiled'
to Evadne, possibly because of a wrong assumption that 'Let's see you walk' is
a rhyming retort to 'Fie, how you talk!' The whole speech belongs to Diphilus,
who 'is speaking as though he were examining a mare whose gait has been
ruined by too hard riding' (Turner), with an obvious sexual implication. There
is no need to incorporate Q1's speech-prefix into the speech as 'Evadne', since
(1) there is another explanation of its presence (as above), (2) Evadne is
consistently addressed as 'sister' by her brothers in this scene.

94. *I ... that*] No editor comments on this, but I am not sure of its
meaning. Perhaps Amintor (accepting Melantius' 'Thou art sad' as true)
thanks him for implicitly suggesting some merriment; or, rather more
probably, (rejecting it as untrue) he thanks him for making so laughable a
remark (as one might reply 'That's a good one!'). The traditional notion of
post-coital sadness is probably relevant in either case.

95. *catch*] 'A short musical composition for three or more voices, which sing
the same melody, the second singer beginning the first line as the first goes on
to the second line, and so on with each successive singer' (*OED*).

Would you had all such wives, and all the world,
That I might be no wonder! Y'are all sad:
What, do you envy me? I walk, methinks,
On water and ne'er sink, I am so light.   105
Melantius. 'Tis well you are so.
Amintor. Well? How can I be other when she looks thus?
    Is there no music there? Let's dance.
Melantius. Why, this is strange, Amintor!
Amintor. I do not know myself; yet I could wish   110
    My joy were less.
Diphilus. I'll marry too, if it will make one thus.
Evadne. (*Aside*) Amintor, hark.
Amintor. [*To her*] What says my love? [*To the others*] I must
    obey.
Evadne. [*Aside to him*] You do it scurvily, 'twill be perceived.   115
Cleon. [*To Amintor*] My lord, the King is here.

                Enter KING *and* LYSIPPUS.

Amintor.   Where?
Strato.   And his brother.
King. Good morrow, all.
    Amintor, joy on joy fall thick upon thee!
    [*To Evadne*] And, madam, you are altered since I saw you;
    I must salute you, you are now another's.   [*Kisses her.*]   120

---

107. Well? How can I] *Q2*; Well? can you *Q1*.   109. Why ... Amintor!] *Q2*
(Why? this is strange, *Amintor.*); Why? this is strange. *Q1*.   110–11. I do ...
less] *so Weber; as prose, Q1, Q2*.   112. marry too] *Q2*; marrie *Q1*.   116. *To
Amintor*] *This ed.; not in Q1, Q2*.   My lord, the King] *Langbaine;* my Lord
the King *Q1, Q2*.   119. And] *Q2*; But *Q1*.   120. *Kisses her.*] *Norland
(subst.); not in Q1, Q2*.

102–3. *Would ... wonder!*] Daniel marks 'and ... wonder' as an aside, but
this breaks the flow of the speech, which reads more naturally as an
extravagant protestation of happiness.
    110–11. *Yet ... less*] Norland marks this as an aside (meaning, presumably,
that Amintor wishes he were unmarried), but Amintor is announcing that his
joy, being extreme, is almost too much for him to endure. His exaggerated
rapture then draws Evadne's rebuke (l. 115).
    115. *scurvily*] badly, i.e., unconvincingly.
    120. *salute*] 'greet (conventionally with a kiss)' (Norland).
    another's] not your own, but your husband's. (Like many other remarks in
the scene, this underlines the irony of the situation.)

How liked you your night's rest?

Evadne.   Ill, sir.

Amintor. Indeed, she took but little.

Lysippus. You'll let her take more and thank her too, shortly.

King. Amintor,
Wert thou truly honest till thou wert married?

Amintor.   Yes, sir.   125

King. Tell me, then,
How shows the sport unto thee?

Amintor.   Why, well.

King. What did you do?

Amintor. No more nor less than other couples use:
You know what 'tis, it has but a coarse name.   130

King. But, prithee, I should think, by her black eye
And her red cheek, she should be quick and stirring
In this same business, ha?

Amintor.   I cannot tell;
I ne'er tried other, sir; but I perceive
She is as quick as you delivered.

King.   Well,   135
You'll trust me then, Amintor, to choose a wife
For you again?

Amintor.   No, never, sir.

King. Why, like you this so ill?

Amintor.   So well I like her;

124–7. Amintor . . . well] *so this ed.; as prose, Q1, Q2.*   126–7. then, / How]
Q2 (then, how); how then *Q1.*   127. unto thee] *Q2*; to you *Q1.*   133–7. I
cannot . . . again?] *so Weber;* I cannot . . . perceiue / She . . . deliuered. / KING.
Well . . . *Amintor,* / To . . . agen. *Q1, Q2.*

---

121. *How . . . sir*] The pause before Evadne's reply is written into the
versification, as are the pauses before Amintor's replies at ll. 127 and 137.

125. *honest*] chaste (*OED*, 3.b). The King's question is a highly charged one
in the circumstances, since he is confident (at this point in the scene) that
Evadne has not allowed Amintor to consummate the marriage.

127. *shows*] seems (*OED*, 30.c).

130. *a coarse name*] 'To fucke' is listed in J. Florio, *A World of Words* (1598),
p. 137, among the equivalents of the Italian *fottere*.

131. *prithee*] i.e., to continue the conversation, if you please.

black] having a dark-brown iris. The combination of black eyes and golden
hair (cf. the bracelet imagery of II.i. 274–6) is found in Sidney, *Astrophil and
Stella*, Sonnets vii and ix, and *Arcadia*, bk. I, chap. 13, p. 90.

135. *delivered*] affirmed (*OED*, 11.b).

138. *this*] this wife of yours.

For this I bow my knee in thanks to you,
And unto heaven will pay my grateful tribute   140
Hourly, and do hope we shall draw out
A long contented life together here,
And die both full of grey hairs in one day,
For which the thanks is yours; but if the powers
That rule us please to call her first away,   145
Without pride spoke, this world holds not a wife
Worthy to take her room.
King. (*Aside*) I do not like this. [*Aloud*] All forbear the room
But you, Amintor, and your lady;

       [*Exeunt* LYSIPPUS, CLEON, STRATO, DIPHILUS
                   and MELANTIUS.]

                  I have some speech with you,
That may concern your after living well.   150
Amintor. [*Aside*] 'A will not tell me that he lies with her? If
   he do,
Something heavenly stay my heart, for I shall be apt
To thrust this arm of mine to acts unlawful.

---

148. *Aside*] *Q1* (*opposite l. 147*); *not in Q2.*   149–50. But ... well] *so this ed.;*
But ... may / Concerne ... well *Q1; as prose, Q2.*   149.1. *Exeunt* ...
MELANTIUS.] *Theobald (subst.); not in Q1, Q2.*   149. speech with you] *Q2;*
speech *Q1.*   150. *Aside*] *Weber; not in Q1, Q2.*   152–3. Something ...
unlawful] *Q2;* For it is apt to thrust this arme of mine to acts vnlawfull *Q1.*

---

139. *this*] this generosity of yours.
141. *Hourly*] (three syllables).
146. *Without pride spoke*] I speak without boasting (of my good fortune).
147. *room*] place.
148. *forbear*] leave.
149. *I have ... you*] I have something to talk with you about. For the idiom
cf. *Wiv.*, II.i.149: 'We have an hour's talk with you.'
150. *your ... well*] your later welfare.
151–3.] Q2 has to be followed here, since it evidently incorporates revision,
and Q1's incomplete sense shows an omission; but the revision is not quite
satisfactory, particularly in the substitution of 'for I shall be apt' for Q1's 'For
it is apt' (where 'it' refers to 'my heart' in the omitted phrase and thus gives
coherence to the sentence), in the vague phraseology of 'something heavenly',
and in the metrical irregularity. I think that at some early stage the lines ran:
''A will not tell me that he lies with her? / If he do, God stay my heart, for it is
apt / To thrust this arm of mine to acts unlawful.' After the statute of 27 May
1606 prohibiting the abuse of God's name in stage-plays (see Chambers, *E.S.*,
IV, 338–9) playwrights were inclined to be sensitive on this matter (though not
consistently so, cf. l. 213), and the revision may reflect this sensitivity, as may
the omission in Q1 (cf. II.i.176–7 n.).
152. *stay*] restrain.

King. You will suffer me to talk with her, Amintor,
    And not have a jealous pang?
Amintor.   Sir, I dare trust my wife   155
    With whom she dares to talk, and not be jealous. [*Retires.*]
King. [*To Evadne*] How do you like Amintor?
Evadne.   As I did, sir.
King. How's that?
Evadne. As one that, to fulfil your will and pleasure,
    I have given leave to call me wife and love.   160
King. I see there is no lasting faith in sin:
    They that break word with heaven will break again
    With all the world, and so dost thou with me.
Evadne. How, sir?
King.   This subtle woman's ignorance
    Will not excuse you; thou hast taken oaths   165
    So great that methought they did misbecome
    A woman's mouth, that thou wouldst ne'er enjoy
    A man but me.
Evadne.   I never did swear so:
    You do me wrong.
King.   Day and night have heard it.
Evadne. I swore indeed that I would never love   170
    A man of lower place, but if your fortune
    Should throw you from this height, I bade you trust
    I would forsake you and would bend to him
    That won your throne. I love with my ambition,
    Not with my eyes. But if I ever yet   175
    Touched any other, leprosy light here
    Upon my face, which for your royalty
    I would not stain.
King. Why, thou dissemblest, and it is in me
    To punish thee.

155. a jealous pang] *Q2;* healous pangs *Q1.*   156. With whom] *Q2;* When
Q1.   156. Retires.] *Weber (subst.); not in Q1, Q2.*   159. your will and] *Q2;*
your *Q1.*   168–9. I . . . wrong] *so Theobald; as one line, Q1, Q2.*

158. *How's that?*] What do you mean? Cf. 'How, sir?' (l. 164).
164. *This . . . ignorance*] this ignorance that women subtly feign.
173. *I . . . ambition*] 'This is the only speech of Evadne's to hint at her
reasons for her liaison with the King' (Gurr).
177. *for your royalty*] in exchange for your royal station.

Evadne.   Why, it is in me, then,   180
  Not to love you, which will more afflict
  Your body than your punishment can mine.
King. But thou hast let Amintor lie with thee.
Evadne. I ha' not.
King.   Impudence, he says himself so.
Evadne. 'A lies.
King.   'A does not.
Evadne.   By this light, he does,   185
  Strangely and basely, and I'll prove it so.
  I did not only shun him for a night,
  But told him I would never close with him.
King. Speak lower; 'tis false.
Evadne.   I am no man,
  To answer with a blow, or, if I were,   190
  You are the King; but urge not, 'tis most true.
King. Do not I know the uncontrollèd thoughts
  That youth brings with him, when his blood is high
  With expectation and desire of that
  He long hath waited for? Is not his spirit,   195
  Though he be temperate, of a valiant strain
  As this our age hath known? What could he do,
  If such a sudden speech had met his blood,

180–2. Why ... mine] *so Daniel;* Why ... will / More ... mine *Q1, Q2.*
185–7. By ... night] *so Theobald;* By ... and / Ile ... night *Q1, Q2.*
189–91. I ... true] *so Theobald;* I ... blow, / Or ... true *Q1, Q2.*

---

184. *Impudence*] impudent woman (impudence personified). The earliest *OED* example is dated 1671.

186. *Strangely*] monstrously.

187. *close*] unite.

189. *Speak lower*] The versification calls for a brief pause between this instruction and the renewal of the dialogue; during it the King may throw a glance towards Amintor.

191. *urge*] importune ('me' understood), *OED*, 3.

193. *youth*] the quality of youth. The personal pronouns are equivalent to modern impersonal pronouns. At the same time 'youth' is not completely abstract, but is a half-personification.

195. *his*] Amintor's.

196. *a valiant strain*] a disposition as valiant.

198. *sudden*] unexpected.

blood] passion.

But ruin thee for ever, if he had not killed thee?
He could not bear it thus: he is as we,   200
Or any other wronged man.
Evadne.   It is dissembling.
King. Take him; farewell. Henceforth I am thy foe,
And what disgraces I can blot thee with, look for.
Evadne. Stay, sir. [*To Amintor*] Amintor! [*To King*] You shall
hear. [*To Amintor*] Amintor!
                              [*Amintor comes forward.*]
Amintor. What, my love?   205
Evadne. Amintor, thou hast an ingenious look,
And shouldst be virtuous: it amazeth me
That thou canst make such base malicious lies.
Amintor. What, my dear wife?
Evadne.   Dear wife! I do despise thee.
Why, nothing can be baser than to sow   210
Dissension amongst lovers.
Amintor.   Lovers? Who?
Evadne. The King and me—
Amintor. O God!
Evadne. Who should live long and love without distaste,
Were it not for such pickthanks as thyself.   215

199–200. But ... thus] *Weber, conj. Mason;* But ruine thee for euer, if he had
not kild thee / He could not beare it thus, *Q1;* But ruine thee for euer? if he had
not kild thee, / He could not beare it thus, *Q2.*   201. It] *Q2;* This *Q1.*
202–5. *King.* Take ... love] *Q2; not in Q1.*   204. hear. Amintor!] *Q6*
(heare, *Amintor.*); heare *Amintor. Q2; not in Q1.*   204.1. *Amintor comes
forward.*] *Weber (subst.); not in Q1, Q2.*   208. canst] *Q2;* should'st *Q1.*
212. me] *Q2;* I *Q1.*   214. live long] *Q1, Q2;* love long *conj. Daniel.*

199–200. *But ... thus*] Brereton defends the punctuation of Qq as meaning
'He could not show such cheerful equanimity if he had not taken vengeance for
such an injury.' But the corollary of this is 'and if he had, then he could', the
absurdity of which justifies Mason's emendation. It is probable that Q1
accidentally omits an interrogation-mark at the end of l. 199, and that Q2's
punctuation is the annotator's attempt to correct Q1's.
    199. *ruin*] disfigure (*OED*, 1, reduce to ruins: figuratively).
    200. *bear it thus*] endure it as calmly as he is doing.
    we] I (the royal plural).
    206. *ingenious*] ingenuous (*OED*, 4).
    214. *live long*] The reading of Qq is correct, implying a life-long love.
    distaste] unpleasantness, annoyance, discomfort (*OED*, 3).
    215. *pickthanks*] tale-bearers.

Did you lie with me? Swear now, and be punished
In hell for this.

Amintor.   The faithless sin I made
To fair Aspatia is not yet revenged:
It follows me. [*To King*] I will not loose a word
To this vile woman, but to you, my king,   220
The anguish of my soul thrusts out this truth:
Y'are a tyrant, and not so much to wrong
An honest man thus, as to take a pride
In talking with him of it.

Evadne. Now, sir, see how loud this fellow lied.   225

Amintor. You that can know to wrong, should know how men
Must right themselves. What punishment is due
From me to him that shall abuse my bed?
Is it not death? Nor can that satisfy,
Unless I send your limbs through all the land   230

216–17. Did ... this] *so Theobald;* Did ... hell / For this *Q1, Q2.*
217. *Amintor.] Q1, Q2; Amintor (aside). Turner.* 220. vile] *Colman* (vild);
wilde *Q1, Q2.* 225. see] *Q1, Q2;* you see *conj. this ed.* lied] *Q2;* lies *Q1.*
226–7. how men / Must] *so Theobald;* how / Men must *Q1, Q2.* 229. Is it
not death?] *Colman;* It is not death, *Q1, Q2.* 230–1. Unless ... myself.]
Q2 (your liues); Vnlesse I show how nobly I haue freed my selfe. *Q1.*
230. limbs] *Theobald, conj. Sympson;* liues *Q2;* not in *Q1.*

---

216. *be punished*] i.e., for perjury.
217–19. *The faithless ... follows me*] Though not addressed directly to
either Evadne or the King, this is an exclamation rather than an aside.
219. *loose*] let go.
222. *Y'are*] Emendation would seem to be required by the metre, but the
similar (and similarly unmetrical) line in *Philaster*, V.iii.78, 'Y'are a tyrant and
a savage monster', urges the retention of 'Y'are', which perhaps represents 'Ye
are'.
225. *see*] 'you see' would not only be metrically preferable but would convey
the sense 'you have had it proved to you', which 'see' alone does not.
226. *know to*] know how to (*OED,* 12).
230. *your limbs*] Colman defends Q2's 'lives' by explaining that Amintor
mean 'to send an account through the land of their vicious mode of life, and
criminal connection'; but Theobald's 'limbs' is preferable because (1) 'What
Amintor had in contemplation, was not to display the justice of his cause, but
the exemplary manner in which he had revenged it' (Mason) and (2) at this
point Amintor is addressing the King and ignoring Evadne (cf. ll. 219–20),
so 'your' should be taken as singular, not plural. A misreading of 'lims' or
'limmes' as 'liues' in Q2 would be easy, and Q1's omission (unless due to eye-
skip) is explainable as expurgation of such regicidal butchery. The notion of

To show how nobly I have freed myself.
                              [*Lays his hand on his sword.*]
King. Draw not thy sword. Thou knowst I cannot fear
          A subject's hand, but thou shalt feel the weight
          Of this, if thou dost rage.   [*Lays his hand on his sword.*]
Amintor.   The weight of that!
          If you have any worth, for heaven's sake think   235
          I fear not swords, for, as you are mere man,
          I dare as easily kill you for this deed
          As you dare think to do it: but there is
          Divinity about you, that strikes dead
          My rising passions. As you are my king,   240
          I fall before you and present my sword
          To cut mine own flesh if it be your will.
          Alas, I am nothing but a multitude
          Of waking griefs! Yet, should I murder you,
          I might before the world take the excuse   245
          Of madness: for compare my injuries,
          And they will well appear too sad a weight
          For reason to endure. But fall I first
          Amongst my sorrows, ere my treacherous hand
          Touch holy things! But why—I know not what   250
          I have to say—why did you choose out me
          To make thus wretched? There were thousands, fools,

231.1. *Lays ... sword.*] *Norland (subst.); not in Q1, Q2.*   234. *Lays ...*
sword.] *This ed.; Draws his sword. Norland; not in Q1, Q2.*   243–4.] *so*
Theobald; Alas ... of / walking ... you. Q1, Q2 (Waking).   244. waking]
Q2; walking Q1.   249. hand] *Q2;* sword *Q1.*   252. were] *Q2;* are *Q1.*
thousands, fools] *Q2;* thousands *Q1.*

---

taking vengeance by hewing the offender in pieces is found in *Philaster*,
III.i.25–8: 'Hew me asunder, and whilst I can think / I'll love those pieces you
have cut away / Better than those that grow, and kiss those limbs / Because you
made 'em so.'
    238–40. *but ... passions*] Theobald compares *Ham.*, IV.v.120–2.
    244. *waking*] unsleeping (*OED*, ppl.a., 1), i.e., continually present to the
mind. Q1's 'walking', i.e., 'that goes about in the semblance of a human being'
(*OED*, ppl.a., 5: this passage cited), would be more acceptable if Amintor
described himself as a walking grief.
    245. *take*] have recourse to.
    247. *sad*] heavy (*OED*, 7), also with its figurative sense, 'causing sorrow'
(*OED*, 5.f).
    248. *fall I*] may I fall dead.

Easy to work on, and of state enough,
Within the island.
Evadne.   I would not have a fool;
It were no credit for me.
Amintor.   Worse and worse!   255
Thou that dar'st talk unto thy husband thus,
Profess thyself a whore and, more than so,
Resolve to be so still, it is my fate
To bear and bow beneath a thousand griefs
To keep that little credit with the world.   260
But there were wise ones too: you might have ta'en
Another.
King.   No, for I believed thee honest
As thou wert valiant.
Amintor.   All the happiness
Bestowed upon me turns into disgrace.
Gods, take your honesty again, for I   265
Am loaden with it! Good my lord the King,
Be private in it.
King.   Thou mayst live, Amintor,
Free as thy king, if thou wilt wink at this,
And be a means that we may meet in secret.
Amintor. A bawd! Hold, hold, my breast! A bitter curse   270
Seize me if I forget not all respects

---

254. island] *Q2* (Iland)*; Land Q1.*   254–5. I ... me] *so Theobald; as one line, Q1, Q2.*   258. it is] *Q2;* is it *Q1.*   fate] *Q2;* fault *Q1.*   261–3. ta'en / Another ... valiant] *so Langbaine;* tane another. / KIN. No ... valiant *Q1, Q2.*   262. believed] *Dyce;* beleeue *Q1;* beleue *Q2.*

253. *state*] dignity.
259. to bear a thousand griefs and bow beneath that burden.
260. *that little credit*] i.e., of yours.
262. *believed*] Dyce's emendation, involving an easy d/e misreading by Q1's compositor, is required for consistency with 'wert' (l. 263). The King is explaining what his motives were when he made the match.
honest] as honest (in the present context, loyal).
267. *it*] i.e., the King's liaison with Evadne; cf. 'this', l. 268.
268. *free*] (adverbial) freely, having full privileges (*OED*, freely, adv., 5).
wink at] close your eyes to.
269. *we*] i.e., the King and Evadne.
270. *Hold ... breast!*] Cf. *Ham.*, I.v.92: 'Hold, hold, my heart!'
Hold] do not burst (with passion).
271–2. *respects ... religious*] considerations enjoined by religion.

That are religious, on another word
Sounded like that, and through a sea of sins
Will wade to my revenge, though I should call
Pains here and after life upon my soul!   275
King. Well, I am resolute you lay not with her,
    And so I leave you.   *Exit* KING.
Evadne.   You must needs be prating,
    And see what follows!
Amintor.   Prithee, vex me not.
    Leave me; I am afraid some sudden start
    Will pull a murder on me.
Evadne.   I am gone;   280
    I love my life well.   *Exit* EVADNE.
Amintor.   I hate mine as much.
    This 'tis to break a troth! I should be glad
    If all this tide of grief would make me mad.   *Exit.*

[ACT III   SCENE ii]
Enter MELANTIUS.

Melantius. I'll know the cause of all Amintor's griefs,
    Or friendship shall be idle.

Enter CALIANAX.

Calianax.   O, Melantius,
    My daughter will die.

---

273. Sounded] *Q2;* Seconded *Q1.*   274. Pains] *Q2;* Plagues *Q1.*   275. lay
not] *Q2;* lay *Q1.*   276–7. You ... follow] *so Theobald; as one line, Q1,
Q2.*   279–80. I am ... well] *so Theobald; as one line, Q1, Q2.*   2–5. O,
Melantius ... slave!] *so Theobald; as prose, Q1, Q2.*

---

274. *wade ... revenge*] Cf. *Ham.,* I.v.31: 'sweep to my revenge'.
274–5. *though ... soul*] though I should render my body liable to torture in
this world and my soul liable to torture in the next.
276. *resolute*] (not in *OED* in this sense) convinced, satisfied (*OED,*
resolved, 2).
277. *prating*] talking (derogatory).
279. *start*] fit of passion (*OED,* 4.d).
282. *troth*] solemn promise (*OED,* 2).
283. *tide of grief*] Cf. *Ham.,* III.i.59: 'sea of troubles'.

2. *idle*] useless.

Melantius.   Trust me, I am sorry;
   Would thou hadst ta'en her room.
Calianax.   Thou art a slave,
   A cut-throat slave, a bloody, treacherous slave!   5
Melantius. Take heed, old man, thou wilt be heard to rave,
   And lose thine offices.
Calianax.   I am valiant grown
   At all these years, and thou art but a slave.
Melantius. Leave!
   Some company will come, and I respect   10
   Thy years, not thee, so much that I could wish
   To laugh at thee alone.
Calianax.   I'll spoil your mirth:
   I mean to fight with thee. There lie, my cloak.
          [*Casts it off, and draws his sword.*]
   This was my father's sword, and he durst fight.
   Are you prepared?
Melantius.   Why, wilt thou dote thyself   15
   Out of thy life? Hence, get thee to bed;
   Have careful looking to, and eat warm things,
   And trouble not me: my head is full of thoughts
   More weighty than thy life or death can be.
Calianax. You have a name in war, where you stand safe   20
   Amongst a multitude, but I will try
   What you dare do unto a weak old man
   In single fight: you'll give ground, I fear.
   Come, draw!
Melantius. I will not draw, unless thou pullst thy death   25

4. room] *Q2;* part *Q1.*   5. bloody, treacherous slave] *Q2;* bloody—*Q1.*
7. offices] *Q2;* office *Q1.*   9. Leave] *Q2 (as first word of l. 10); not in Q1.*
12–15. I'll ... prepared?] *so Theobald;* Ile ... thee, / There ... sword, / And
... prepar'd? *Q1, Q2.*   13.1. Casts ... sword.] *This ed.; not in Q1, Q2.*
15–19. Why ... be] *so Theobald; as prose, Q1, Q2.*   16. to bed] *Q1, Q2;* to
thy bed *Theobald.*

4. *ta'en her room*] died in her place.
   7. *offices*] Cf. IV.ii.220, 241, 268. Calianax has at least two, i.e., Lord
Chamberlain of the Household (I.ii.16 n.) and Keeper of the Fort (ll. 287–9,
302, etc.).
   9. *Leave!* Cf. II.i.190.
   15–16. *dote ... life*] get yourself killed through your foolishness.
   17. *looking to*] attendance.
   20. *name*] reputation.

Upon thee with a stroke: there's no one blow
That thou canst give hath strength enough to kill me.
Tempt me not so far, then; the power of earth
Shall not redeem thee.

Calianax. [*Aside*]   I must let him alone;
He's stout and able, and, to say the truth,   30
However I may set a face and talk,
I am not valiant. When I was a youth
I kept my credit, with a testy trick
I had, 'mongst cowards, but durst never fight.

Melantius. I will not promise to preserve your life   35
If you do stay.

Calianax. [*Aside*]   I would give half my land
That I durst fight with that proud man a little.
If I had men to hold him, I would beat him
Till he asked me mercy.

Melantius.   Sir, will you be gone?

Calianax. [*Aside*] I dare not stay, but I will go home and beat   40
my servants all over for this.   *Exit* CALIANAX.

Melantius. This old fellow haunts me.
But the distracted carriage of mine Amintor
Takes deeply on me. I will find the cause:
I fear his conscience cries he wronged Aspatia.   45

---

27. hath] *Q2;* hast *Q1.*   to] *Q2;* can *Q1.*   28. not so far, then;] *Q1* (not
so far then), *Q2;* not so, for then *conj. this ed.*   29. Aside] *Weber; not in Q1,*
Q2.   34. 'mongst] *Q1* (mongst); Amongst *Q2* (I had,/Amongst).   35–9. I
will ... mercy] *so Theobald; as prose, Q1, Q2.* 36. Aside] *Dyce; not in Q1, Q2.*
39. asked] *Q1* (askt); aske *Q2.*   40. Aside] *Dyce; not in Q1, Q2.*   go home
and beat] *Q2;* beat *Q1.*

25–6. *unless ... stroke*] i.e., unless, by striking a blow at me, you
provoke my fatal retaliation.
28–9. *the power ... not*] no power on earth shall.
31. *set a face*] adopt a grim expression.
33. *credit*] reputation (of valour).
testy trick] 'a trick of showing irascibility' (Spencer).
38. *If ... hold him*] Tamburlaine's cowardly son Calyphas declares himself
ready to be valiant under the same circumstances: 'If any man will hold him, I
will strike' (*2 Tamburlaine*, I.iii.102).
41.] Calianax's humiliation is reinforced by his having to pick up his cloak as
well as sheathe his sword.
43. *carriage*] behaviour.
44. *Takes ... me*] has a deep effect on me; cf. I.ii.198 n.
45. *I fear ... Aspatia*] This remark, naturally prompted by his encounter
with Calianax, draws attention to his complete ignorance of 'the cause'.

Enter AMINTOR.

Amintor. [*Aside*] Men's eyes are not so subtle to perceive
My inward misery: I bear my grief
Hid from the world. How art thou wretched then?
For aught I know, all husbands are like me,
And every one I talk with of his wife   50
Is but a well dissembler of his woes,
As I am; would I knew it, for the rareness
Afflicts me now.
Melantius. Amintor, we have not enjoyed our friendship of late,
For we were wont to change our souls in talk.   55
Amintor. Melantius, I can tell thee a good jest
Of Strato and a lady the last day.
Melantius. How was't?
Amintor. Why, such an odd one!
Melantius.   I have longed to speak with you,
Not of an idle jest that's forced, but of matter   60
You are bound to utter to me.
Amintor. What is that, my friend?
Melantius.   I have observed your words
Fall from your tongue wildly, and all your carriage
Like one that strove to show his merry mood
When he were ill disposed. You were not wont   65
To put such scorn into your speech, or wear
Upon your face ridiculous jollity.

46. Aside] *Dyce; not in Q1, Q2.*   Men's] *Q2;* Mans *Q1.*   not so] *Q2;* not
Q1.   54–61. Amintor ... to me] *Langbaine (54–5 only), Weber; as prose,
Q1, Q2.*   55. change] *Theobald;* charge *Q1, Q2.*   62–3. I ... carriage] *so
Weber;* I ... tongue / Wildely ... carriage *Q1, Q2.*   64. strove] *Q2;* striues
Q1.   66. speech, or wear] *Q2;* speech—yow weare *Q1.*

51. *a well ... woes*] a skilful concealer of his wretchedness.
52. *rareness*] i.e., of my situation.
55. *change*] exchange. Theobald's emendation is right, for the point is the
reciprocity; he compares *A King and No King*, I.i.368–70: 'should I chuse a
companion ... for honesty to enterchange my bosome with, it would be you'.
Editors who retain 'charge' gloss it as 'load' or 'fill (render replete)', But the
word usually has the sense 'overload', 'burden' (e.g., *Caes.*, II.iii.2; *Mac.*,
V.i.59), which is contrary to the sense here.
63. *wildly*] in a disordered fashion.
67. *ridiculous jollity*] The phrase had been used contemptuously, of his
mockers, by the hero of Chapman's *Bussy D'Ambois*, I.ii.177.

Some sadness sits here, which your cunning would
Cover o'er with smiles, and 'twill not be:
What is it?
Amintor.   A sadness here? What cause   70
Can fate provide for me to make me so?
Am I not loved through all this isle? The King
Rains greatness on me. Have I not received
A lady to my bed, that in her eye
Keeps mounting fire, and on her tender cheeks   75
Inevitable colour, in her heart
A prison for all virtue? Are not you,
Which is above all joys, my constant friend?
What sadness can I have? No, I am light,
And feel the courses of my blood more warm   80
And stirring than they were. 'Faith, marry too,
And you will feel so unexpressed a joy
In chaste embraces that you will indeed
Appear another.
Melantius.   You may shape, Amintor,
Causes to cozen the whole world withal,   85
And yourself too, but 'tis not like a friend
To hide your soul from me. 'Tis not your nature

68. cunning would] *Q2;* tongue would *Q1;* cunning tongue / Would *conj. this
ed.*   76. Inevitable] *Q2;* Immutable *Q1;* Inimitable *Theobald.*   86. but]
Q2; and *Q1.*

───────────────────────────────

68.] The metre of Q1 is plainly defective and that of Q2 suspect: 'would'
does not look like the last, stressed, word of a line. Perhaps Q2's 'cunning' was
intended as an addition (not as a substitution), restoring the original reading of
Q1's copy and thus giving 'your cunning tongue / Would cover o'er.'
    here] i.e., in your breast.
    70.] The pause in the line reflects Amintor's attempt to collect himself
before replying.
    75. *mounting fire*] fire that leaps up.
    76. *inevitable*] 'irresistible' (Mason, who compares Dryden, 'Palamon and
Arcite', 1, 232: 'Th'inevitable charms of Emily'). Sidney, with the same
meaning, has 'the unevitable Philoclea' (*Arcadia*, bk. 1, chap. 14, p. 94).
Theobald emends Q1's 'immutable' to 'inimitable' (i.e., which art cannot
imitate).
    80. *courses*] runnings, flowings.
    82. *unexpressed*] inexpressible.
    84. *Appear another*] seem a changed man, as I do.
    85. *Causes*] reasons (i.e., for your alleged happiness).

To be thus idle: I have seen you stand
As you were blasted 'midst of all your mirth,
Call thrice aloud, and then start, feigning joy   90
So coldly. World, what do I here? A friend
Is nothing. Heaven! I would ha' told that man
My secret sins. I'll search an unknown land,
And there plant friendship; all is withered here.
Come with a compliment! I would have fought,   95
Or told my friend 'a lied, ere soothed him so.
Out of my bosom!
Amintor. But there is nothing.
Melantius.   Worse and worse! Farewell!
From this time have acquaintance, but no friend.
Amintor. Melantius, stay! You shall know what that is.   100
Melantius. See how you played with friendship! Be advised
How you give cause unto yourself to say
You ha' lost a friend.
Amintor.   Forgive what I ha' done,
For I am so o'ergone with injuries
Unheard of, that I lose consideration   105
Of what I ought to do;—oh!—oh!   [*Weeps.*]
Melantius. Do not weep. What is't ? May I once but know the
        man

96. friend] *Q2;* friends *Q1.*   100. that] *Q1, Q2;* it *Theobald.*   101. played]
Q2 (plaid); plead *Q1;* play *conj. Daniel.*   104. injuries] *Q2;* miseries *Q1.*
106. *Weeps.*] *This ed; not in Q1, Q2.*   107. Do ... man] *so this ed.;* Doe ...
ist ? / May ... man *Q1, Q2.*

88. *idle*] out of your mind (*OED,* 2.b).
89. *blasted*] thunderstruck (*OED,* 1).
91. *World*] in the world's name.
91-2. *A friend / Is nothing*] A friend is (I, your friend, am) of no account.
93. *search*] go and discover (*OED,* 11).
95. *Come ... compliment!*] How dare you come to me with a mere
compliment! (alluding to ll. 77-8).
96. *soothed*] blandished (*OED,* 5).
97. *Out ... bosom!*] figurative, though Dyce took it literally and compared
III.i.55, which he also misinterpreted as breaking away from an embrace.
99. *have ... friend*] have acquaintance with me, but be no friend of mine.
100. *that*] the matter. This seems not to be idiomatic, and so Theobald's
emendation, though not accepted by recent editors, may be right.
101. *played*] trifled.
Be advised] take consideration (in future).
104. *o'ergone*] overwhelmed (*OED,* overgo, 5).

Hath turned my friend thus—
Amintor.   I had spoke at first,
     But that—
Melantius.   But what?
Amintor.   I held it most unfit
     For you to know; 'faith, do not know it yet.   110
Melantius. Thou seest my love, that will keep company
     With thee in tears. Hide nothing, then, from me,
     For when I know the cause of thy distemper,
     With mine old armour I'll adorn myself,
     My resolution, and cut through thy foes   115
     Unto thy quiet, till I place thy heart
     As peaceable as spotless innocence.
     What is it?
Amintor.   Why, 'tis this—it is too big
     To get out; let my tears make way awhile.
Melantius. Punish me strangely, heaven, if he scape   120
     Of life or fame, that brought this youth to this!
Amintor. Your sister—
Melantius.   Well said.
Amintor.   You'll wish't unknown
     When you have heard it.
Melantius.   No.
Amintor.   —is much to blame,

108–9. I ... that—] *so Theobald; as one line, Q1, Q2.*   122–3. You'll ...
heard it] *so Theobald (*You will ... heard it*); as one line, Q1, Q2.*

---

   108. *turned*] changed, i.e., into such a miserable being.
   110. *you*] emphatic, the point being the guilt of Melantius' sister.
   'faith] For the use of the interjection "faith" with an imperative verb (not
recorded in *OED*), cf. Suckling, *The Sad One*, III.iv.33: 'Forget her, faith
forget her' (*Works. The Plays*, ed. L. A. Beaurline, Oxford, 1971).
   111–2.] Melantius (unlike Amintor, who audibly sobs. l. 106) has tears in
his eyes.
   113. *distemper*] disordered state of mind (*OED*, 4).
   144. *mine old armour*] my armour familiar from of old (*OED*, 7.c), i.e., 'My
resolution', l. 115; cf. I.i.122–3.
   116. *place*] establish.
   120. *strangely*] in some unprecedented way.
   120–1. *scape / Of*] escape with.
   121. *fame*] reputation.
   122. *Well said*] Cf. I.ii.3; here equivalent to 'Good; go on.' Followed by an
expectant pause.

And to the King has given her honour up,
And lives in whoredom with him.
Melantius.   How's this?   125
Thou art run mad with injury indeed;
Thou couldst not utter this else. Speak again,
For I forgive it freely. Tell thy griefs.
Amintor. She's wanton; I am loth to say a whore,
Though it be true.   130
Melantius. Speak yet again, before mine anger grow
Up beyond throwing down. What are thy griefs?
Amintor. By all our friendship, these.
Melantius.   What, am I tame?
After mine actions, shall the name of friend
Blot all our family, and strike the brand   135
Of whore upon my sister, unrevenged?
My shaking flesh, be thou a witness for me
With what unwillingness I go to scourge
This railer, whom my folly hath called friend!
I will not take thee basely: [*Draws his sword.*] thy sword   140
Hangs near thy hand; draw it, that I may whip
Thy rashness to repentance. Draw thy sword!
Amintor. Not on thee, did thine anger go as high
As troubled waters. Thou shouldst do me ease
Here and eternally, if thy noble hand   145
Would cut me from my sorrows.
Melantius.   This is base
And fearful: they that use to utter lies
Provide not blows but words, to qualify

---

133. tame] *Q2;* tane *Q1.*   135. strike] *Q2;* stick *Q1.*   140. *Draws his sword.*] *Dyce; not in Q1, Q2.*

---

125. *How's this?*] Note the astonished pause before these words.

129. *wanton*] licentious. Amintor has already used the word 'whoredom' (l. 125), and shrinks from repeating it.

131-2. *grow ... down*] shoot up so high that it will be too big to throw down.

135-6. *strike ... upon*] a common metaphor derived from the branding of criminals with the initial letter of their offence.

139. *railer*] reviler.

145. *Here and eternally*] here, in ridding me of my life, and eternally, in freeing me from the mortal sin of suicide.

147. *fearful*] cowardly.

148. *qualify*] appease (*OED*, 9).

The men they wronged. Thou hast a guilty cause.

Amintor. Thou pleasest me, for so much more like this   150
　　Will raise my anger up above my griefs,
　　Which is a passion easier to be borne,
　　And I shall then be happy.

Melantius.　　　　　　　　Take, then, more
　　To raise thine anger. 'Tis mere cowardice
　　Makes thee not draw, and I will leave thee dead   155
　　However; but if thou art so much pressed
　　With guilt and fear as not to dare to fight,
　　I'll make thy memory loathed and fix a scandal
　　Upon thy name for ever.

Amintor. [*Drawing his sword*] Then I draw,
　　As justly as our magistrates their swords   160
　　To cut offenders off. I knew before
　　'Twould grate your ears, but it was base in you
　　To urge a weighty secret from your friend
　　And then rage at it. I shall be at ease
　　If I be killed, and if you fall by me   165
　　I shall not long outlive you.

Melantius.　　　　　　　　Stay awhile.
　　The name of friend is more than family
　　Or all the world besides. I was a fool.
　　Thou searching human nature, that didst wake
　　To do me wrong, thou art inquisitive,   170
　　And thrusts me upon questions that will take
　　My sleep away. Would I had died ere known
　　This sad dishonour! Pardon me, my friend.
　　　　　　　　　　[*Sheathes his sword.*]

---

152. borne] *Q2*; knowne *Q1*.　153. happy] *Q2*; blessed *Q1*.　153–5. Take
... dead] *so Theobald;* Take ... meere / Cowardise ... dead *Q1, Q2*.
158. scandal] *Q2*; farewell *Q1*.　159. *Drawing his sword*] *Dyce; not in Q1,
Q2.*　169. wake] *Q2*; make *Q1*.　173. *Sheathes his sword.*] *Dyce; not in Q1,
Q2.*

---

156. *However*] one way or another (*OED*, 2); i.e., I will run you through,
whether you will draw or not. Melantius then changes his mind and declares
that if Amintor will not fight he will denounce him as a coward.
　pressed] oppressed.
166. *I ... you*] Amintor contemplates suicide, cf. ll. 180–2.
169. *searching*] given to searching (*OED*, 2), over-curious.
　wake] be aroused (*OED*, 7.e), rather than be watchful (*OED*, 4.b).
170. *inquisitive*] seeking dangerous knowledge (*OED*, 1.b).
171. *thrusts*] thrustest (shortened for ease of pronunciation).

If thou wilt strike, here is a faithful heart;
Pierce it, for I will never heave my hand 　　　　175
To thine. Behold the power thou hast in me.
I do believe my sister is a whore,
A leprous one. Put up thy sword, young man.
Amintor. [*Sheathing his sword*] How should I bear it, then, she
　　　　being so?
　　I fear, my friend, that you will lose me shortly, 　　　　180
　　And I shall do a foul act on myself
　　Through these disgraces.
Melantius. 　　　　　　　Better half the land
Were buried quick together. No, Amintor,
Thou shalt have ease. O, this adulterous King,
That drew her to't! Where got he the spirit 　　　　185
To wrong me so?
Amintor. 　　　　　What is it then to me,
　　If it be wrong to you?
Melantius. 　　　　　　Why, not so much:
The credit of our house is thrown away.
But from his iron den I'll waken Death
And hurl him on this King; my honesty 　　　　190
Shall steel my sword, and on my horrid point
I'll wear my cause, that shall amaze the eyes
Of this proud man, and be too glittering
For him to look on.
Amintor. 　　　　　I have quite undone my fame.
Melantius. Dry up thy watery eyes, 　　　　195

---

179. *Sheathing his sword*] Dyce; *not in Q1, Q2.*　184. ease. O, this] *Q2* (ease:
Oh this)*; ease of this *Q1.*　187–8. Why … away] *so Theobald;* Why …
house / Is … away *Q1, Q2.*

---

176. *thine*] thy heart.
Behold … me] referring to what Melantius is about to declare.
178. *leprous*] disfigured with moral disease.
183. *quick*] alive.
186–7. *What … me?*] How much greater, then, is the injury to me? A
rhetorical question, which receives an unexpected reply.
188. *house*] family.
189. *iron*] Iron is figuratively 'a type of extreme hardness' (*OED*, 3), and is
here applied to Death's den to emphasise the merciless revenge that Melantius
contemplates.
191. *horrid*] causing horror.
192. *amaze*] terrify (*OED*, 3).

And cast a manly look upon my face,
For nothing is so wild as I thy friend
Till I have freed thee; still this swelling breast.
I go thus from thee, and will never cease
My vengeance till I find thy heart at peace.   200
Amintor. It must not be so. Stay! Mine eyes would tell
How loth I am to this, but, love and tears,
Leave me awhile, for I have hazarded
All that this world calls happy. Thou hast wrought
A secret from me, under name of friend,   205
Which art could ne'er have found, nor torture wrung
From out my bosom. Give it me again,
For I will find it wheresoe'er it lies
Hid in the mortal'st part; invent a way
To give it back.
Melantius.   Why would you have it back?   210
I will to death pursue him with revenge.
Amintor. Therefore I call it back from thee, for I know
Thy blood so high that thou wilt stir in this
And shame me to posterity. Take to thy weapon.
                              [*Draws his sword.*]
Melantius. Hear thy friend, that bears more years than thou.   215
Amintor. I will not hear, but draw, or I—
Melantius.   Amintor!

200. thy] *Q1;* my *Q2.*   206. wrung] *Q2;* wrong *Q1.*   207. my] *Q2;* this
Q1.   212. it back from] *Q2;* it from *Q1.*   213–4. Thy ... weapon] *so
Theobald; as one line, Q2;* Thy blood so high, that thou wilt stir in this, take to
thy weapon *Q1.*   214. *Draws his sword.*] *Dyce; not in Q1, Q2.*   215. Hear]
Q1, Q2; Hear thou *Theobald.*

───────────────────────────────────────

197. *wild*] fierce (*OED,* 8).
198. *this*] i.e., Amintor's, swelling with grief (cf. l. 195).
200. *thy*] Q2's 'my' seems to be a mistaken attempt at correction by the
annotator.
201. *would*] are trying to.
204. *wrought*] dug out, as from a mine or quarry (*OED,* work (of which
'wrought' is a past tense), 12.b).
206. *art*] skilful questioning.
209. *the ... part*] i.e., of thee (i.e., the heart).
invent] devise (implying the impossibility of doing so).
212. *back*] not introduced in error into Q2, making the line hypermetrical
(as Turner thinks), but omitted from Q1; the metre is correct if 'for I' is elided
(as, e.g., 'to thy' must be in l. 214).
213. *blood so high*] rage so strong.

Amintor. Draw, then, for I am full as resolute
    As fame and honour can enforce me be.
    I cannot linger. Draw!
Melantius. [*Drawing his sword*] I do. But is not
    My share of credit equal with thine   220
    If I do stir?
Amintor.   No; for it will be called
    Honour in thee to spill thy sister's blood
    If she her birth abuse, and on the King
    A brave revenge; but on me, that have walked
    With patience in it, it will fix the name   225
    Of fearful cuckold—O, that word! Be quick.
Melantius. Then join with me.
Amintor.   I dare not do a sin,
    Or else I would. Be speedy.
Melantius. Then dare not fight with me, for that's a sin.
    [*Aside*] His grief distracts him. [*To him*] Call thy thoughts
        again,   230
    And to thyself pronounce the name of friend,
    And see what that will work. I will not fight.
                                    [*Sheathes his sword.*]
Amintor. You must.

---

218. me be] *Q2*; me *Q1*.   219. *Drawing his sword*] *Dyce; not in Q1, Q2*.
220. equal with thine] *Q1, Q2*; equal then with thine *Theobald*; equal with
thine own *Dyce*.   226.] *so Q2*; Of ... word, / Be quick. *Q1*.   227–8. I ...
speedy] *so Theobald; as one line, Q1, Q2*.   228. would. Be] *Q2* (would: be);
would be *Q1*.   230. *Aside*] *Weber; not in Q1, Q2*.   232. *Sheathes his sword.*]
Dyce (at l. 233), Norland; not in Q1, Q2.

---

220. *My ... thine*] metrically defective and certainly corrupt; for alternative
restorations see collation. The possessives are no doubt authentic, but the
sense implies their transposition, since Melantius means that Amintor's share
of credit would equal Melantius' if Melantius took revenge.
221–4. *it will be ... revenge*] i.e., to kill your sister for defiling the family
name will be called an honourable act, and to kill the King for seducing her
will be called a fine act of revenge. Gurr interprets the revenge on the King as
the killing of Evadne; but Melantius has twice stated his intention to have his
revenge on the King by killing him (ll. 189–94, 211).
222. *to ... blood*] Melantius has not in fact proposed to kill Evadne.
224–5. *walked ... in't*] endured their adultery patiently (rather than
'patiently acquiesced in your revenge').
226. *fearful*] cowardly.
    cuckold] husband of an adulterous wife.

Melantius.   I will be killed first; though my passions
      Offered the like to you, 'tis not this earth
      Shall buy my reason to it. Think awhile,   235
      For you are (I must weep when I speak that)
      Almost besides yourself.
Amintor. [*Sheathing his sword*] O, my soft temper!
      So many sweet words from thy sister's mouth,
      I am afraid, would make me take her,
      To embrace and pardon her. I am mad indeed,   240
      And know not what I do; yet have a care
      Of me in what thou dost.
Melantius.   Why, thinks my friend
      I will forget his honour, or to save
      The bravery of our house will lose his fame
      And fear to touch the throne of majesty?   245
Amintor. A curse will follow that; but rather live
      And suffer with me.
Melantius.   I will do what worth
      Shall bid me, and no more.

235. buy] *Q2;* by *Q1.*   236. when I speak that] *Q2;* when I speak it *Q1;* when that I speak it *conj. this ed.*   237. *Sheathing his sword*] *Dyce; not in Q1, Q2.*   239. her] *Q1, Q2;* her to me *Theobald.*   241. yet] *Q2;* but *Q1.*   242–3. Why ... save] *so Theobald; as one line, Q1, Q2.*   244. our] *Q2;* your *Q1.*   lose] *Q2;* loose *Q1.*   247–51. I ... you] *so Theobald;* I ... bid me. / AMIN. Faith ... hope, / Yet ... ease. / MEL. Come ... you *Q1;* I ... more. / *Amin.* Faith ... hope, / Yet ... ease. / *Mel.* Come ... you *Q2.*

236. that] Q2's 'that' is better than Q1's unmetrical (because unstressed) 'it', but is less idiomatic than either 'it' or 'this' (since Melantius has not yet pronounced the reason for his tears), and I conjecture that in Q2 an intended insertion (to give 'I must weep when that I speak it') was treated as a substitution.

237. besides] beside (*OED*); cf. V.iii.101.
soft temper] yielding disposition (cf. II.ii.12).

239. I ... her] another corrupt line. Theobald's emendation (see collation) is better than 'back' or 'home' (cf. V.iii.155) would be.

242–5. Why ... majesty?] Melantius replies to Amintor's vague injunction as though Amintor had urged him to take revenge and was afraid that he would not.

244. bravery] splendour (*OED*, 3), here with a derogatory implication, i.e., the material benefits deriving from Evadne's secret liaison with the King.
lose his fame] destroy (*OED*, 2) his reputation, i.e., allow it to be blasted by letting Evadne's liaison continue.

246. that] i.e., regicide.

247. worth] moral worthiness, virtue.

Amintor. [*Leaning on Melantius*] 'Faith, I am sick,
    And desperately, I hope; yet leaning thus
    I feel a kind of ease.
Melantius.   Come, take again   250
    Your mirth about you.
Amintor.   I shall never do't.
Melantius. I warrant you. Look up; we'll walk together;
    Put thine arm here. All shall be well again.
Amintor. Thy love (O wretched I!), thy love, Melantius—
    Why, I have nothing else.
Melantius.   Be merry then.   255
                              Exeunt.

           Enter MELANTIUS *again.*

Melantius. This worthy young man may do violence
    Upon himself, but I have cherished him
    As well as I could, and sent him smiling from me
    To counterfeit again. Sword, hold thine edge;
    My heart will never fail me.

           Enter DIPHILUS.

                Diphilus,   260
    Thou com'st as sent.
Diphilus.   Yonder has been such laughing!
Melantius. Betwixt whom?

248. me, and no more.] *Q2;* me. *Q1.*   *Leaning on Melantius*] *This ed.; not in*
Q1, Q2.   254. love ... thy] *Turner;* loue, o wretched, I thy *Q1, Q2;* love
(O wretched!) Ay, thy *Theobald.*

---

249. *desperately*] incurably (*OED*, 3).
hope] think (*OED*, 4), though perhaps implying desire (*OED*, 3.b).
253. here] either in Melantius' arm or around Melantius' shoulder.
255.2. Enter *MELANTIUS* again.] 'Perhaps a new scene should here be
marked' (Daniel). Melantius' immediate re-entry is strangely inept in an
otherwise carefully constructed play, and belies ll. 252 ('we'll walk together')
and 257–9. But there is no likelihood that a formal interval (e.g., with music)
was observed here, for (1) the action of ll. 256–328 is an immediate sequel to
that of ll. 1–255, and (2) the play's act-divisions are clear, and any intervals
might be expected to be confined to those points. Nevertheless, the modern
productions by the Citizens' Theatre, Glasgow, and the Royal Shakespeare
Company, both having a single interval, placed it here.
256. *young man*] stressed like the single word 'youngman' (*OED*), as in
Rom., I.ii.26.
261. *as sent*] as if heaven-sent in response to my wish.

Diphilus.   Why, our sister and the King.
   I thought their spleens would break; they laughed us all
   Out of the room.
Melantius.   They must weep, Diphilus.
Diphilus. Must they?
Melantius.   They must.   265
   Thou art my brother, and if I did believe
   Thou hadst a base thought, I would rip it out,
   Lie where it durst.
Diphilus.   You should not; I would first
   Mangle myself and find it.
Melantius.   That was spoke
   According to our strain. Come, join thy hands to mine,   270
   And swear a firmness to what project I
   Shall lay before thee.
Diphilus.   You do wrong us both;
   People hereafter shall not say there passed
   A bond more than our loves to tie our lives
   And deaths together.   275
Melantius. It is as nobly said as I would wish.
   Anon I'll tell you wonders, we are wronged.
Diphilus. But I will tell you now, we'll right ourselves.
Melantius. Stay not; prepare the armour in my house,

263-4. I ... room] *so Weber;* Why ... King, / I ... breake, / They ...
roome *Q1, Q2.*   265-6. They ... believe] *so Theobald; as one line, Q1, Q2.*
268-9. You ... find it] *so Theobald; as one line, Q1, Q2.*   269-70. That ...
mine] *so Theobald; as one line, Q1, Q2.*   270. hands to mine] *Q2;* hands *Q1.*

---

263. *I ... break*] The spleen was considered as the seat of various passions,
including mirth (cf. *Meas.,* II.ii.122-3) and anger (cf. l. 291).
   268. *Lie ... durst*] i.e., even in thy heart.
   269. *Mangle myself*] hack myself to pieces.
   270. *strain*] family, i.e., its moral integrity.
   to mine] an authorial addition (cf. I.i.13), probably springing from the
realisation that 'join thy hands' might be wrongly understood as 'join thy
hands together'. At I.ii.107 the King orders 'Calianax, join hands' (i.e., with
Melantius).
   273-5. *People ... together*] i.e., It shall not be said hereafter that we needed
to take an oath to live and die together; our mutual love was all the assurance
that we needed. Theobald compares *Caes.,* II.i.113-40 ('No, not an oath',
etc.).
   279. *Stay not*] do not delay.
   the armour] At l. 114 Melantius' armour was figurative, but by now he
has formed his plan of killing the King (not yet necessarily by Evadne's hand)
and retiring with his adherents to the safety of the fort.

And what friends you can draw unto our side,   280
Not knowing of the cause, make ready too.
Haste, Diphilus, the time requires it. Haste!

                                        Exit DIPHILUS.

I hope my cause is just; I know my blood
Tells me it is, and I will credit it.
To take revenge and lose myself withal   285
Were idle; and to scape, impossible,
Without I had the fort, which (misery!)
Remaining in the hands of my old enemy
Calianax—but I must have it.

                    Enter CALIANAX.

                    See
Where he comes shaking by me. [*To him*] Good my lord,   290
Forget your spleen to me: I never wronged you,
But would have peace with every man.
Calianax.   'Tis well.
If I durst fight, your tongue would lie at quiet.
Melantius. Y'are touchy without all cause.
Calianax.   Do, mock me.
Melantius. By mine honour, I speak truth.
Calianax.   Honour! Where is't?   295
Melantius. See what starts you make
Into your idle hatred, to my love

287. which (misery!) *Theobald;* which miserie *Q1, Q2.*   296–300. See ...
sir] *so Dyce;* See what starts you make into your idle hatred, / I am come with
resolution to obtaine a sute / Of you. / CAL. A sute of me, tis very like it should
be granted sir *Q1;* See what starts you make into your hatred to my loue and
freedome to you. / I come with resolution to obtaine a sute / Of you. / *Cal.* A
sute of me? tis very like it should be granted sir *Q2.*   297. idle hatred] *Q1;*
hatred *Q2.*   297–8. to my ... to you] *Q2; not in Q1.*

---

281. *not ... cause*] relating to 'friends'. Diphilus does not know the cause
either, but may be supposed to infer it from Melantius' remarks, ll. 264, 277.
283. *hope*] think (cf. l. 249 n.).
blood] passion (*OED*, 5).
285. *lose*] destroy.
287. *Without*] unless.
291. *spleen*] anger (cf. l. 263 n.).
292. *'Tis well*] Cf. I ii.65 n.
294. *touchy*] irritable.
Do, mock me] i.e., with your pretence of wanting to be friends.
296. *starts*] startings aside, deviations (*OED*, start, sb.^{2}, 7).
297. *to*] in response to.

And freedom to you. I am come with resolution
To obtain a suit of you.
Calianax.   A suit of me?
'Tis very like it should be granted, sir.   [*Going*]   300
Melantius. Nay, go not hence!
'Tis this: you have the keeping of the fort,
And I would wish you, by the love you ought
To bear unto me, to deliver it
Into my hands.
Calianax.   I am in hope thou art mad,   305
To talk to me thus.
Melantius.   But there is a reason
To move you to it; I would kill the King,
That wronged you and your daughter.
Calianax. Out, traitor!   [*Going*]
Melantius.   Nay, but stay; I cannot scape,
The deed once done, without I have this fort.   310
Calianax. And should I help thee? Now thy treacherous mind
Betrays itself.
Melantius.   Come, delay me not.
Give me a sudden answer, or already
Thy last is spoke. Refuse not offered love
When it comes clad in secrets.
Calianax. [*Aside*]   If I say   315
I will not, he will kill me; I do see't
Writ in his looks; and should I say I will,

---

298. I am come] *Q1;* I come *Q2.*   300. *Going*] *This ed.; not in Q1, Q2.*
305–8. I am ... daughter] *so Weber;* I ... thus./MEL. But ... would /
Kill ... daughter *Q1, Q2.*   309. *Going*] *This ed.; not in Q1, Q2.*
309. 10. Nay ... fort] *so Theobald;* Nay ... done / Without ... fort *Q1,
Q2.*   311–12. And ... itself] *so Theobald; as prose, Q1, Q2.*   313. or
already] *Q2;* already *Q1.*   314. Thy] *Q2;* The *Q1.*   not] *Q2;* my *Q1.*
315. *Aside*] *Weber; not in Q1, Q2.*   315–20. If ... think] *so Theobald; as
prose (with capitals at* In, King, But), *Q1, Q2.*

---

305. *I ... hope*] It's my belief; cf. l. 249 n.
306. *me*] (stressed); me, of all people.
309. *Out*] an interjection 'expressing abhorrence, reproach, or indignation'
(Onions, *Shakespeare Glossary*).
312. *Come*] In the pause before this word, Melantius may lay his hand on his
sword.
313. *sudden*] immediate.
314. *last*] last word.

He'll run and tell the King. [*To him*] I do not shun
Your friendship, dear Melantius, but this cause
Is weighty; give me but an hour to think.   320
Melantius. Take it. [*Aside*] I know this goes unto the King,
But I am armed.   *Exit* MELANTIUS.
Calianax.   Methinks I feel myself
But twenty now again. This fighting fool
Wants policy: I shall revenge my girl,
And make her red again. I pray my legs   325
Will last that pace that I will carry them;
I shall want breath before I find the King.   [*Exit.*]

321. Take it. [*Aside*] I know] *Q1, Q2 (subst.:* Take it,—I know).   327. *Exit.*]
Weber; not in Q1, Q2.

322. *armed*] i.e., with resolution; also , as IV.ii will show, with a defence.
324. *Wants policy*] lacks calculation.
325. *make her red again*] bring back her healthy colour.
326. *Will ... them*] will stand the pace at which I will make them go.
327. *want breath*] be out of breath.

Act IV

ACT IV [SCENE i]

Enter MELANTIUS, EVADNE, *and* Ladies.

Melantius. God save you!

Evadne.　　　　　　Save you, sweet brother!

Melantius.　　　　　　　　　　　　　In my blunt eye
　　Methinks you look, Evadne—

Evadne.　　　　　　　　　Come, you would make me blush.

Melantius. I would, Evadne; I shall displease my ends else.

Evadne. You shall if you commend me; I am bashful.
　　Come, sir, how do I look?　　　　　　　　　　　　　5

Melantius. I would not have your women hear me break
　　Into a commendation of you; 'tis not seemly.

Evadne. [*To Ladies*] Go wait me in the gallery.

　　　　　　　　　　　　　　　Exeunt Ladies.
　　　　　　　　　　　　　　　Now speak.

Melantius. I'll lock the door first.　　　[*Locks the door.*]

Evadne.　　　　　　　Why?

Melantius. I will not have your gilded things, that dance　　10

ACT IV] *Q1, Q2 (Actus Quartus.).*　6.1. *and* Ladies] *Weber; and a Lady Q1,
Q2.*　1. God save] *Q1*; Saue *Q2.*　1–2. In . . . Evadne] *so Theobald; as one
line, Q1, Q2.*　2. Evadne—] *Theobald*; Euadne. *Q1, Q2.*　would] *Q1, Q2;*
will *Weber.*　4. commend] *Theobald*; command *Q1, Q2.*　6–7. I . . .
seemly] *so Norland;* I . . . me / Breake . . . seemely *Q1, Q2.*　7. Into a
commendation] *Turner*; Into a commendations *Q1*; Into commendations *Q2*;
Into commendation *Q3.*　9. the door] *Q2*; your dores *Q1.*　Locks the door.]
This ed.; not in Q1, Q2.

---

2. *look, Evadne*—] For the punctuation cf. l. 5, which shows that Evadne
has interrupted Melantius here.

2. *you . . . blush*] you want to make me blush (with modesty, by a
compliment).

3. *I would*] I do want to (make you blush; with guilt, by a denunciation).
displease] offend (i.e., frustrate); *OED*, 2.

4. *commend*] praise (cf. l. 14). Melantius, who means to show her her fault,
uses the noun 'commendation' with secret irony at ll. 7 and 15.

8. *gallery*] a long room on to which other rooms open.

10. *your*] those (derogatory).
gilded things] men dressed in clothes covered with gold embroidery. Daniel
compares *Valentinian*, II.ii.26–36: 'Were there not men came hither too?' . . .

In visitation with their Milan skins,
Choke up my business.

Evadne.   You are strangely disposed, sir.

Melantius. Good madam, not to make you merry.

Evadne. No, if you praise me, 'twill make me sad.

Melantius. Such a sad commendation I have for you.

Evadne.   Brother,   15
The court has made you witty, and learned to riddle.

Melantius. I praise the court for't; has it learned you nothing?

Evadne. Me?

Melantius.   Ay, Evadne; thou art young and handsome,
A lady of a sweet complexion
And such a flowing carriage that it cannot   20
Choose but inflame a kingdom.

Evadne.   Gentle brother!

Melantius. 'Tis yet in thy repentance, foolish woman,
To make me gentle.

Evadne.   How is this?

Melantius.   'Tis base,
And I could blush at these years, through all

---

15. commendation] *Q6;* commendations *Q1, Q2.*   15–16. Brother . . . riddle]
so Dyce; Brother . . . wittie, / And . . . riddle *Q1, Q2.*   16. learned] *This ed.;*
learne *Q1, Q2.*   17. has it] *Q2;* has *Q1.*

'I fear me Bawdes' . . . 'Saving the reverence of their guilded doublets / And
Millan skins . . . They shew'd to me directly / Court crabbs, that creepe a side
way for their living.'

10–11. *dance / In visitation*] move affectedly as they enter to pay their visits.

11. *Milan skins*] ('Milan' accented, as usual, on the first syllable) 'Some
article of fashionable dress. I think they were fine gloves manufactured at
Milan' (R. Nares, *Glossary,* 1859 ed., II, 568). Spencer draws attention to the
fact that 'gloves were often perfumed' and to 'Choke up' in l. 12.

12. *Choke up*] smother.

15. *sad*] sorrowful (taking up Evadne's word in l. 14, where it was opposed
to 'merry' in l. 13); with the additional sense of 'serious' (*OED,* 4).

16. *learned*] taught you (*OED,* 4.b). Melantius' rejoinder shows that Evadne
has used the verb in this transitive sense. Qq's 'learne' is a d/e misreading error
for 'learnd'; cf. their spelling 'learnd' in l. 17.

19. *complexion*] (four syllables).

20. *flowing*] graceful (*OED,* 3.b).

21. *Gentle*] courteous (*OED,* 3.c).

23. *gentle*] mild (*OED,* 8).

24. *And . . . all*] The defective metre suggests that the line is corrupt, either
by printing 'through' for 'thorough' or by omitting a word, in which case 'And

My honoured scars, to come to such a parley.   25

Evadne. I understand ye not.

Melantius.   You dare not, fool;
They that commit thy faults fly the remembrance.

Evadne. My faults, sir? I would have you know I care not
If they were written here, here in my forehead.

Melantius. Thy body is too little for the story,   30
The lusts of which would fill another woman,
Though she had twins within her.

Evadne.   This is saucy;
Look you intrude no more. There's your way.

Melantius. Thou art my way, and I will tread upon thee
Till I find truth out.

Evadne.   What truth is that you look for?   35

Melantius. Thy long-lost honour. Would the gods had set me
Rather to grapple with the plague, or stand

---

33. There's] *Q1, Q2* (theres); there lies *Q3.*

I could blush, I [= ay] at these yeares' or 'And I could blush at these yeares
through all these [i.e., the scars on his face, indicating them]' may have been
the reading of the original.

29. *forehead*] (The pronunciation required is fŏrr′ed, not fore′head').
Offenders were sometimes exhibited in public wearing 'papers' (*OED*, 7.b)
specifying their offence, usually on their backs but sometimes on their breasts.
For the idea of a forehead similarly papered cf. *All's W.*, IV.iii.216–17: 'He
shall be whipt through the army with this rhyme in's forehead'). Aspatia says
'Write on my brow my fortune' (II.i.105), without any implication of guilt. In
the present context Evadne seems rather to be imagining, figuratively, her
faults written upon her forehead itself for all to read; Melantius' retort (ll.
30–2) reinforces this interpretation.

31. *The ... which*] the lusts recorded in which.

31–2. *would ... her*] would, if written down, cover your whole body and
another woman's as well, even one enlarged by being about to give birth to
twins. Colman, explaining this, comments: 'It must be allowed, the thought
and expression are rather uncouth.'

32. *saucy*] presumptuous, insolent.

33. *Look*] take care.

There's] The pause (with appropriate gesture) before this word fills the
apparent gap in the line's metre. Q3's emendation 'There lies' is wrong, for
Melantius' retort depends on Evadne's having used the verb 'to be'.

34–5. *and ... out*] a double metaphor, (1) of journeying to Truth's abode,
(2) of crushing the truth out of Evadne.

35. *that*] that which.

37. *stand*] withstand.

    One of their loudest bolts! Come, tell me quickly,
    Do it without enforcement, and take heed
    You swell me not above my temper.
Evadne.   How, sir!   40
    Where got you this report?
Melantius.   Where there was people:
    In every place.
Evadne. They and the seconds of it are base people;
    Believe them not, they lied.
Melantius. Do not play with mine anger, do not, wretch!   45
                               [*Seizes her.*]
    I come to know that desperate fool that drew thee
    From thy fair life: be wise and lay him open.
Evadne. Unhand me and learn manners; such another
    Forgetfulness forfeits your life.
Melantius. [*Releasing her*] Quench me this mighty humour,
    and then tell me   50
    Whose whore you are, for you are one, I know it.
    Let all mine honours perish but I'll find him,
    Though he lie locked up in thy blood. Be sudden;
    There is no facing it. And be not flattered:

40–1. How ... report?] *so Weber; as one line,* Q1, Q2.   41–2. Where ...
place] *so Weber; as one line,* Q1, Q2.   44. they lied] *Q2;* theile lie *Q1.*
45.1. Seizes her.] *Weber; not in* Q1, Q2.   50. *Releasing her*] *This ed.; not in*
Q1, Q2.   53. Be sudden] *Q2;* come tell me *Q1.*

---

   38. bolts] thunderbolts. Cf. Chapman, *Bussy D'Ambois* (Q1, 1607), IV.ii.13–
17: 'He had better / Ventured his breast in the consuming reach / Of the hot
surfeits cast out of the clouds, / Or stood the bullets that, to wreak the sky, /
The Cyclops ram in Jove's artillery.'
   40. swell] i.e., with impatience.
   43. seconds] upholders (*OED*, 8).
   base] contemptible (probably in both senses, morally and socially).
   46. know] learn the name of.
   desperate] made extremely reckless by despair (*OED*, 4); probably with the
consequential sense 'suicidal', since Melantius intends to kill him, and so the
sinner will have caused his own death.
   50. Quench me] Quench, I tell you. For this use of the pronoun see E. A.
Abbott, *Shakespearian Grammar* (1870 ed.), pp. 146–8 (section 220).
   mighty humour] affectation of mightiness.
   53. Though ... blood] i.e., though I have to kill you to get his name from
you.
   54. facing it] either (1) braving the matter out (*OED*, 1) or (2) dissembling
the matter (*OED*, 1.c).
   flattered] self-deceived.

The burnt air when the Dog reigns is not fouler   55
Than thy contagious name, till thy repentance
(If the gods grant thee any) purge thy sickness.
Evadne. Begone! You are my brother, that's your safety.
Melantius. I'll be a wolf first. 'Tis, to be thy brother,
An infamy below the sin of coward.   60
I am as far from being part of thee
As thou art from thy virtue. Seek a kindred
'Mongst sensual beasts, and make a goat thy brother:
A goat is cooler. Will you tell me yet?
Evadne. If you stay here and rail thus, I shall tell you   65
I'll ha' you whipped. Get you to your command,
And there preach to your sentinels, and tell them
What a brave man you are. I shall laugh at you.
Melantius. Y'are grown a glorious whore: where be your
       fighters?
What mortal fool durst raise thee to this daring,   70
And I alive? By my just sword, h'ad safer
Bestrid a billow when the angry north
Ploughs up the sea, or made heaven's fire his food!
Work me no higher. Will you discover yet?

---

63. brother] *Q2;* father *Q1.*   67–8. And ... at you] *so Theobald;* And ...
Centinels, / And ... you *Q1, Q2.*   71–2. Y'are ... daring] *so Theobald;*
Y'are ... your / Fighters ... daring *Q1, Q2.*   71. h'ad] *Q1;* ha'd *Q2.*
72. Bestrid] *Theobald;* Bestride *Q1, Q2.*   73. food] *Q2;* foe *Q1.*

---

55. *The burnt ... reigns*] The dog-days (*OED,* 'the days about the time of
the heliacal rising of the Dog-star, noted from ancient times as the hottest and
most unwholesome period of the year') are generally assigned to most of July
and the first half of August.
   56. *contagious*] i.e., infecting her whole family with her dishonour.
   57. *If ... any*] i.e., if you are not struck down in your sins.
   59. *I'll ... first*] I'd rather be a wolf.
   63. *goat*] a type of lustfulness; cf. *Oth.,* III.iii.403.
   66–8. *Get ... are*] Cf. *Caes.,* IV. iii. 43–4: 'Go show your slaves how
choleric you are, / And make your bondmen tremble.'
   68. *brave man*] fine fellow.
   69. *glorious*] proud, haughty (*OED,* 1).
   fighters] champions, bullies (*OED,* 1.b).
   73. *made ... food*] swallowed a thunderbolt. The extravagant image is
appropriate to the passionate tone (cf. Webster, *The White Devil,* III.iii.128:
'H'had as good met with his fist a thunderbolt.'). Q1's 'foe' presumably
resulted from misreading 'food' in secretary hand as 'fooe'.
   74. *discover*] reveal (i.e., your lover's name).

Evadne. The fellow's mad. Sleep, and speak sense.   75
Melantius. Force my swoll'n heart no further. I would save
    thee.
    Your great maintainers are not here, they dare not;
    Would they were all, and armed! I would speak loud;
    Here's one should thunder to 'em. Will you tell me?
    Thou hast no hope to scape: he that dares most,   80
    And damns away his soul to do thee service,
    Will sooner snatch meat from a hungry lion
    Than come to rescue thee; thou hast death about thee.
    He has undone thine honour, poisoned thy virtue,
    And of a lovely rose left thee a canker.   85
Evadne. Let me consider.
Melantius.   Do, whose child thou wert,
    Whose honour thou hast murdered, whose grave opened,
    And so pulled on the gods that in their justice
    They must restore him flesh again and life
    And raise his dry bones to revenge this scandal.   90

76–9. Force ... tell me?] *so Langbaine; as prose, Q1, Q2.*   80–5. Thou ...
canker] *so Langbaine; as prose, Q2; not in Q1.*   84. He has] *Langbaine;* has
Q2; Who has *Colman;* H'as *Norland; not in Q1.*   85. canker.] *Q2;* canker?
Colman; not in Q1.

---

77. *maintainers*] supporters (in your wrongdoing: *OED*, 3.b); cf. 'your
fighters', l. 69. An additional sense of 'maintainer' (*OED*, 5) is 'one who keeps
a mistress'; cf. *The Woman Hater*, II.i.76–9: 'and wheresoever you remoove,
your great maintainer and you shal have your lodgings directly opposite, it is
but putting on your night-gowne, and your slippers'. The 'he' of ll. 80 and 84
is her 'maintainer' in this sense.
    dare not] i.e., come in my presence.
    79. *thunder*] utter terrible menace (*OED*, 3).
    82. *Will ... lion*] The incident in Peele's *Battle of Alcazar* (II.iii.538) where
Muly Mahamet does this was well-known and parodied in *2H4*, II.iv.169, and
elsewhere (see A. R. Humphreys's note in the Arden *2H4*).
    84. *He has*] The emendation is metrically necessary, and the omission is
easily explained, as the whole passage is set as prose without full stops ('thee',
the last word in the previous line, is followed by a colon).
    85 *canker*] a rose eaten into holes by a canker-worm (not in this sense in
OED). A canker (*OED*, 4), or canker-worm, is 'a caterpillar, or any insect
larva, which destroys the buds and leaves of plants'. The line is probably
influenced by *1H4*, I.iii.176–7: 'To put down Richard, that sweet lovely rose,
/ And plant this thorn, this canker, Bolingbroke' (where, however, 'canker' is a
wild rose or brier, *OED*, 5).
    88. *pulled on*] provoked (*OED*, pull on, 'induce'). This use with a personal
object is not recorded in *OED*.

Evadne. The gods are not of my mind: they had better
    Let 'em lie sweet still in the earth; they'll stink here.
Melantius. Do you raise mirth out of my easiness?
    Forsake me then, all weaknesses of nature
    That make men women!
        [*Draws his sword, and forces her to the ground.*]
                  Speak, you whore, speak truth,   95
    Or, by the dear soul of thy sleeping father,
    This sword shall be thy lover; tell, or I'll kill thee!
    And when thou hast told all, thou wilt deserve it.
Evadne. You will not murder me!
Melantius. No, 'tis a justice, and a noble one,   100
    To put the light out of such base offenders.
Evadne. Help!
Melantius. By thy foul self,
    No human help shall help thee if thou criest.
    When I have killed thee   105
    (As I have vowed to do if thou confess not)
    Nak'd as thou hast left thine honour will I leave thee,
    That on thy branded flesh the world may read
    Thy black shame and my justice. Wilt thou bend yet?

95.1. *Draws ... ground.*] *This ed.; Draws his sword. Dyce; not in Q1, Q2.*
103–7. By ... thee] *This ed.;* By ... help thee, / If ... haue / Vow'd ... left /
Thine ... thee *Q1, Q2.*   107. Nak'd] *This ed.;* naked *Q1, Q2.*

---

93. *easiness*] gentleness (*OED*, 5).

95.1.] This stage direction, natural to the sudden rise in tension, is necessary in order that Melantius may say 'Up' at l. 111 (contrast Dyce's directions, which make Evadne kneel at l. 110—taking 'bend' too literally—and rise, with incongruous rapidity, the next moment).

97. *This sword ... lover*] i.e., by penetrating her body? But the literal threat is surely to stab her through the heart, not in the genitals (as the stage business in the Royal Shakespeare Company production of 1982 suggested, in which Melantius was armed with a dagger and not with a sword).

98. *when ... it*] i.e., I do not promise to spare your life when you have confessed.

99. *You ... me!*] Cf. *Ham.*, III.iv.21. Cf. also l. 117, 'What shall I do?' with *Ham.*, III.iv.180.

101. *put ... out*] extinguish the life; cf. *Oth.*, V.ii.7.

107. *Nak'd*] monosyllabic: cf. II.i.2, and Introduction, p. 36.

thou hast] The verse requires elision: 'thou'st' (cf. l. 134, where 'thou hadst' becomes 'thou'dst').

108. *branded*] (figuratively) marked with infamy.

109. *bend*] yield (*OED*, 10).

Evadne. Yes.   110
Melantius. [*Raising her*] Up, and begin your story.
Evadne. O, I am miserable!
Melantius.   'Tis true, thou art; speak truth still.
Evadne. I have offended, noble sir, forgive me.
Melantius. With what secure slave?
Evadne.   Do not ask me, sir;
   Mine own remembrance is a misery   115
   Too mighty for me.
Melantius.   Do not fall back again;
   My sword's unsheathèd yet.
Evadne.   What shall I do?
Melantius. Be true, and make your fault less.
Evadne.   I dare not tell.
Melantius. Tell, or I'll be this day a-killing thee.
Evadne. Will you forgive me then?   120
Melantius. Stay, I must ask mine honour first.
   I have too much foolish nature in me; speak.
Evadne. Is there none else here?
Melantius. None but a fearful conscience; that's too many.
   Who is't?
Evadne.   O, hear me gently! It was the King.   125
Melantius. No more. My worthy father's and my services
   Are liberally rewarded. King, I thank thee;
   For all my dangers and my wounds thou hast paid me

110. Yes.] *Q1, Q2; Yes. (Kneels.) Dyce.*   111. *Raising her*] *Dyce; not in
Q1, Q2.*   116–17. Do not ... yet] *so Theobald; as one line, Q1, Q2.*
117. unsheathèd] *Q1, Q2 (vnsheathed).*   121–2. Stay ... speak] *so Weber;
as prose, Q1, Q2.*   123. none else] *Q2; no more Q1.*   125. O, hear ...
King] *Q2; The King Q1.*   126. No more.] *Q2; not in Q1.*

---

112. *miserable*] distressed. Melantius, in his reply, implies the sense 'in a
state of wretchedness'.
   114. *secure*] over-confident (*OED*, 1).
   116. *fall ... again*] i.e., to concealment.
   118. *true*] truthful.
   119. *this day*] all this day; cf. *Oth.*, IV.i.174: 'I would have him nine years
a-killing.'
   120. *then*] when I have told the truth.
   122. *I ... speak*] an affirmative reply. In the pause before this line Melantius has deliberated and probably brushed away a tear (cf. III.ii.111–12).
   126. *No more*] Say no more; i.e., that is all I need to know.
   128–9. *thou hast ... metal*] You have paid me in steel (i.e., by figuratively
stabbing me).

In mine own metal: these are soldiers' thanks.
How long have you lived thus, Evadne?   130
Evadne. Too long.
Melantius.   Too late you find it. Can you be sorry?
Evadne. Would I were half as blameless!
Melantius. Evadne, thou wilt to thy trade again.
Evadne. First to my grave.
Melantius.   Would gods thou hadst been so bless'd!
Dost thou not hate this King now? Prithee, hate him.   135
Couldst thou not curse him? I command thee, curse him;
Curse till the gods hear and deliver him
To thy just wishes. Yet I fear, Evadne,
You had rather play your game out.
Evadne.   No, I feel
Too many sad confusions here to let in   140
Any loose flame hereafter.
Melantius. Dost thou not feel, amongst all those, one brave
anger
That breaks out nobly and directs thine arm
To kill this base King?
Evadne.   All the gods forbid it!
Melantius. No, all the gods require it: 145
They are dishonoured in him.
Evadne.   'Tis too fearful.
Melantius. Y'are valiant in his bed, and bold enough

---

131. Too long ... you] *Q2;* Too long, too late I finde it. / *Mel.* Can you *Q1.*   131. be sorry] *Q2;* be very sorry *Q1.*   133. Evadne ... to] *Q2;* Woman thou wilt not to *Q1.*   134. bless'd] *Q1, Q2* (blest).   136. Couldst thou not curse him] *Q3;* Could'st thee not curse him *Q2;* Has sunke thy faire soule *Q1.*   145–6. No ... him] *so Weber; as one line, Q1, Q2.*

---

129. *soldiers' thanks*] the thanks that soldiers expect; bitterly ironical.
132. *half as blameless*] i.e., as I am sorry.
134. *so bless'd*] i.e., so blessed as to have died before you first fell from virtue.
140. *confusions*] agitations of mind (*OED*, 3).
here] in my heart (with the appropriate gesture).
142. *amongst*] (one syllable: "mongst')
144. *forbid it!*] not a statement (Qq 'forbid it.') but an exclamation. The force of Melantius' retort comes from his treating it as a statement. Cf. Tourneur, *The Atheist's Tragedy*, V.ii.246–7: '*Judge.* God forbid. / *D'Amville.* Forbid? You lie, judge; he commanded it.'

To be a stale whore, and have your madam's name
Discourse for grooms and pages; and hereafter,
When his cool majesty hath laid you by,   150
To be at pension with some needy sir
For meat and coarser clothes:
Thus far you knew no fear. Come, you shall kill him.
Evadne. Good sir!
Melantius. And 'twere to kiss him dead, thou'dst smother him.   155
Be wise and kill him. Canst thou live and know
What noble minds shall make thee, see thyself
Found out with every finger, made the shame
Of all successions, and in this great ruin
Thy brother and thy noble husband broken?   160
Thou shalt not live thus. Kneel and swear to help me
When I shall call thee to it, or, by all
Holy in heaven and earth, thou shalt not live
To breathe a full hour longer, not a thought.
Come, 'tis a righteous oath. [*Evadne kneels.*] Give me thy
        hand,   165

150. cool] *Q1, Q2;* cool'd *conj. Daniel.*   152–3. For . . . him] *so this ed.;* For
. . . feare. / Come . . . him *Q1, Q2.*   153. knew] *Q2;* had *Q1.*   157. thee,
see thyself] *Weber;* thee see thy selfe, *Q1, Q2.*   159. this great] *Q2;* this thy
Q1.   163. shalt] *Q1;* shall *Q2.*   164. full] *Q2;* foule *Q1.*   165. *Evadne
kneels.*] *Norland; Dyce (at l. 168); not in Q1, Q2.*

---

148. *stale*] having lost the vigour or attractiveness of youth (*OED*, 4).
Evadne is still in her prime, but Melantius is combining the present and the
future in this speech.
    madam's] ladyship's.
149. *Discourse*] a subject of gossip.
    grooms and pages] i.e., palace servants in general.
150. *cool*] satiated (his lust being quenched). Daniel's conjecture 'cool'd'
(involving an easy d/e misreading) is attractive and may be correct; but Qq's
'coole' gives the same sense and is therefore retained.
151. *be at pension*] take lodging.
152. *meat*] food.
153. *knew*] have known.
155. *And*] if.
157. *make thee*] regard you as being.
158. *found . . . finger*] pointed at, as an object of universal scorn.
159.. *successions*] succeeding ages.
160. *broken*] destroyed (continuing the image in 'ruin', which is of a mansion
falling, not of a business failing).
164. *a thought*] i.e., a moment, the time needed to think a thought.
165. *Give . . . hand*] i.e., in confirmation.

And, both to heaven held up, swear by that wealth
This lustful thief stole from thee, when I say it,
To let his foul soul out.

Evadne.   Here I swear it,
And all you spirits of abusèd ladies
Help me in this performance!   170

Melantius. Enough. [*Raising her*] This must be known to none
But you and I, Evadne, not to your lord,
Though he be wise and noble, and a fellow
Dare step as far into a worthy action
As the most daring, ay, as far as justice.   175
Ask me not why. Farewell.   *Exit* MELANTIUS.

Evadne. Would I could say so to my black disgrace!
Gods, where have I been all this time, how friended,
That I should lose myself thus desperately,
And none for pity show me how I wandered?   180
There is not in the compass of the light
A more unhappy creature; sure, I am monstrous,
For I have done those follies, those mad mischiefs,
Would dare a woman. O, my loaden soul,
Be not so cruel to me, choke not up   185
The way to my repentance.

---

171. *Raising her*] Dyce; not in *Q1, Q2.*

---

166. *both . . . up*] Melantius raises the hand he holds, and Evadne raises the other, in the pause in l. 168.

that wealth] i.e., of reputation.

169. *abusèd*] misused.

174. *Dare*] that dare.

175. *justice*] executing justice.

177. *say so*] say farewell.

178. *friended*] befriended. 'Friend' often means a close relative, but Diphilus (Evadne's only relative at court) did not know of her guilt; nor, apparently, did any of her friends the ladies. The point seems to be her present sense of her past moral isolation.

181. *in . . . light*] in all that the sun goes round, i.e., the world.

182. *monstrous*] a monster.

183. *mischiefs*] evil-doings (*OED*, 6).

184. *dare*] daunt (*OED*, 6).

184–6. *O, my . . . repentance*] Evadne fears that her sense of guilt may drive her to despair.

185. *cruel*] (two syllables).

Enter AMINTOR.

O, my lord!

Amintor. How now?

Evadne. My much abusèd lord!   *Kneel.*

Amintor.   This cannot be.

Evadne. I do not kneel to live; I dare not hope it;
The wrongs I did are greater. Look upon me,   190
Though I appear with all my faults.

Amintor.   Stand up.
This is a new way to beget more sorrows;
Heaven knows I have too many. Do not mock me:
Though I am tame and bred up with my wrongs,
Which are my foster-brothers, I may leap   195
Like a hand-wolf into my natural wildness,
And do an outrage. Prithee, do not mock me.

Evadne. My whole life is so leprous it infects
All my repentance. I would buy your pardon
Though at the highest set, even with my life: 200
That slight contrition, that's no sacrifice
For what I have committed.

Amintor.   Sure, I dazzle.
There cannot be a faith in that foul woman
That knows no god more mighty than her mischiefs.

---

192. a new] *Q1;* no new *Q2.*   sorrows] *Q1;* sorrow *Q2.*   201. That ...
that's no sacrifice] *Q3 (subst.:* That ... thats; no sacrifice*);* That ... that; no
sacrifice *Q1, Q2;* That ... that no-sacrifice *conj. Brereton;* That's ... that; no
sacrifice *conj. Daniel.*

---

188. Kneel.] Stage directions in the imperative indicate the hand either of
the theatre's book-keeper or (as probably here) of an author familiar with
theatrical practice.
   This ... be] I cannot believe that this is happening.
   191. *with*] i.e., disfigured by.
   196. *hand-wolf*] a wolf that has been made hand-tame; not in *OED*. Cf. *Lr.,*
III.vi.18–19: 'He's mad that trusts in the tameness of a wolf', an idea perhaps
proverbial (see D. R. Klinck in *Notes and Queries,* n.s., XXIV (1977), 113–14).
   200. *set*] stake (*OED,* 24).
   201. *That ... contrition*] that insignificant thing contrition.
   202. *dazzle*] am confused (*OED,* 2).
   204. *That ... mischiefs*] that recognises no higher law than her own
wickedness.

Thou dost still worse, still number on thy faults,   205
To press my poor heart thus. Can I believe
There's any seed of virtue in that woman
Left to shoot up, that dares go on in sin
Known, and so known as thine is? O, Evadne,
Would there were any safety in thy sex,   210
That I might put a thousand sorrows off
And credit thy repentance; but I must not;
Thou hast brought me to that dull calamity,
To that strange misbelief of all the world
And all things that are in it, that I fear   215
I shall fall like a tree and find my grave,
Only remembering that I grieve.

Evadne.   My lord,
Give me your griefs; you are an innocent,
A soul as white as heaven; let not my sins
Perish your noble youth. I do not fall here   220
To shadow my dissembling with my tears
(As all say women can) or to make less

221. my dissembling] *This ed.;* by dissembling *Q1, Q2.*

---

205. *number on*] add to.
206. *press*] oppress.
209. *Known . . . is*] i.e., sin which she knows to be a sin, and such a heavy
one.
201. *safety . . . sex*] reliability in womankind.
213. *dull calamity*] state of distress (*OED,* calamity, 1) in which one is
physically or emotionally insensible (*OED,* dull, 2).
216. *like a tree*] i.e., where I stand; also, as insensible as a tree (to anything
but my own griefs, l. 217).
218. *Give . . . griefs*] Let me take the burden of your sorrows.
220. *Perish*] destroy (*OED,* 3).
fall here] kneel before you.
221. *my*] The emendation is necessary. If Qq's 'by' is retained, the sense of
the main clause has to be 'to shadow . . . or to make less what my hot will hath
done', which is open to objection because (1) 'make less' must here mean
'make *seem* less', (2) it substantially duplicates 'shadow', and (3) 'shadow'
(*OED,* 6: conceal) is inapplicable because Evadne's sin is already beyond
concealment from Amintor. If 'by' is emended to 'my', the sense is 'to
dissemble [contrition] and screen my dissimulation from your knowledge by
my tears (as all say women can), or to make less [by my genuine contrition] the
sin that I have committed'.
222. *As all . . . can*] Cf. *Arcadia,* bk. III, chap. 15, pp. 244–5: 'she could not
onely sigh when she would, as all can doo, & weep when she would, as (they
say) some can doo'.

What my hot will hath done, which heaven and you
Knows to be tougher than the hand of time
Can cut from man's remembrance; no, I do not.   225
I do appear the same, the same Evadne,
Dressed in the shames I lived in, the same monster.
But these are names of honour to what I am:
I do present myself the foulest creature,
Most poisonous, dangerous, and despised of men,   230
Lerna e'er bred or Nilus. I am hell,
Till you, my dear lord, shoot your light into me,
The beams of your forgiveness. I am soul-sick,
And wither with the fear of one condemned
Till I have got your pardon.
Amintor.   Rise, Evadne.   235
Those heavenly powers that put this good into thee
Grant a continuance of it! I forgive thee.
Make thyself worthy of it, and take heed,
Take heed, Evadne, this be serious:
Mock not the powers above, that can and dare   240
Give thee a great example of their justice

---

225. Can] *Q2;* Shall *Q1.*

---

224. *Knows*] The singular form of the verb agrees with 'heaven', the sense
being 'which heaven knows (and you know too)'.

228. *these*] i.e., such names as 'monster'; anticipating ll. 229–31.

to what I am] The stress falls on 'I'.

231. *Lerna*] a marsh harbouring the hydra, a many-headed serpent killed by
Hercules.

Nilus] the Nile, productive of crocodiles; cf. l. 247.

hell] i.e., an evil place of total darkness.

232. *lord*] husband (as elsewhere in the scene, ll. 172, 186, 188, 217, 251,
279; always printed 'Lord' in Qq). Gurr's suggestion that 'Amintor's reproof
[l. 240] is not simply a warning that she must repent sincerely but an implied
reproof against her using the image of Amintor as her "Lord", Jesus-like
casting light into her hell' is therefore unconvincing.

234. *condemned*] in a state of impending damnation.

235. *Rise*] Evadne does not rise until Amintor has again bidden her do so,
l. 261.

238. *it*] forgiveness.

239. *this*] this repentance of yours.

240. *Mock not*] do not try to deceive; cf. Gal.vi.7: 'God is not mocked.'
dare] i.e., will not hesitate to.

241–2. *Give ... ages*] present thee, to all future times, as a notable example
of their just punishing of sin.

To all ensuing ages, if thou playst
With thy repentance, the best sacrifice.
Evadne. I have done nothing good to win belief,
My life hath been so faithless. All the creatures   245
Made for heaven's honours have their ends, and good
     ones,
All but the cozening crocodiles, false women.
They reign here like those plagues, those killing sores
Men pray against; and when they die, like tales
Ill told and unbelieved they pass away   250
And go to dust forgotten. But, my lord,
Those short days I shall number to my rest
(As many must not see me) shall, though too late,
Though in my evening, yet perceive I will,
Since I can do no good because a woman,   255
Reach constantly at something that is near it.
I will redeem one minute of my age,
Or like another Niobe I'll weep
Till I am water.

---

242. ages] *Dyce, conj. Weber;* eies *Q1, Q2.*   if] *Q1, Q2;* if that *Theobald.*
244. win] *Q2;* get *Q1.*   246. honours] *Q1, Q2;* honour *conj. Mason.*
253. too late] *Q1, Q2;* late *Theobald.*   254. I] *Q7;* a *Q1, Q2.*

---

242. *ages*] Weber's emendation restores the metre and improves the sense:
ensuing ages could know of Evadne's punishment, but ensuing eyes could not
see it. Q1's compositor presumably misread 'ages' as 'eyes', though he spelled
it 'eies' (the usual spelling in Qq) when he set it.
playst] Cf. III.ii.101 n.
243. *best*] most pleasing to heaven.
246. *for heaven's honours*] to do honour to heaven (*OED*, honour, sb., 6).
ends] purposes (in heaven's design).
247. *cozening*] i.e., by the tears with which they attract their prey.
false women] i.e., women, who are without exception false; cf. l. 255.
248. *sores*] i.e., of bubonic plague, periodically prevalent in London.
249. *Men*] people.
252. *rest*] death.
253. *many*] many days.
253–6. *shall, though ... near it*] The sense is 'my few remaining days of life
shall witness that—though my time is all too short—I will steadfastly strive
towards something like goodness, even though true goodness is beyond my
power because I am a woman.'
257. *age*] lifetime (*OED*, 2).
258. *Niobe*] Niobe boasted that her six sons and six daughters were fairer
offspring than Leto's children Apollo and Artemis, who thereupon slew all
Niobe's children with their arrows. She thus became a type of sorrowful

Amintor.   I am now dissolved;
   My frozen soul melts. May each sin thou hast   260
   Find a new mercy! Rise, I am at peace.   [*Evadne rises.*]
   Hadst thou been thus, thus excellently good,
   Before that devil King tempted thy frailty,
   Sure thou hadst made a star. Give me thy hand.
   From this time I will know thee, and, as far   265
   As honour gives me leave, be thy Amintor.
   When we meet next I will salute thee fairly,
   And pray the gods to give thee happy days;
   My charity shall go along with thee,
   Though my embraces must be far from thee.   270
   I should ha' killed thee, but this sweet repentance
   Locks up my vengeance, for which thus I kiss thee:
                        [*Kisses her.*]
   The last kiss we must take; and would to heaven
   The holy priest that gave our hands together
   Had given us equal virtues! Go, Evadne;   275
   The gods thus part our bodies. Have a care
   My honour falls no further: I am well then.
Evadne. All the dear joys here, and above hereafter,
   Crown thy fair soul! Thus I take leave, my lord,
   And never shall you see the foul Evadne   280
   Till she have tried all honoured means that may
   Set her in rest, and wash her stains away.
                   Exeunt [*severally*].

259. am now] *Q2;* am *Q1.*   261.1. *Evadne rises.*] *Dyce; not in Q1, Q2.*
264. hadst] *Q1, Q2;* hadst been *conj. this ed.*   272.1. *Kisses her.*] *Dyce; not in*
Q1, Q2.   282.1. *Exeunt* [*severally*].] *Theobald; Exeunt. Q1, Q2.*

---

bereavement (cf. *Ham.*, I.ii.149: 'Like Niobe, all tears'). She was finally
changed to a weeping statue (cf. II.ii.38–9 n.).
   262. *thus, thus . . . good*] like this, so excellently good.
   264. *thou . . . made*] thou wouldst have become (*OED*, make, 28). But I
conjecture that 'been' has been omitted ('Sure thou'dst been made a star'
would, with elision, be the metre), since the idea of being stellified involves not
active development but passive metamorphosis.
   265. *know*] acknowledge (as wife); not 'know' carnally (cf. l. 270).
   267. *salute*] greet; not kiss (cf. l. 273).
   269. *charity*] loving kindness.
   271. *should ha' killed*] meant to kill.
   273–5. *and would . . . virtues!*] i.e., if only, when we married, you had been
as chaste as I was!
   282. *rest*] spiritual calm.

[ACT IV SCENE ii]

Hautboys play within. [A] banquet [brought forth by two Servants.
Exeunt Servants]. *Enter* KING, [*and*] CALIANAX.

King. I cannot tell how I should credit this
From you that are his enemy.
Calianax.   I am sure
He said it to me, and I'll justify it
What way he dares oppose, but with my sword.
King. But did he break, without all circumstance,   5
To you his foe, that he would have the fort
To kill me and then scape?
Calianax.   If he deny it
I'll make him blush.
King.   It sounds incredibly.
Calianax. Ay, so does everything I say of late.
King. Not so, Calianax.
Calianax.   Yes, I should sit   10
Mute whilst a rogue with strong arms cuts your throat.
King. Well, I will try him, and if this be true
I'll pawn my life I'll find it; if't be false,
And that you clothe your hate in such a lie,
You shall hereafter dote in your own house,   15
Not in the court.
Calianax.   Why, if it be a lie,

0.1. *A banquet* ... Servants.] *This ed.; Banquet. Q1, Q2.*   2–3. I ... it] *so
Theobald, as one line, Q1, Q2.*   7–8. If ... blush] *so Theobald; as one line,
Q1, Q2.*

0.1. banquet] 'A course of sweetmeats, fruit, and wine, served either as a
separate entertainment, or as a continuation of a principal meal, but in the
latter case usually in a different room; a dessert' (*OED*, 3). For the stage
direction cf. *Thomas Lord Cromwell*, III.iii.0.1: '*The Musick playes, they bring
out the banquet. Enter* Sir Christopher Hales, *and* Cromwell, *and two seruants.*'
(*Shakespeare Apocrypha*, p. 178).
    1. *I cannot* ... *this*] I do not know how I can believe this (i.e., this
accusation).
    4. *with my sword*] in a trial by combat; cf. ll. 37–40.
    5. *break*] disclose (*OED*, 22).
    without all circumstance] abruptly (*OED*, circumstance, 7).
    15. *dote*] play the fool; C. Leech, *The John Fletcher Plays* (1962), p. 124,
compares *Ham.*, III.i.132–3: 'that he [i.e., Polonius] may play the fool
nowhere but in's own house'.

Mine ears are false, for I'll be sworn I heard it.
Old men are good for nothing: you were best
Put me to death for hearing and free him
For meaning it; you would ha' trusted me   20
Once, but the time is altered.
King.   And will still
Where I may do with justice to the world.
You have no witness.
Calianax.   Yes, myself.
King.   No more,
I mean, there were that heard it.
Calianax.   How, no more?
Would you have more? Why, am not I enough   25
To hang a thousand rogues?
King.   But so you may
Hang honest men too, if you please.
Calianax.   I may;
'Tis like I will do so! There are a hundred
Will swear it for a need too if I say it.
King. Such witnesses we need not.
Calianax.   And 'tis hard   30
If my word cannot hang a boisterous knave.
King. Enough. Where's Strato?

Enter STRATO.

Strato. Sir?
King. Why, where's all the company? Call Amintor in,
Evadne; where's my brother, and Melantius?   35
Bid him come too, and Diphilus; call all

17. I'll be sworn] *Q2;* I besworne *Q1.*   21–31. And ... knave] *so Theobald;
as prose, Q1, Q2.*   34–5. Call ... where's] *Theobald (subst.);* call *Amintor* in /
Euadne, wheres *Q1, Q2, Q3;* call *Amintor* in. / *Euadne,* wheres *Q4;* call *Amintor*
and / *Evadne,* wheres *Turner.*

17. *false*] liars.
19. *hearing*] hearing it.
23. *You ... witness*] This, and the King's next speech, are not questions but
statements, as Calianax's emphatic replies make clear.
27–8. *I ... so!*] ironical.
31. *boisterous*] violently fierce (*OED,* 9a).
34–5. *Call ... Evadne*] call in Amintor and Evadne.

That are without there.

Exit STRATO.

If he should desire
The combat of you, 'tis not in the power
Of all our laws to hinder it, unless
We mean to quit 'em.

Calianax.   Why, if you do think   40
'Tis fit an old man, and a counsellor,
To fight for what he says, then you may grant it.

Enter AMINTOR, EVADNE, MELANTIUS, DIPHILUS,
LYSIPPUS, CLEON, [*and*] STRATO.

King. Come, sirs. Amintor, thou art yet a bridegroom,
And I will use thee so: thou shalt sit down.
Evadne, sit, and you, Amintor, too;   45
This banquet is for you, sir.

[*Evadne and Amintor sit at the table.*]
Who has brought
A merry tale about him to raise laughter
Amongst our wine? Why, Strato, where art thou?
Thou wilt chop out with them unseasonably
When I desire 'em not.   50

Strato. 'Tis my ill luck, sir, so to spend them then.

King. Reach me a bowl of wine, Melantius.

42. To] *Q1, Q2*; Do *Theobald.*   42.1–2.] *Q1 (Enter Amintor, Euadne,
Melant. Diph. Lysip. Cle. Stra.); Enter Amint. Euad. Melant. Diph. Lisip. Cle.
Stra. Diag. Q2.*   46.1.] *This ed.; not in Q1, Q2.*   49. chop] *Q2*; chopt *Q1.*
52–3. Reach ... sad] *so Dyce; as one line, Q1, Q2.*   wine, Melantius. / [*To
Amintor.*] Thou art sad] *This ed.;* wine, *Melantius* thou art sad *Q1;* wine:
Melantius thou art sad *Q2.*

37–8. *desire ... you*] demand that you oppose him in a trial by combat.
40. *quit*] abandon.
42. *To*] The syntax is loose but natural, and there is no need to emend to
'Do'.
42.1–2.] Q2 incongruously includes Diagoras, a servant, at this select
banquet where the nobles serve themselves. His name was probably added by
the annotator because the prominent catchword *Diagoras* on sig. I2 in Q1 made
it seem that he was present. See l. 192 n.
46. *you*] Amintor.
49. *chop out with*] come out with, blurt out (*OED*, chop, 8.b).
52–5.] Q1's habitual omission of punctuation led the compositor himself to
think that 'thou art sad' was addressed to Melantius, whereupon he changed
the next speech prefix. In Q2 the speech prefix was corrected but Q1's faulty
punctuation was retained.

[*To Amintor*] Thou art sad.

Amintor.   I should be, sir, the merriest here,
    But I ha' ne'er a story of mine own
    Worth telling at this time.

King.   Give me the wine.   55
                    [*Melantius gives him the bowl.*]
    Melantius, I am now considering
    How easy 'twere for any man we trust
    To poison one of us in such a bowl.

Melantius. I think it were not hard, sir, for a knave.

Calianax. [*Aside*] Such as you are.   60

King. I' faith, 'twere easy. It becomes us well!
    To get plain-dealing men about ourselves,
    Such as you all are here. Amintor, to thee
    And to thy fair Evadne.   [*Drinks.*]

Melantius. (*Aside* [*to Calianax*]) Have you thought
    Of this, Calianax?

Calianax.   Yes, marry, have I.   65

Melantius. And what's your resolution?

Calianax.   Ye shall have it;
    [*Aside*] Soundly, I warrant you.

King. Reach to Amintor, Strato.
                    [*Strato gives the bowl to Amintor, who
                    drinks to Evadne and gives her the bowl.*]

Amintor.   Here, my love;
    This wine will do thee wrong, for it will set
    Blushes upon thy cheeks, and till thou dost   70
    A fault 'twere pity.

                              [*Evadne drinks.*]

53. Amintor.] *Q2 (Amint.); Mel. Q1.   55.1.] This ed; not in Q1, Q2.*
60. Aside] *Weber; not in Q1, Q2.   64. Drinks.] Dyce; not in Q1, Q2.   Aside
[to Calianax]] Q2 (aside); not in Q1.   64-5. Have ... Calianax?] so
Theobald; as one line, Q1, Q2.   66-7. Ye ... you] so Weber; as one line Q1,
Q2.   have it; / [Aside] Soundly] Colman (subst.); haue it soundly Q1, Q2.
68.1-2.] Dyce (subst.); not in Q1, Q2.   71.1.] This ed.; not in Q1, Q2.*

---

53. *I ... here*] i.e., being the bridegroom.

56-8.] It now becomes clear why the King asked Melantius to hand him a
bowl of wine at l. 52. He can pretend to the company that his meaningful
remark is merely a casual thought.

65. *this*] the matter that we talked of (i.e., the proposal about the fort,
III.ii.301-10).

66. *have it*] (1) get the fort, (2) meet your fate (cf. *Rom.*, III.i.105: 'I have it,
and soundly too—Your houses!').

King.   Yet I wonder much
     Of the strange desperation of these men
     That dare attempt such acts; here in our state
     He could not scape that did it.
Melantius.   Were he known,
     Unpossible.
King.   It would be known, Melantius.   75
Melantius. It ought to be. If he got then away
     He must wear all our lives upon his sword.
     He need not fly the island, he must leave
     No one alive.
King.   No, I should think no man
     Could kill me, and scape clear, but that old man.   80
Calianax. But I? Heaven bless me! I? Should I, my liege?
King. I do not think thou wouldst, but yet thou mightst,
     For thou hast in thy hands the means to scape,
     By keeping of the fort. He has, Melantius,
     And he has kept it well.
Melantius.   From cobwebs, sir.   85
     'Tis clean swept: I can find no other art
     In keeping of it now; 'twas ne'er besieged
     Since he commanded.
Calianax.   I shall be sure
     Of your good word; but I have kept it safe
     From such as you.
Melantius.   Keep your ill temper in.   90
     I speak no malice; had my brother kept it

72. Of] *Q1, Q2;* At *Theobald.*   73–4. acts; here in our state / He] *This ed.;*
acts here in our state, / He *Q1, Q2.*   74–5. Were ... Unpossible] *so*
Theobald; as one line, Q1, Q2.   87. besieged] *Q1 (subst.:* beseidge *[sic]),*
Q2.   88. commanded] *Q1, Q2;* commanded it *Theobald.*   shall] *Q1, Q2;*
shall still *conj. this ed.*

----

    72. *Of*] at; cf. *Tp.,* II.i.76: 'You make me study of that.'
    73.] The re-punctuation is necessary. The King is not saying that desperate
assassinations are attempted in Rhodes but that they are desperate anywhere
and in Rhodes particularly so (it being an island, l. 78).
    75. *Unpossible*] impossible.
    It] i.e., who the assassin was.
    77. *wear ... sword*] run us all through, one after another. The image is of a
sword on which numerous opponents' bodies are spitted.
    88–9. *I ... word*] ironical; cf. *Cor.,* I.i.164: 'We have ever your good
word.' Perhaps 'still' has been omitted (as might easily be done after setting
'shall'): the idea of habitual detraction is implied.

I should ha' said as much.
King. [*To those at the table*]   You are not merry.
Brother, drink wine. Sit you all still. (*Aside* [*to Calianax*])
Calianax,
I cannot trust thus. I have thrown out words
That would have fetched warm blood upon the cheeks   95
Of guilty men, and he is never moved:
He knows no such thing.
Calianax.   Impudence may scape
When feeble virtue is accused.
King.   'A must,
If he were guilty, feel an alteration
At this our whisper whilst we point at him: 100
You see he does not.
Calianax.   Let him hang himself!
What care I what he does? This he did say.
                    [*King beckons Melantius to join them.*]
King. Melantius, you can easily conceive
What I have meant, for men that are in fault
Can subtly apprehend when others aim   105
At what they do amiss; but I forgive
Freely before this man; heaven do so too!
I will not touch thee so much as with shame
Of telling it; let it be so no more.
Calianax. [*Aside*] Why, this is very fine!
Melantius.   I cannot tell   110
What 'tis you mean; but I am apt enough

92–3. You ... Calianax] *so Theobald;* You ... wine, / Sit ... *Calianax Q1, Q2.* merry. / Brother] *Theobald* (*subst.*); merry, brother *Q1, Q2.*
94. thus] *Q1, Q2;* this *Dyce;* to't thus *conj. this ed.;* thee *conj. J. R. Mulryne.*
97–8. Impudence ... accused] *so Theobald; as one line, Q1, Q2.* 98–9. 'A must ... alteration] *so Theobald; as one line, Q1, Q2.* 102.1.] *This ed.; not in Q1, Q2.* 104. fault] *Q2;* faults *Q1.* 110. Aside] *Turner; not in Q1, Q2.*

---

94. *thus*] on the basis of this test. Dyce's 'this' (i.e., this accusation of yours) is not closely enough related to the context. But it is possible that the original read 'I cannot trust to't [i.e., to your accusation] thus. I have [elided to 'I've'] thrown out words.' J. R. Mulryne (privately) conjectures that 'thus' may be a misreading of 'thee', pointing out that at l. 98 Calianax says that he is 'accused' (i.e., of falsehood).
99. *alteration*] distemper, discomfort (*OED*, 3).
108. *touch*] hurt (*OED*, 12.b), i.e., punish.
109. *telling it*] mentioning it (i.e., to you).

Rudely to thrust into an ignorant fault.
But let me know it; happily 'tis nought
But misconstruction, and where I am clear
I will not take forgiveness of the gods,   115
Much less of you.

King.   Nay, if you stand so stiff,
I shall call back my mercy.

Melantius.   I want smoothness
To thank a man for pardoning of a crime
I never knew.

King. Not to instruct your knowledge, but to show you 120
My ears are everywhere, you meant to kill me
And get the fort to scape.

Melantius.   Pardon me, sir,
(My bluntness will be pardoned) you preserve
A race of idle people here about you,
Eaters and talkers, to defame the worth   125
Of those that do things worthy. The man that uttered this
Had perished without food, be't who it will,

---

112. thrust into an] *Theobald;* thrust into *Q1, Q2;* thrust me into *conj.*
Brereton.   116–17. Nay ... mercy] *so Theobald; as one line, Q1, Q2.*
120–2. Not ... scape] *so Langbaine; as prose, Q1, Q2.*   122–3. Pardon ...
preserve] *so Weber; as one line, Q1, Q2.*   125. Eaters] *Q2;* Facers *Q1.*
worth] *Q2;* world *Q1.*

---

112. *an*] Some emendation is necessary, and Theobald's is acceptable,
though Brereton's is just as good.

ignorant fault] Cf. *Oth.,* IV.ii.71: 'ignorant sin'.

113. *happily*] haply, perhaps.

114. *misconstruction*] misunderstanding (of yours).

clear] innocent.

115. *I ... gods*] I do not concede that even the gods have a right to 'forgive'
me.

116. *stand so stiff*] persist in being so obstinate (*OED,* stiff, 8.b).

117. *want*] lack.

123. *will*] demands to.

125. *Eaters*] 'idle servants or hangers-on' (Turner, comparing Jonson,
Epicoene, III.v.34); not recorded in this sense in *OED.* Q1's 'Facers' (i.e.,
braggarts) is an easy misreading.

126. an unusually irregular line. I conjecture that its original form was 'Of
those that do. The man that uttered this' ('do' being in emphatic contrast with
'eat' and 'talk'), and that Beaumont added 'things worthy' for the sake of
clarity; cf. similar additions at I.i.14 and III.ii.270.

127. *without food*] through starvation (i.e., in a blockade). Melantius insists
at ll. 165–6 that all the inhabitants of Rhodes have 'fed' through his valour; cf.
'this arm', l. 128.

But for this arm that fenced him from the foe.
And if I thought you gave a faith to this,
The plainness of my nature would speak more.   130
Give me a pardon (for you ought to do't)
To kill him that spake this.
Calianax. [Aside]   Ay, that will be
The end of all, then I am fairly paid
For all my care and service.
Melantius.   That old man,
Who calls me enemy, and of whom I   135
(Though I will never match my hate so low)
Have no good thought, would yet, I think, excuse me,
And swear he thought me wronged in this.
Calianax.   Who, I?
Thou shameless fellow, didst thou not speak to me
Of it thyself?
Melantius.   O, then it came from him?   140
Calianax. From me! Who should it come from but from me?
Melantius. Nay, I believe your malice is enough.
But I ha' lost my anger. [To King] Sir, I hope
You are well satisfied.
King. [To those at the table] Lysippus, cheer
Amintor and his lady: there's no sound   145
Comes from you. I will come and do't myself.
Amintor. You have done already, sir, for me, I thank you.
King. [To Melantius] Melantius, I do credit this from him,
How slight soe'er you make't.
Melantius.   'Tis strange you should.
Calianax. 'Tis strange 'a should believe an old man's word   150
That never lied in's life!

---

132. Aside] Daniel; not in Q1, Q2.   132-4. Ay ... service] so Theobald;
I ... all, / Then ... seruice Q1, Q2.   134-5. That ... I] so Theobald;
as one line, Q1, Q2.   138-40. Who ... thyself?] so Theobald; Who I,
thou shamelesse Fellow that hast spoke to me / Of it thy selfe. Q1; Who I,
thou shamelesse Fellow, didst thou not speake to me of it thy selfe? Q2.
144-5. Lysippus ... sound] so Theobald; as one line, Q1, Q2.

---

133. fairly] handsomely (ironical).
136. match ... low] set my hatred against so insignificant an opponent.
147.] Amintor's reply courteously asserts that the King has been a good
host, though it also carries an ironical allusion to what the King has done for
his benefit (i.e., in marrying him to Evadne).

Melantius.   I talk not to thee.
    [*To King*] Shall the wild words of this distempered man,
    Frantic with age and sorrow, make a breach
    Betwixt your majesty and me? 'Twas wrong
    To harken to him; but to credit him,   155
    As much, at least, as I have power to bear.
    But, pardon me (whilst I speak only truth,
    I may commend myself), I have bestowed
    My careless blood with you, and should be loth
    To think an action that would make me lose   160
    That and my thanks too. When I was a boy
    I thrust myself into my country's cause
    And did a deed that plucked five years from time
    And styled me man then, and for you my King
    [I still have laboured]; your subjects all have fed   165
    By virtue of my arm: this sword of mine
    Hath ploughed the ground and reaped the fruit in peace,
    And you yourself have lived at home in ease.
    So terrible I grew that without swords
    My name hath fetched you conquest; and my heart   170
    And limbs are still the same, my will as great
    To do you service. Let me not be paid
    With such a strange distrust.
King.   Melantius,

164–7. and for ... peace,] *This ed.;* and for you my king / Your Subiects all
haue fed by vertue of my arme, *Q1;* and for you my King / Your Subiects all
haue fed by vertue of my arme, / This sword of mine hath plowd the ground, /
And reapt the fruit in peace; / *Q2.*   173–4. Melantius ... believe] *so*
Theobald; as one line, Q1, Q2.

---

    156. *As much ... as*] is as much as, if not more than.
    158–9. *bestowed ... you*] spent my uncared-for blood in your service (*OED*,
bestow, 5.b; careless, 4.a).
    160. *To think*] even to think; cf. l. 328.
    161. *That*] my blood.
    165.] Something is omitted here in Q1. I conjecturally supply 'I still have
laboured' ('still' accounting for the Q1 compositor's eye-skip from 'styled'
('stil'd') in l. 164, and 'laboured' preparing for the ploughing-and-reaping
metaphor). In Qq's text 'and for you my King', if it means anything, has to
mean 'and, as for you, my King', which is quite superfluous to the next phrase.
Q2 restored 'this sword ... in peace' (also omitted from Q1, for whatever
reason, but evidently always a part of the speech because it maintains the
metre), but failed to restore the omission at l. 165.
    169–70. *without ... conquest*] Cf. *1H6*, I.ii.79–81.
    173. *strange*] unnatural.

  I held it great injustice to believe
  Thine enemy, and did not; if I did,   175
  I do not: let that satisfy. [*To those at the table*] What, struck
  With sadness all? More wine!   [*Goes to them.*]
Calianax. [*To Melantius*]   A few fine words
  Have overthrown my truth. Ah, th'art a villain!
Melantius. (*Aside* [*to him*]) Why, thou wert better let me have
   the fort;
  Dotard, I will disgrace thee thus for ever: 180
  There shall no credit lie upon thy words.
  Think better and deliver it.
Calianax. [*To King*]   My liege,
  He's at me now again to do it. [*To Melantius*] Speak;
  Deny it if thou canst. [*To King*] Examine him
  Whilst he is hot, for if he cool again   185
  He will forswear it.
King.   This is lunacy,
  I hope, Melantius.
Melantius.   He hath lost himself
  Much, since his daughter missed the happiness
  My sister gained, and though he call me foe
  I pity him.
Calianax. Ha, pity? A pox upon you!   190
Melantius. Mark his disordered words; and at the masque
  Diagoras knows he raged and railed at me,
  And called a lady 'whore' so innocent
  She understood him not. But it becomes
  Both you and me to forgive distraction.   195

175. and did not] *Q2*; and did *Q1*. 177. *Goes to them.*] *This ed.; not in Q1,
Q2.* 177–8. A few ... villain] *so Theobald; as prose, Q1;* A few ... truth, /
A ... Villaine *Q2.* 178. Ah] *Q1* (a), *Q2* (A). 179. *Aside [to him]*] *Q2*
(aside); *not in Q1.* 182–3. My ... speak] *so Theobald; as one line, Q1, Q2.*
190. Ha, pity?] *Q1, Q2* (A pittie); Pity! *Q3;* 'A pity! *Norland.* 195. and me
to] *Q1, Q2;* and me too, to *Q3;* and me, sir, to *conj. this ed.*

---

  187. *hope*] believe; cf. III.ii.249 and l. 228 below.
  187–8. *lost ... Much*] become much distracted.
  190. *Ha, pity?*] I take the 'A' of Qq's 'A pittie' to resemble that in l. 178 ('a
th'art a Villaine') and modernise both spellings according to context.
  192. *Diagoras knows*] i.e., Diagoras is my witness. This does not imply his
presence now (cf. l. 42.2 n.)—rather his absence.
  195.] Something is omitted, unless (as is improbable) we are to elide 'to
forgive' and make four syllables of 'distraction'. Q3's emendation has value as
showing how a contemporary heard the rhythm, but it is weak ('too' being

    Pardon him as I do.
Calianax.   I'll not speak for thee,
    For all thy cunning. [*To King*] If you will be safe,
    Chop off his head, for there was never known
    So impudent a rascal.
King. [*Pointing to Calianax*] Some that love him
    Get him to bed. Why, pity should not let   200
    Age make itself contemptible; we must be
    All old. Have him away.
Melantius.   Calianax,
    The King believes you. Come, you shall go home
    And rest; you ha' done well. [*Aside to him*] You'll give it up
    When I have used you thus a month, I hope.   205
Calianax. [*To King*] Now, now 'tis plain, sir; he does move me
      still:
    He says he knows I'll give him up the fort
    When he has used me thus a month. I am mad,
    Am I not, still?
All [*those at the table*]. Ha, ha, ha!   210
Calianax. I shall be mad indeed if you do thus.
    Why should you trust a sturdy fellow there,
    That has no virtue in him, all's in his sword,
    Before me? Do but take his weapons from him
    And he's an ass; and I am a very fool   215
    Both with 'em and without 'em, as you use me.
All [*those at the table*]. Ha, ha, ha!
King. 'Tis well, Calianax, but if you use
    This once again I shall entreat some other
    To see your offices be well discharged.   220

196–204. I'll ... it up] *so Theobald; as prose, Q1, Q2.*   204. *Aside to him*]
Weber (subst.); not in Q1, Q2.   210, 217. *All those at the table*] *Q1, Q2 (subst.:*
Omnes.).   216. with 'em, and without 'em] *Dyce;* with him, and without him
Q1, Q2.   218. 'Tis] *Q2;* Too *Q1.*

---

tautologous after 'both'). I conjecture that the original had 'Both you and me,
sir, to forgive distraction.' Melantius has addressed the King as 'sir' at ll. 59,
85, 122 and 143.

    203. *The ... you*] Melantius pretends to humour Calianax's madness (in a
manner calculated to infuriate him).

    204. *it*] the fort.

    206. *move*] solicit.

    218–19. *use / This*] behave in this way.

[*To those at the table*] Be merry, gentlemen. It grows
  somewhat late;
Amintor, thou wouldst be abed again.
Amintor. Yes, sir.
King.   And you, Evadne. Let me take
  Thee in my arms, Melantius; and believe,
  Thou art, as thou deserv'st to be, my friend   225
  Still and for ever. Good Calianax,
  Sleep soundly, it will bring thee to thyself.
           Exeunt [all except] Melantius and Calianax.
Calianax. Sleep soundly! I sleep soundly now, I hope;
  I could not be thus else. How dar'st thou stay
  Alone with me, knowing how thou hast used me?   230
Melantius. You cannot blast me with your tongue,
  And that's the strongest part you have about ye.
Calianax. I do look for some great punishment for this,
  For I begin to forget all my hate,
  And take't unkindly that mine enemy   235
  Should use me so extraordinarily scurvily.
Melantius. I shall melt too if you begin to take

223–5. And ... friend] *so Theobald; as prose, Q1, Q2.* 224. arms] *Q2;* arme
Q1. and believe] *Q2; not in Q1.* 227.1.] *Q1, Q2 (subst.: Exeunt omnes.
Manent Mel. & Cal.).* 231–2.] *so Langbaine;* You ...strongest / Part ... ye
Q1; You ... tongue, / And ... you *Q2.* 232. about ye] *Q1;* about you *Q2.*
233–4. I do ... hate] *Q2;* Dost not thou looke for some great punishment for
this? I feele / My selfe beginne to forget all my hate *Q1.* 236. extra-
ordinarily] *Q2;* extremely *Q1.* 237. melt] *Q2;* meet *Q1.*

227. *to thyself*] to thy right mind.
228. *I sleep ... now*] i.e., I am dreaming.
229. *thus*] in this situation.
231–2.] Cf. Sidney, *Arcadia,* bk. I, chap. 4, p. 27: 'nature loves to exercise
that part [of old men] most, which is least decayed, and that is our tongue.'
231. *blast*] strike, as with lightning (*OED,* 7).
233. *I ... this*] Q2 restores the reading which Q1's compositor evidently
found incomprehensible and therefore altered. Calianax means that because he
begins to soften towards the traitor Melantius he expects heaven to punish
him.
235. *unkindly*] with dissatisfaction or resentment (*OED,* adv., 4). Calianax
probably weeps; cf. l. 237, 'I shall melt too'.
236. *extraordinarily*] This must be an authorial revision (Q2 would hardly
substitute it otherwise), but it is metrically inferior to Q1's 'extremely'.
Possibly the irregularity is intended to promote a semi-comic effect connected
with Calianax's tendency, from this point onwards, to cry; cf. l. 248, V.iii.275.
237. *melt*] soften (into tears).

Unkindnesses: I never meant you hurt.
Calianax. Thou'lt anger me again. Thou wretched rogue,
  Meant me no hurt! Disgrace me with the King,   240
  Lose all my offices, this is no hurt,
  Is it? I prithee, what dost thou call hurt?
Melantius. To poison men because they love me not;
  To call the credit of men's wives in question;
  To murder children betwixt me and land: 245
  This I call hurt.
Calianax.   All this thou thinkst is sport,
  For mine is worse; but use thy will with me,
  For betwixt grief and anger I could cry.
Melantius. Be wise then and be safe. Thou mayst revenge.
Calianax. Ay, o' the King: I would revenge of thee.   250
Melantius. That you must plot yourself.
Calianax.   I am a fine plotter!
Melantius. The short is, I will hold thee with the King
  In this perplexity till peevishness
  And thy disgrace have laid thee in thy grave;
  But if thou wilt deliver up the fort,   255
  I'll take thy trembling body in my arms
  And bear thee over dangers. Thou shalt hold
  Thy wonted state.
Calianax.   If I should tell the King,
  Canst thou deny't again?
Melantius.   Try, and believe.
Calianax. Nay, then thou canst bring anything about.   260

---

238. Unkindnesses] *Q2*; Vnkindnesse *Q1*.   240. hurt] *Q2*; wrong *Q1*.
250. o' the] *Q1*, *Q2* (subst.: oth'the).   254. And thy] *Q2*; And his *Q1*.
258-9. If ... again?] *so Theobald; as one line, Q1, Q2*.

237-8. *take / Unkindnesses*] take my actions to heart as unkind ones (*OED*, unkindness, 3.b).
  243-5.] Melantius' instances are typical and do not relate to anything in the play; l. 244 recalls the behaviour of Iago, and l. 245 that of Richard III.
  245. *betwixt me and land*] who stand between me and the inheritance of some land.
  247. *mine*] the injury that you do me.
  251. *I am ... plotter!*] ironical: 'I am not, as you are, a plotter.'
  253. *perplexity*] distress (*OED*, 1.b).
  258. *state*] exalted position.

Melantius, thou shalt have the fort.
Melantius.   Why, well.
Here let our hate be buried, and this hand
Shall right us both. Give me thy agèd breast
To compass.   [*Offers to embrace him.*]
Calianax.   Nay, I do not love thee yet.
I cannot well endure to look on thee,   265
And if I thought it were a courtesy
Thou shouldst not have it. But I am disgraced;
My offices are to be ta'en away,
And if I did but hold this fort a day,
I do believe the King would take it from me   270
And give it thee, things are so strangely carried.
Ne'er thank me for't, but yet the King shall know
There was some such thing in't I told him of,
And that I was an honest man.
Melantius.   He'll buy
That knowledge very dearly.

Enter DIPHILUS.

                              Diphilus,   275
What news with thee?
Diphilus.   This were a night indeed
To do it in: the King hath sent for her.
Melantius. She shall perform it then. Go, Diphilus,
And take from this good man, my worthy friend,
The fort; he'll give it thee.
Diphilus.   Ha' you got that?   280
Calianax. Art thou of the same breed? Canst thou deny
This to the King too?

---

261. Melantius, thou] *Q1*; Thou *Q2*.   261–3. Why ... breast] *so Theobald;*
Why ... and / This ... brest *Q1, Q2*.   264.] *This ed.; not in Q1, Q2.*
274. He'll ... Diphilus] *so Theobald; as one line, Q1, Q2.*

---

271. *carried*] handled.
275.1.] The movements of the three characters, though not precise enough
to be formulated as stage directions, must be as follows. At the end of his
speech (l. 274) Calianax turns away from Melantius, whose comment is
therefore not a true aside. Diphilus enters by one of the doors and comes
down-stage to Melantius, who takes him across to Calianax at l. 278 (where
'Go' means 'Go to the fort with Calianax').

Diphilus.   With a confidence
  As great as his.
Calianax.   'Faith, like enough.
Melantius. Away, and use him kindly.
                    [*Diphilus offers to embrace Calianax.*]
Calianax. [*To Diphilus*]   Touch not me:
  I hate the whole strain. If thou follow me   285
  A great way off, I'll give thee up the fort,
  And hang yourselves.
Melantius. [*To Diphilus*] Be gone.
Diphilus.   He's finely wrought.
                    Exeunt CALIANAX [*and*] DIPHILUS.
Melantius. This is a night, spite of astronomers,
  To do the deed in. I will wash the stain
  That rests upon our house off with his blood.   290

              Enter AMINTOR [*with his sword drawn*].

Amintor. Melantius, now assist me; if thou be'st
  That which thou sayst, assist me. I have lost
  All my distempers, and have found a rage
  So pleasing: help me!
Melantius. [*Aside*]   Who can see him thus,
  And not swear vengeance? [*To him*] What's the matter,
      friend?   295
Amintor. Out with thy sword, and hand in hand with me
  Rush to the chamber of this hated King,
  And sink him with the weight of all his sins
  To hell for ever.
Melantius.   'Twere a rash attempt,

282-3. With . . . his] *so Theobald; as one line, Q1, Q2.*   284.1.] *This ed.; not in Q1, Q2.*   284-7. Touch . . . yourselves] *so Weber; as prose, Q1, Q2.* 290.1. *with his sword drawn*] *This ed.; not in Q1, Q2; Draws his sword. Dyce (after l. 308).*   294. Aside] *Dyce; not in Q1, Q2.*

---

282. *confidence*] boldness (*OED*, 3).
283. *his*] Melantius'.
287. *He's finely wrought*] He has been worked round finely.
288. *spite of astronomers*] despite astrologers; i.e., even if astrologers had declared it inauspicious. 'When astrologer and astronomer began to be differentiated, the relation between them was, at first, the converse of the present usage' (*OED*, astrologer, 1).
290. *his*] the King's.

Not to be done with safety. Let your reason   300
　　Plot your revenge, and not your passion.
Amintor. If thou refusest me in these extremes,
　　Thou art no friend. He sent for her to me,
　　By heaven, to me, myself! And I must tell ye
　　I love her as a stranger, there is worth   305
　　In that vile woman, worthy things, Melantius,
　　And she repents. I'll do't myself alone,
　　Though I be slain. Farewell!
Melantius. [*Aside*]   He'll overthrow
　　My whole design with madness. [*To him*] Amintor,
　　Think what thou dost. I dare as much as valour,   310
　　But 'tis the King, the King, the King, Amintor,
　　With whom thou fightest. (*Aside*) I know he's honest,
　　And this will work with him.
Amintor. [*Letting fall his sword*] I cannot tell
　　What thou hast said, but thou hast charmed my sword
　　Out of my hand, and left me shaking here   315
　　Defenceless.
Melantius.   I will take it up for thee.
　　　　[*Takes up the sword, and gives it to Amintor.*]
Amintor. What a wild beast is uncollected man!
　　The thing that we call honour bears us all
　　Headlong unto sin, and yet itself is nothing.

---

306. vile] *Q1, Q2* (vild).   308. Aside] *Dyce; not in Q1, Q2*.   308–9. He'll
... Amintor] *so Theobald; as one line, Q1, Q2*.   313. *Letting fall his sword*]
Dyce; not in Q1, Q2.   316.1. *Takes up the sword, and gives it to Amintor.*]
Dyce; not in Q1, Q2.

---

301. *passion*] (three syllables).
302. *extremes*] extremities, straits (*OED*, 4.b).
305. *as a stranger*] Cf. IV.i.269–70.
309. *Amintor*] In the pause before uttering his name, Melantius intercepts
Amintor, who is in the act of leaving.
310. *valour*] valour personified.
312. *honest*] loyal; cf. III.i.262.
314. *What ... said*] i.e., what magic words you have used.
316. *I ... thee*] What meaning this has beyond the literal is ambiguous.
Melantius may mean that he will take it up in Amintor's defence (cf. 'defenceless') or that he will do so in Amintor's revenge.
317. *uncollected*] distracted, without control over his thoughts and feelings
(*OED*, collect, v., 3).
319. *nothing.*] i.e., a mere word.

Melantius. Alas, how variable are thy thoughts!   320
Amintor. Just like my fortunes. I was run to that
   I purposed to have chid thee for. Some plot
   I did distrust thou hadst against the King
   By that old fellow's carriage. But take heed:
   There's not the least limb growing to a king   325
   But carries thunder in't.
Melantius.   I have none
   Against him.
Amintor.   Why, come then, and still remember
   We may not think revenge.
Melantius.   I will remember.   *Exeunt.*

322–3. I purposed ... King] *Q1;* I purpos'd ... for. / Some ... King *Q2.*
322. for. Some] *Q2* (for. / Some); for some *Q1.*   326–8. I ... revenge] *so
Theobald; as prose, Q1, Q2.*

---

   321. *was run*] had run.
   323. *distrust*] suspect (*OED,* 1).
   324. *that old fellow's*] Calianax's.
   326. *none*] no plot; cf. l. 322.
   328. *We ... revenge*] We must not even contemplate revenge (much less
execute it).

Act V

ACT V [SCENE i]

Enter EVADNE *and a* Gentleman.

Evadne. Sir, is the King abed?
Gentleman.   Madam, an hour ago.
Evadne. Give me the key then, and let none be near;
    'Tis the King's pleasure.
Gentleman. I understand you, madam: would 'twere mine!
    I must not wish good rest unto your ladyship.   5
Evadne. You talk, you talk.
Gentleman. 'Tis all I dare do, madam, but the King
    Will wake, and then—
Evadne. Saving your imagination, pray, good night, sir.
Gentleman. A good night be it, then, and a long one, madam.   10
    I am gone.   *Exit.*
Evadne. The night grows horrible, and all about me
    Like my black purpose. O, the conscience
    Of a lost virgin, whither wilt thou pull me?
    To what things dismal as the depth of hell   15
    Wilt thou provoke me? Let no woman dare
    From this hour be disloyal, if her heart
    Be flesh, if she have blood and can fear. 'Tis a daring

ACT V] *Q1, Q2 (Actus 5.)*.   2. and let] *Q2;* and Sir let *Q1*.   7-8. 'Tis
... then—] *so Theobald; as prose, Q1, Q2*.   8. then—] *Q2* (then.)*; then
me thinkes. Q1*.   10-11. A ... gone] *so Theobald; as prose, Q1, Q2*.
11. *Exit.*] *Q1, Q2; Exeunt severally. Weber*.   12.] *so Q1, Q2;* SCENE ii
Weber.   14. virgin] *Q2;* virtue *Q1*.   18. daring] *Q2;* madnesse *Q1*.

---

2. *Give ... key*] This dramatically establishes the privacy of the King's
chamber, and does not imply any later business with the stage doors; cf. l.
24.1 n.

11. *Exit.*] Weber, substituting *Exeunt severally*, begins a new scene after
this, but the action is continuous and Evadne does not leave the stage.

14. *lost*] ruined.

17-18.] The lineation of Qq is followed, 'disloyal' in l. 17 being three
syllables and the stresses in l. 18 falling on 'flesh', 'she', 'blood', 'fear' and the
first syllable of 'daring'.

Above that desperate fool's that left his peace
And went to sea to fight; 'tis so many sins   20
An age cannot repent 'em, and so great
The gods want mercy for, yet I must through 'em:
I have begun a slaughter on my honour,
And I must end it there.   [*Discovers*] *King abed.*
                              'A sleeps: O God,
Why give you peace to this untemperate beast   25
That hath so long transgressed you? I must kill him,
And I will do't bravely: the mere joy
Tells me I merit in it. Yet I must not
Thus tamely do it as he sleeps: that were
To rock him to another world; my vengeance   30
Shall take him waking, and then lay before him

---

19. fool's] *Q2* (fooles); mans *Q1*.   21. repent 'em] *Q1*; preuent 'm *Q2*.
24. King abed.] *Q1* (K. a bed.), *Q2* (King a bed.), *opposite l. 13*.   O God] *Q1*;
good heauens *Q2*.   26. hath so long] *Q2*; has so farre *Q1*.   28. Tells . . . in
it] *Q2*; Confirmes me that I merit *Q1*.   30. rock] *Q2*; rake *Q1*.   31. take]
Q2; seaze *Q1*.

19-20. *that . . . fight*] not a particular allusion but a general one in keeping
with recent events, e.g., Essex's expedition against Cadiz in 1596 and to the
Azores in 1597; Donne's poems 'The Storm', 'The Calm', and Satire III (ll.
17-19) record the dangers and hardships of those who served on such
expeditions.
  22. *for*] for them.
  24. *there*] in the King's bedroom, which she is approaching.
  S.D.] The direction *K. a bed.* (Q1; *King a bed.* Q2) is placed opposite l. 13.
This may mean either (1) that the King, in his curtained bed, is to be pushed
on to the stage through one of the doors, or (2) that the King, in his bed, is to
be ready to be 'discovered' by Evadne in a 'discovery space' under the acting
area 'above'. I think the first interpretation is right. Evadne's tying of the
King's arms to the bed ensures that he does not leave it. It ought therefore to
be placed near the spectators so that they can see and hear clearly. At l. 24
Evadne opens the curtains of the bed. At the end of the scene the bed can be
pushed off while attention is drawn to Melantius and others appearing 'above'
to begin V.ii. For a review of stage directions about beds 'thrust out' and
'drawn in' see Chambers, *E.S.*, III, 112-14.
  25. *untemperate*] intemperate.
  27. *mere*] absolute.
  28. *I merit*] I acquire merit, become entitled to reward, gratitude or
commendation (*OED*, 5). Evadne may mean this simply in the ethical sense,
or she may mean it in the religious sense, i.e., become worthy of salvation.
  31. *take*] In support of Q1's reading, 'seize', Gurr suggests that Q2's
compositor set 'take' in error because he had corrected Q1's 'rake' to 'rock'

The number of his wrongs and punishments.
I'll shape his sins like furies till I waken
His evil angel, his sick conscience,
And then I'll strike him dead. King, by your leave,   35
                    Ties his arms to the bed.
I dare not trust your strength; your grace and I
Must grapple upon even terms no more.
So; if he rail me not from my resolution
I shall be strong enough.
My lord the King; my lord! [*Aside*] 'A sleeps   40
As if he meant to wake no more. [*Aloud*] My lord!
[*Aside*] Is he not dead already? [*Aloud*] Sir! My lord!
King. Who's that?
Evadne. O, you sleep soundly, sir.
King.   My dear Evadne!
I have been dreaming of thee; come to bed.   45
Evadne. I am come at length, sir, but how welcome?
King. What pretty new device is this, Evadne?
What, do you tie me to you? By my love,
This is a quaint one. Come, my dear, and kiss me.
I'll be thy Mars; to bed, my Queen of Love,   50

---

35. I'll] *Q2* (Ile); *I Q1.*   strike] *Q1*; strick *Q2.*   36. your grace] *Q1* (your Grace); you Grace *Q2.*   39. I ... enough.] *Q2*; As I beleeue I shall not, I shall fit him. *Q1.*   46. I am] *Q1*, *Q2*; Ay, I am *conj. this ed.*   48. to you? By my love,] *Q2* (to you, by my loue,); to you by my loue? *Q1.*

---

immediately above this word. But Q2's reading may be an authorial revision in order to concentrate attention not on the verb but on the participial adjective 'waking'.
      waking] awake.
    33. *furies*] avenging infernal spirits (*OED*, 5).
    34. *evil angel*] The King's 'sick conscience' is called his evil angel because it will present to his mind the 'punishments' (l. 32) due to his soul in hell, as the Evil Angel does to Faustus's sight in Marlowe, *Doctor Faustus*, xix.116–32.
      conscience] (three syllables).
    37. *grapple*] wrestle (alluding to their sexual grappling in the past).
    46.] The incomplete metre may indicate a long pause before 'but how welcome?', but possibly the original read 'I [i.e., Ay; cf. ll. 60, 96 in Qq], I am come', and the first 'I' was overlooked by the compositor.
    50–2.] Alluding to Vulcan's capture of his wife Venus (the 'Queen of Love') and her lover Mars in a net to expose them to the gods' derision (and not, as here, to their envy). 'The King acknowledges the adulterous aspect of the parallelism' (Gurr).

Let us be caught together, that the gods may see
And envy our embraces.

Evadne.   Stay, sir, stay:
You are too hot, and I have brought you physic
To temper your high veins.

King. Prithee, to bed then; let me take it warm;   55
Here thou shalt know the state of my body better.

Evadne. I know you have a surfeited foul body,
And you must bleed.

King. Bleed!

Evadne. Ay, you shall bleed. Lie still, and if the devil   60
Your lust will give you leave, repent. [*Draws a knife.*] This
          steel
Comes to redeem the honour that you stole,
King, my fair name, which nothing but thy death
Can answer to the world.

King.   How's this, Evadne?

Evadne. I am not she, nor bear I in this breast   65
So much cold spirit to be called a woman:
I am a tiger; I am any thing

51. see] *Q2;* looke *Q1.*   56. Here] *Q1;* There *Q2.*   61. *Draws a knife.*]
Dyce (at l. 58); not in Q1, Q2.   64. How's this] *Q2;* How *Q1.*

---

53. *hot*] (1) eager, (2) heated in your blood (as with a fever).

54. *temper*] cure (*OED*, 5).

high] violent (*OED*, 10). With ll. 53–4 cf. Jonson, *Volpone*, III.vii.157–8: 'I
am now as fresh, / As hot, as high, and in as jovial plight ...' (Volpone
soliciting Celia).

55.] The King interprets 'physic' (medicine, which could be taken either
cold or warm) as a metaphor for Evadne's body.

56. *know ... better*] applicable to Evadne (1) as a physician, (2) as a mistress.

57–8. *I know ... must bleed*] Cf. *2H4*, IV.i.54–7, where the Archbishop
of York, justifying his rebellion, speaks metaphorically of the state of the
nation: 'we are all diseas'd, / And with our surfeiting and wanton hours /
Have brought ourselves into a burning fever, / And we must bleed for it.'

58. *bleed*] (1) be let blood, (2) be stabbed to death.

61. *knife*] Cf. V.iii.105.1, 124. Evadne's knife may be a dagger (cf. *Mac.*,
I.v.16, 76; II.i.33–47) or an all-purpose knife such as Hieronimo kills himself
with in Kyd, *The Spanish Tragedy*, IV.iv.199: 'Oh, he would have a knife to
mend his pen.'

63. *King*] For this aggressive use of the vocative, cf. *Philaster*, I.i.269, and
also *R2*, I.iii.226; *Lr.*, I.i.159.

66. *cold spirit*] timidity.

67. *tiger*] a type of ferocity and pitilessness; cf. *3H6*, I.iv.137: 'O tiger's
heart wrapp'd in a woman's hide!'

That knows not pity. Stir not; if thou dost,
I'll take thee unprepared, thy fears upon thee,
That make thy sins look double, and so send thee   70
(By my revenge, I will) to look those torments
Prepared for such black souls.
King. Thou dost not mean this, 'tis impossible;
Thou art too sweet and gentle.
Evadne.   No, I am not,
I am as foul as thou art, and can number   75
As many such hells here. I was once fair,
Once I was lovely, not a blowing rose
More chastely sweet, till thou, thou, thou foul canker,
(Stir not!) didst poison me. I was a world of virtue
Till your curs'd court and you (hell bless you for't),   80
With your temptations on temptations,
Made me give up mine honour; for which, King,
I am come to kill thee.
King.   No!
Evadne.   I am.
King.   Thou art not!
I prithee, speak not these things; thou art gentle,
And wert not meant thus rugged.
Evadne.   Peace, and hear me.   85
Stir nothing but your tongue, and that for mercy
To those above us, by whose lights I vow,
Those blessèd fires that shot to see our sin,
If thy hot soul had substance with thy blood
I would kill that too, which being past my steel,   90
My tongue shall reach. Thou art a shameless villain,
A thing out of the overcharge of nature,

---

71. *look*] seek (*OED*, 6.d).
76. *here*] i.e., in my heart (with the appropriate gesture).
77. *blowing*] blooming, in bloom (*OED*, ppl.a.²).
78. *canker*] canker-worm; cf. IV.i.85 n.
81. *temptations*] (three syllables the first time, four the seond).
85. *rugged*] ungentle, harsh (*OED*, 6).
87. *those*] the gods.
lights] i.e., the stars.
89. *had substance with*] were consubstantial with, were as material as.
90. *past*] out of reach of.
92. *A thing ... nature*] a monster produced by nature's being over-
loaded (*OED*, overcharge, sb., 1).

      Sent like a thick cloud to disperse a plague
      Upon weak catching women; such a tyrant
      That for his lust would sell away his subjects,   95
      Ay, all his heaven hereafter.
King.   Hear, Evadne,
      Thou soul of sweetness, hear! I am thy King.
Evadne. Thou art my shame. Lie still; there's none about you
      Within your cries; all promises of safety
      Are but deluding dreams. Thus, thus, thou foul man,   100
      Thus I begin my vengeance.   *Stabs him.*
King.   Hold, Evadne!
      I do command thee, hold!
Evadne.   I do not mean, sir,
      To part so fairly with you; we must change
      More of these love-tricks yet.
King.   What bloody villain
      Provoked thee to this murder?
Evadne.   Thou, thou monster!   *Stabs him.* 105
King. O!
Evadne. Thou keptst me brave at court, and whored me, King,
      Then married me to a young noble gentleman,
      And whored me still.
King.   Evadne, pity me!
Evadne. Hell take me then! [*Stabbing him*] This for my lord
      Amintor,   110
      This for my noble brother, and this stroke

---

101. *Stabs him.*] *Q2; not in Q1.*   104. villain] *Q1 (subst.:* villanie [*sic*]), *Q2*
(villaine).   105. *Stabs him.*] *Q1; not in Q2.*   110. *Stabbing him*] *Dyce*
(*subst.*); *not in Q1, Q2.*

---

93. *disperse*] spread abroad (*OED*, 6).
97. *soul of*] personification of (*OED*, 4.b).
99. *Within*] within hearing of.
   promises] self-assurances (*OED*, 4.b).
103. *fairly*] gently (*OED*, 5).
   change] exchange.
104. *love-tricks*] not in *OED*; cf. Donne, 'Epithalamion made at Lincoln's
Inn', l. 53, where the bride is promised 'Other love trickes than glancing with
the eyes'.
106. *brave*] showily dressed.
110-12. *This ... women*] Cf. Marston, *Antonio's Revenge*, V.v.77-9:
'*Antonio.* This for my father's blood! / *Pandulpho.* This for my son! *Alberto.*
This for them all! / And this, and this; sink to the heart of hell!'

For the most wronged of women!   *Kills him.*
King.   O, I die!
Evadne. Die all our faults together! I forgive thee.   *Exit.*

    Enter two [Gentlemen] *of the Bed-chamber.*

1 Gentleman. Come, now she's gone, let's enter; the King
    expects it, and will be angry.   115
2 Gentleman. 'Tis a fine wench; we'll have a snap at her one of
    these nights as she goes from him.
1 Gentleman. Content. How quickly he had done with her! I see
    kings can do no more that way than other mortal people.
2 Gentleman. How fast he is! I cannot hear him breathe.   120
1 Gentleman. Either the tapers give a feeble light
    Or he looks very pale.
2 Gentleman. And so he does; pray heaven he be well!
    Let's look. Alas! he's stiff, wounded and dead.
    Treason, treason!   125
1 Gentleman. Run forth and call.
                                      Exit [2] Gentleman.
2 Gentleman. [*Within*] Treason, treason!
1 Gentleman. This will be laid on us: who can believe
    A woman could do this?

        Enter CLEON *and* LYSIPPUS.

Cleon.   How now? Where's the traitor?
1 Gentleman. Fled, fled away, but there her woeful act   130
    Lies still.
Cleon.   Her act! A woman!
Lysippus.   Where's the body?

---

113. *Exit.*] F2; *Exeunt Q1, Q2.*   121–2. Either ... pale] *so Theobald; as
prose, Q1, Q2.*   123. And ... well!] *Q2; not in Q1.*   125. Treason,
treason!] *Q2;* Treason. *Q1.*   127. *Within*] *Turner; not in Q1, Q2.*

    115. *will be angry*] i.e., if we are late.
    116. *snap*] snatch (*OED*, 5).
    120. *fast*] sound asleep.
    128. *laid*] blamed.
    129.1.] Though Qq do not direct 2 Gentleman to re-enter, he should
perhaps do so. 'Sirs, which way went she?' (l. 138) can then most naturally be
addressed to both gentlemen; otherwise it has to be addressed to 1 Gentleman
and to the entering Strato.
    131. *Lies still*] still lies.

1 Gentleman. There.

Lysippus. Farewell, thou worthy man. There were two bonds
    That tied our loves, a brother and a king,
    The least of which might fetch a flood of tears;   135
    But such the misery of greatness is,
    They have no time to mourn; then pardon me.

Enter STRATO.

    Sirs, which way went she?
Strato.   Never follow her,
    For she, alas, was but the instrument.
    News is now brought in that Melantius   140
    Has got the fort, and stands upon the wall,
    And with a loud voice calls those few that pass
    At this dead time of night, delivering
    The innocence of this act.
Lysippus.   Gentlemen,
    I am your King.
Strato.   We do acknowledge it.   145
Lysippus. I would I were not. Follow all, for this
    Must have a sudden stop.   *Exeunt.*

[ACT V SCENE ii]

Enter MELANTIUS, DIPHILUS, [*and*] CALIANAX *on the walls.*

Melantius. If the dull people can believe, I am armed.
    Be constant, Diphilus; now we have time

136. greatness] *Q1, Q2* (greatnesse); great ones *conj. this ed.*   142. calls] *Q2;*
cals to *Q1.*   144–5. Gentlemen ... king] *so Weber; as one line, Q1, Q2.*
146–7. I would ... stop] *so Theobald; as prose, Q1, Q2.*   1. armed.] *Q2*
(arm'd.); arm'd, *Q1.*

---

136. *greatness*] If this Qq reading is correct, it is evidently synonymous with
'the great' since it is followed by a plural verb. But this usage is not recorded in
OED, so perhaps it is an error for 'great ones' (misread as 'greatnes'); cf. *Oth.*,
III.iii.277: 'Yet 'tis the plague of great ones.'

137. *then pardon me*] i.e., for ending my speech of mourning so soon.
Perhaps Lysippus closes the curtain of the King's bed after these words.

147. *Must ... stop*] The half-line ending suits the abrupt departure.

0.1. on the walls] In the upper playing area 'above' the stage. The phrase is
common in stage directions, many of which are quoted by Chambers, *E.S.*,
III, 53, 54–5.

  Either to bring our banished honours home
  Or to create new ones in our ends.
Diphilus.   I fear not;
  My spirit lies not that way. Courage, Calianax!   5
Calianax. Would I had any, you should quickly know it.
Melantius. Speak to the people; thou art eloquent.
Calianax. 'Tis a fine eloquence to come to the gallows.
  You were born to be my end, the devil take you!
  Now must I hang for company. 'Tis strange   10
  I should be old, and neither wise nor valiant.

Enter LYSIPPUS, DIAGORAS, CLEON, [*and*] STRATO, [*with a*] Guard.

Lysippus. See where he stands as boldly confident
  As if he had his full command about him.
Strato. He looks as if he had the better cause, sir.
  Under your gracious pardon let me speak it,   15
  Though he be mighty-spirited and forward
  To all great things, to all things of that danger
  Worse men shake at the telling of, yet certainly
  I do believe him noble, and this action
  Rather pulled on than sought: his mind was ever   20

---

14. sir.] *This ed.;* Sir, *Q1, Q2.* 15. speak it,] *Q1, Q2;* speak it. *Theobald.*
18. certainly] *Q2;* certaine *Q1.*

---

 1. *believe*] i.e., understand my reasons for my action. Gurr draws attention
to 'the appeal to the political power of the masses familiar in most of the
dramas of the collaboration', but points out that in *Philaster* 'the people' have
an active part to play, as they do not here.
 armed] fortified, in a strong position.
 2–3. *now . . . home*] Cf. *1H4,* I.iii.180–2: 'No; yet time serves wherein you
may redeem / Your banish'd honours, and restore yourselves / Into the good
thoughts of the world again.'
 4. *create . . . ends*] achieve new honours by the courage with which we can
die.
 5. *that way*] in the direction of fear.
 6. *Would . . . it*] Calianax probably means that he would kill them for getting
him into this trouble.
 11.1. *Guard*] a number of soldiers.
 13. *full command*] whole troop.
 14. *better*] not 'better than yours' but 'better than if he showed less
confidence'. Strato proceeds to beg pardon (cf. IV.ii.157) for inferring that the
King must have been guilty.
 20. *pulled on*] forced on him.

As worthy as his hand.
Lysippus.   'Tis my fear too.
Heaven forgive all! Summon him, lord Cleon.
Cleon. Ho, from the walls there!
Melantius.   Worthy Cleon, welcome.
We could ha' wished you here, lord; you are honest.
Calianax. (*Aside*) Well, thou art as flattering a knave, though I   25
dare not tell thee so.
Lysippus. Melantius!
Melantius. Sir?
Lysippus. I am sorry that we meet thus; our old love
Never required such distance. Pray to heaven   30
You have not left yourself and sought this safety
More out of fear than honour. You have lost
A noble master, which your faith, Melantius,
Some think might have preserved; yet you know best.
Calianax. [*Aside*] When time was, I was mad; some that dares
fight,   35
I hope, will pay this rascal.
Melantius. Royal young man, those tears look lovely on thee;
Had they been shed for a deserving one
They had been lasting monuments. Thy brother,
Whilst he was good, I called him King, and served him   40

30. distance. Pray to] *Q1* (distance, pray to); distance, pray *Q2*.   34. Some
think] *Q2*; I'm sure *Q1*.   34–6. yet … rascal] *Q2; not in Q1*.   35. *Aside*]
Dyce; not in Q1, Q2.   35–6. When … rascal] *so Theobald;* When … dares /
Fight … rascall *Q2; not in Q1*.

---

21. *'Tis … too*] i.e., that the King may have provoked his own murder.
25. *as … knave*] i.e., as flattering a knave as he (i.e., Cleon) is an honest
man.
30. *Pray to heaven*] not an imperative but equivalent to 'I pray to heaven' or
(more shortly) 'pray heaven' (as Q2 unmetrically reads, probably because of an
accidental omission rather than a deliberate alteration).
31. *left yourself*] deserted your nature.
32. *lost*] destroyed (*OED*, 2).
33. *which*] whom.
faith] loyalty.
35. *When … mad*] There was a time (*OED*, time, 49) when I was believed
mad.
dares] (plural).
36. *pay*] reward, i.e., punish (*OED*, 3.b).
39. *lasting monuments*] everlasting commemorations, i.e., of the
virtues of the dead man.

With that strong faith, that most unwearied valour,
Pulled people from the farthest sun to seek him
And buy his friendship. I was then his soldier.
But since his hot pride drew him to disgrace me,
And brand my noble actions with his lust   45
(That never-cured dishonour of my sister,
Base stain of whore, and, which is worse,
The joy to make it still so), like myself
Thus I have flung him off with my allegiance,
And stand here mine own justice, to revenge   50
What I have suffered in him, and this old man
Wronged almost to lunacy.
Calianax. Who, I? You would draw me in. I have had no
        wrong;
    I do disclaim ye all.
Melantius.   The short is this:
    'Tis no ambition to lift up myself   55
Urgeth me thus; I do desire again
To be a subject, so I may be free;
If not, I know my strength, and will unbuild
This goodly town; be speedy, and be wise,
In a reply.
Strato.   Be sudden, sir, to tie   60
    All up again. What's done is past recall,
    And past you to revenge; and there are thousands

43. buy] *Q2;* begge *Q1.*   47. whore] *Q1, Q2;* whore in her *Theobald.*
50. to revenge] *Q2;* for reuenge *Q1.*   59–60. This . . . reply] *so Theobald;*
as one line, Q1, Q2.

42. *Pulled*] that pulled.
from . . . sun] from the opposite side of the globe.
46–8.] The defective metre of l. 47 indicates corruption, and Theobald's
emendation does not remove all the difficulty: 'Base stain of whore', considered as in apposition to 'dishonour', makes awkward syntax. I conjecture
that 'sister,' (with comma) should be 'sister's' (without comma), giving the
sense 'That never-cured dishonour [of mine] of my sister's base stain of
whore', and that the remainder of l. 47 should read 'and which is worse than
so' (cf. III.i.257). The phrase 'The joy to make it still so' seems to mean 'his
pleasure in making her whoredom continual', i.e., he not only seduced her but
delighted in maintaining her as his mistress after marrying her to Amintor.
50. *justice*] magistrate (in a general sense: *OED,* 8).
53. *in*] i.e., into your treacherous conspiracy.
57. *so*] provided that.

That wait for such a troubled hour as this.
Throw him the blank.
Lysippus. [*Throwing Melantius a scroll of paper*] Melantius, write
       in that
   Thy choice; my seal is at it.   65
Melantius. It was our honours drew us to this act,
   No gain, and we will only work our pardons.
Calianax. Put my name in too.
Diphilus.   You disclaimed us all
   But now, Calianax.
Calianax.   That's all one;
   I'll not be hanged hereafter by a trick: 70
   I'll have it in.
Melantius.   You shall, you shall.
   [*To Lysippus*] Come to the back gate, and we'll call you
       King,
   And give you up the fort.
Lysippus.   Away, away!   *Exeunt.*

[ACT V SCENE iii]

Enter ASPATIA *in man's apparel.*

Aspatia. This is my fatal hour. Heaven may forgive
   My rash attempt, that causelessly hath laid
   Griefs on me that will never let me rest,
   And put a woman's heart into my breast.

---

64. *Throwing . . . paper*] Weber (subst.); *not in* Q1, Q2.   64–5. Melantius . . .
at it] *so Theobald; Melantius . . .* choice, / My . . . at it Q1, Q2.   67. No] Q1,
Q2; Not Q6.   68–9. You . . . Calianax] *so Weber; as one line,* Q1, Q2.
72. call you] Q2; call the Q1.   73. *Exeunt.*] Q1, Q2 (*subst.: Exeunt omnes.*)

---

64. *Throw . . . blank*] The urgent imperative is in keeping with the speech
(and with Strato's forthright character). Since the words form a half-line of
verse (completed by 'Melantius, write in that') they are not a mistakenly
incorporated stage direction.
   blank] a blank document, or a document with blank spaces left in it, to be
filled up at the recipient's pleasure (*OED*, 6).
   67. *No gain*] i.e., no desire of gain. A more emphatic expression than Q6's
'Not gain'.
   work] achieve.
   1. *may*] may justly.
   2. *that*] The antecedent is 'Heaven'.

It is more honour for you that I die,   5
For she that can endure the misery
That I have on me, and be patient too,
May live and laugh at all that you can do.

Enter Servant.

God save you, sir.
Servant.   And you sir. What's your business?
Aspatia. With you, sir, now, to do me the fair office   10
To help me to your lord.
Servant.   What, would you serve him?
Aspatia. I'll do him any service, but, to haste,
For my affairs are earnest, I desire
To speak with him.
Servant. Sir, because you are in such haste, I would be loth to   15
delay you longer: you cannot.
Aspatia. It shall become you, though, to tell your lord.
Servant. Sir, he will speak with nobody.
Aspatia.   This is most strange.
Art thou gold-proof? [*Gives money.*] There's for thee: help
me to him.
Servant. Pray be not angry, sir; I'll do my best.   *Exit.*   20
Aspatia. How stubbornly this fellow answered me!
There is a vile dishonest trick in man,
More than in women. All the men I meet

---

5. die] *Q2;* doe *Q1.*   9. God] *Q1;* Cod *Q2.*   18. nobody.] *Q2* (no body.);
no body, but in particular, I haue in charge about no waightie matters. *Q1.*

---

5. *you*] heaven; the gods.
12. *to haste*] to make haste, to be brief.
18. *Sir ... strange*] As Gurr notes, the Servant's short speech in Q2 makes
adequate sense, and the remainder of his speech in Q1 is too considerable to
have been accidentally omitted by Q2's compositor. He therefore attributes the
deletion to authorial revision. It may be further noted that l. 18 is a whole line
of verse. As for Aspatia's reply, in Q1 it most probably refers to Amintor's
reported instructions to the Servant, while in Q2 it most probably refers to the
Servant's own brusque manner (cf. l. 21). If the deletion is an authorial
revision, the motive may either have been to remove absurdity ('he will speak
with nobody' makes what follows redundant, and what follows admits the
possibility that Amintor might speak about trivial matters) or to bring out what
was perhaps always intended, i.e., that Aspatia's reply referred to the Servant's
behaviour.

Appear thus to me, are harsh and rude,
And have a subtlety in everything,   25
Which love could never know; but we fond women
Harbour the easiest and the smoothest thoughts,
And think all shall go so. It is unjust
That men and women should be matched together.

Enter AMINTOR *and* Servant.

Amintor. Where is he?
Servant.   There, my lord.
Amintor. [*To Aspatia*]   What would you, sir?   30
Aspatia. Please it your lordship to command your man
     Out of the room, I shall deliver things
     Worthy your hearing.
Amintor. [*To Servant*]   Leave us.

                              [*Exit* Servant.]
Aspatia. (*Aside*)   O, that that shape
     Should bury falsehood in it!
Amintor.   Now, your will, sir?
Aspatia. When you know me, my lord, you needs must guess   35
     My business, and I am not hard to know,
     For till the chance of war marked this smooth face
     With these few blemishes, people would call me
     My sister's picture, and her mine: in short,
     I am the brother to the wronged Aspatia.   40
Amintor. The wronged Aspatia! Would thou wert so too
     Unto the wronged Amintor! Let me kiss

29.1. *Enter* AMINTOR *and* Servant.] *Q1, Q2 (subst.: Enter Amintor and his man.).*   33.1. *Exit* Servant.] *Langbaine; not in Q1, Q2.*   33–4. O ... it] *so Theobald; as one line, Q1, Q2.*

24. *Appear*] (three syllables).
26. *fond*] foolish.
29. *matched*] i.e., in opposition.
38. *blemishes*] Aspatia has marked her face in some way—or, at this point, the audience is to imagine so. Dyce added to the opening stage direction the words 'and with artificial scars on her face'. Melantius also speaks of his facial scars (IV.i.24–5), and it is not absolutely necessary that they should be represented by make-up.
41. *so*] brother, i.e., brother-in-law. Amintor regrets that he did not marry Aspatia instead of Evadne.
42–3. *Let ... thine*] Probably Amintor seizes his visitor's hand at the end of l. 40 and now presses it to his lips.

That hand of thine in honour that I bear
Unto the wronged Aspatia. Here I stand
That did it; would I could not! Gentle youth,   45
Leave me, for there is something in thy looks
That calls my sins in a most hideous form
Into my mind, and I have grief enough
Without thy help.
Aspatia.   I would I could with credit.
Since I was twelve years old I had not seen   50
My sister till this hour I now arrived.
She sent for me to see her marriage,
A woeful one, but they that are above
Have ends in everything. She used few words,
But yet enough to make me understand   55
The baseness of the injuries you did her.
That little training I have had is war:
I may behave myself rudely in peace;
I would not, though. I shall not need to tell you
I am but young, and would be loth to lose   60
Honour that is not easily gained again.
Fairly I mean to deal. The age is strict

---

44. I stand] *Q1, Q2;* he stands *conj. Heath.*   45. I] *Turner, conj. Daniel;* he
Q1, Q2.   47. hideous] *Q2;* odious *Q1.*

44–5. *Here . . . not!*] Grammatical consistency requires that we read either
'I . . . I . . .' with Turner or 'he . . . he . . .' with Heath. The use of 'I' and
'thou' by Amintor in III.ii.46–53 (cited by Dyce in defence of the Qq reading
here) is not analogous. As Turner notes, ' "I" and "he" may resemble one
another in the secretary hand', so Q1's error may come from a misreading;
alternatively it may come from imperfectly following a correction in
manuscript, in which case 'I stand . . . I could . . .' was probably the corrected
form.
    45. *it*] the wrong.
    49. *I . . . credit*] I wish I could [leave you] without losing honour [which
requires me to challenge you].
    52. *marriage*] (three syllables).
    53. *one*] i.e., occasion.
    53–4. *but they . . . everything*] but the gods have their purposes in everything
that happens.
    61. *easily*] (two syllables).
    62. *Fairly*] justly.
    62–4. *The age . . . published*] In March 1610 the House of Commons
recognised that 'His Majesty's care of men's bodies and lives was eminent and
of great merit in the matter of duels which devoured worthy persons upon

For single combats, and we shall be stopped
If it be published. If you like your sword,
Use it; if mine appear a better to you,   65
Change: for the ground is this, and this the time
To end our difference.

Amintor.   Charitable youth,
If thou be'st such, think not I will maintain
So strange a wrong, and, for thy sister's sake,
Know that I could not think that desperate thing   70
I durst not do; yet, to enjoy this world,
I would not see her, for, beholding thee,
I am I know not what. If I have aught
That may content thee, take it and be gone,
For death is not so terrible as thou: 75
Thine eyes shoot guilt into me.

Aspatia.   Thus she swore
Thou wouldst behave thyself, and give me words
That would fetch tears into my eyes, and so
Thou dost indeed, but yet she bade me watch
Lest I were cozened, and be sure to fight   80
Ere I returned.

Amintor.   That must not be with me.
For her I'll die directly, but against her
Will never hazard it.

Aspatia.   You must be urged.

83–5. You ... as you] *so Theobald; as prose, Q1, Q2.*

trifling and unworthy causes' (*Proceedings in Parliament, 1610,* ed. E. R.
Foster, New Haven and London, 1966, II, 42). There is, of course, good
dramatic reason for this duel's being immediate and unseconded.

   64. *published*] made public.
   66. *ground*] place.
   68. *such*] i.e., charitable; but also applicable (with unconscious irony) to
'youth'.
   69. *strange*] unnatural.
   69–71. *for ... do*] Let me tell you that for your sister's sake I would dare to
undertake any dangerous action.
   71–2. *to ... her*] I would not see her for the world.
   73. *I ... what*] i.e., I feel a strange effect upon me.
   79. *watch*] take care.
   80. *cozened*] tricked.
   82. *directly*] immediately, i.e., without hesitation.
   83. *urged*] goaded.

I do not deal uncivilly with those
That dare to fight, but such a one as you   85
Must be used thus.   *She strikes him.*

Amintor.   I prithee, youth, take heed.
Thy sister is a thing to me so much
Above mine honour that I can endure
All this—good gods! A blow I can endure—
But stay not, lest thou draw a timeless death   90
Upon thyself.

Aspatia.   Thou art some prating fellow,
One that has studied out a trick to talk
And move soft-hearted people; to be kicked, *She kicks him.*
Thus to be kicked! (*Aside*) Why should he be so slow
In giving me my death?

Amintor.   A man can bear   95
No more and keep his flesh. Forgive me, then;
I would endure yet if I could. Now show
The spirit thou pretendest, and understand
Thou hast no hour to live.

              They fight [:Amintor wounds Aspatia].
                      What dost thou mean?
Thou canst not fight: the blows thou mak'st at me   100
Are quite besides, and those I offer at thee

99.1. *Amintor wounds Aspatia.*] Weber (subst.); *not in Q1, Q2.*   99–103. What
... defenceless] *so Q1;* What ... fight: / The ... besides, / And ... armes /
And ... defencelesse *Q2.*

---

86. *thus*] probably with a blow on the face from her hand. She is not wearing
gloves (ll. 42–3, 219–22).
90. *timeless*] untimely.
93. *kicked*] i.e., on the buttocks; cf. Bacurius' kicking of the two
'swordmen' in *A King and No King*, V.ii.75, 98–9.
95–6. *A man ... flesh*] i.e., flesh and blood will not endure any more
of this treatment; cf. II.i.214, 341–2.
98. *The ... thou pretendest*] the courage that you lay claim to.
99. *no hour*] not another hour.
99–103. *What ... defenceless!*] Amintor has wounded Aspatia in the chest
(l. 102), and lowers his sword before speaking these lines. The fight is difficult
to stage, for despite ll. 143 and 204 it is inconceivable that Amintor would
repeatedly wound an unresisting opponent. Contrast the fight between
Amphialus and Parthenia (Appendix A), where the woman, though desiring a
fatal wound, also desires to wound the slayer of her husband.
101. *besides*] by the side (*OED*, 4), so as to miss.

     Thou spreadst thine arms and tak'st upon thy breast,
     Alas, defenceless!
Aspatia.   I have got enough,
     And my desire. There is no place so fit
     For me to die as here.   [*Falls.*]   105

       Enter EVADNE, *her hands bloody, with a knife.*

Evadne. Amintor, I am loaden with events
     That fly to make thee happy; I have joys
     That in a moment can call back thy wrongs
     And settle thee in thy free state again.
     It is Evadne still that follows thee,   110
     But not her mischiefs.
Amintor. Thou canst not fool me to believe again,
     But thou hast looks and things so full of news
     That I am stayed.
Evadne. Noble Amintor, put off thy amaze;   115
     Let thine eyes loose, and speak. Am I not fair?
     Looks not Evadne beauteous with these rites now?

---

102. thy] *Q2*; thine *Q1*.   105. *Falls.*] *Dyce; not in Q1, Q2.*   105.1.] *Q2*;
Ent. Euadne. Q1.   113. looks] *Q1 (corrected)* (lookes), *Q2*; bookes *Q1*
(uncorrected).   114. stayed] *Q2* (staid); stald *Q1*.

103. *enough*] i.e., to kill me.
105. *here*] at Amintor's feet.
107. *fly*] hasten.
108. *call back*] undo.
109. *free*] unburdened with injuries.
111. *mischiefs*] evil-doings (*OED*, 6).
112. *believe again*] After believing Evadne's repentance (IV.i.259–77; cf. IV.ii.304–7), Amintor now thinks that she has reverted to her adultery (though IV.ii. did not indicate that he knew she was going to the King's chamber).
113. *things*] Cf. ll. 122–4.
114. *stayed*] made to stay and hear you.
115. *put ... amaze*] discard your amazement (OED, amaze, sb., 4).
116. *Let ... loose*] look at me.
117. *rites*] attributes (i.e., the bloody knife and hands and the unbound hair). Not in *OED* in this sense. Cf. Chapman, *Bussy D'Ambois*, IV.ii.24; 'I have put on these exorcising rites' (i.e., these robes appropriate to the conjuring-up of spirits); this is in the 1607 text of Chapman's play, the 1641 text of which (entirely re-written at this point) also includes 'rites' in this sense ('To assume these magic rites').

Were these hairs half so lovely in thine eyes
When our hands met before the holy man?
I was too foul within to look fair then;   120
Since I knew ill I was not free till now.
Amintor. There is presage of some important thing
About thee which it seems thy tongue hath lost:
Thy hands are bloody, and thou hast a knife.
Evadne. In this consists thy happiness and mine.   125
Joy to Amintor, for the King is dead!
Amintor. Those have most power to hurt us that we love;
We lay our sleeping lives within their arms.
Why, thou hast raised up mischief to his height,
And found one to out-name thy other faults.   130
Thou hast no intermission of thy sins,
But all thy life is a continued ill.
Black is thy colour now, disease thy nature.
Joy to Amintor? Thou hast touched a life

---

118. these hairs] *This ed.;* those houres *Q1, Q2.*   130. found one] *Q1, Q2;*
found out one *Q6.*

---

118. *these hairs*] these loose, unbound tresses. Qq's 'those houres' (the Q1
compositor's misreading of 'these haires' or 'these heares') makes no sense: the
marriage service cannot have lasted for hours, and the context shows that
Evadne is asking Amintor to look at her appearance. The point is that at the
marriage ceremony 'the bride wore her hair down, and was crowned with a
garland of wheat-ears or flowers' (*Shakespeare's England*, II, 146); cf. 'loose as
a bride's hair', Webster, *The White Devil*, IV.i.2). The hair was, of course, also
worn loose in the bedroom (cf. II.i.274–7: 'Or by those hairs ... I'll drag thee
to my bed'), and it is thus that Evadne will have visited the King's chamber in
V.i, from which the present scene shows her as directly coming.
  121. *knew ill*] could distinguish evil from good.
  free] innocent, acquitted (*OED*, 7).
  122. *presage*] (accented on second syllable) an ominous sign.
  important thing] matter of the utmost seriousness.
  127–9. *Those ... arms*] 'The quiet reflective tone ... is extraordinarily
effective in the circumstances and makes a brilliant contrast to the bitter
denunciation which follows' (Eugene M. Waith, *The Pattern of Tragicomedy in
Beaumont and Fletcher* (New Haven, 1952), p. 178.
  129. *his*] its.
  130. *found*] Q6's emendation ('found out') is attractive, with its implication
'sought out', and may be correct ('out-name' later in the line may have
confused the Q1 compositor); with the elision 't'out-name' it makes good
versification.
  one ... faults] a sin whose name is worse than your others', i.e., regicide; cf.
ll. 134–6.

The very name of which had power to chain   135
Up all my rage, and calm my wildest wrongs.
Evadne. 'Tis done, and since I could not find a way
To meet thy love so clear as through his life,
I cannot now repent it.
Amintor. Couldst thou procure the gods to speak to me,   140
To bid me love this woman and forgive,
I think I should fall out with them. Behold,
Here lies a youth whose wounds bleed in my breast,
Sent by his violent fate to fetch his death
From my slow hand; and to augment my woe   145
You now are present, stained with a king's blood
Violently shed. This keeps night here,
And throws an unknown wilderness about me.
Aspatia. O, O, O!
Amintor. [*To Evadne*] No more; pursue me not.   [*Going*]
Evadne.   Forgive me, then,   150

136. calm] *Q2;* tame *Q1.*   145-7. and to ... shed] *Q2; not in Q1.*
146. present, stained] *Q2* (present, stain'd); *not in Q1;* present-stain'd *conj.*
Daniel.   147. Violently shed] *Q2; not in Q1;* Most violently shed *conj.*
Theobald; Violently shed by thee *conj. this ed.*   150. Going] *This ed.; not in*
Q1, Q2.   150-1. Forgive ... part] *so Theobald;* Forgiue ... bed, / We ...
part *Q1, Q2.*

___

137. *way*] path.
138. *clear*] free from obstructions (*OED*, 20).
141. *love ... forgive*] i.e., in these very words; 'this woman' is otherwise
awkward after 'Couldst thou'.
143. *whose ... breast*] whose wounds make my own heart bleed.
145. *slow*] reluctant (*OED*, 3).
145-7. *and ... shed*] These lines, omitted in Q1 (probably because of their
vivid reference to regicide), must always have been part of the text. Amintor
means that his situation after the duel was bad enough, but that Evadne's
revelation has increased his grief and plunged him into 'night' and
'wilderness'.
147. *Violently ... here*] This line looks incomplete. The following line is
complete (and is so printed in Qq), so enjambement of 'And throws' is not
appropriate. Theobald's 'Most violently' is weak. I conjecture 'Violently shed
by thee'; in secretary hand 'ly shed' and 'by thee' are sufficiently alike to make
the omission of the latter a possible error. Though Amintor uses 'you' at l. 146,
he uses 'thou' throughout the rest of the dialogue.
148. *unknown*] strange, unfamiliar (*OED*, 1), i.e., one in which I do not
know my way.
wilderness] desolate region (*OED*, 2). Used metaphorically, like 'night',
l. 147.
150. Going] I take Amintor's 'No more; pursue me not' to mean 'I will hear

And take me to thy bed; we may not part.   [*Holds him.*]
Amintor. Forbear, be wise, and let my rage go this way.
Evadne. 'Tis you that I would stay, not it.
Amintor.   Take heed;
   It will return with me.
Evadne.   If it must be,
   I shall not fear to meet it. Take me home.   155
Amintor. Thou monster of cruelty, forbear!
Evadne. For heaven's sake look more calm: thine eyes are
      sharper
   Than thou canst make thy sword.   [*Kneels.*]
Amintor.   Away, away!
   Thy knees are more to me than violence;
   I am worse than sick to see knees follow me   160
   For that I must not grant. For God's sake, stand.

---

151. *Holds him.*] *This ed.; not in Q1, Q2; Kneels. Weber.*   153–5. Take heed
... home] *so Theobald;* Take ... me. / *Euad.* If ... it, / Take me home *Q1,*
Q2.   156. of cruelty] *Q1, Q2* (of crueltie); of all cruelty *Theobald;* of
crudelity *conj. this ed.*   157–9. For ... violence] *so Theobald;* For ... calme,
/ Thine ... sword. / *Amint.* Away ... violence *Q1, Q2.*   157. sharper] *Q2;*
crueller *Q1.*   158. *Kneels.*] *This ed.; not in Q1, Q2.*

---

you no more. I am now going; do not pursue me', and to be followed by his
move, whereupon Evadne tries to 'stay' him (l. 153). Turner, who adds to
l. 148 the direction '*Offers to go. Evadne followes.*', takes 'pursue me not' to
mean 'cease pursuing me'.

   151. *Holds him.*] Previous editors make Evadne kneel at this point, but this
is premature. At l. 159 Amintor indicates that she has just knelt (rather than
that she is still kneeling), and that she has hitherto been holding him by
'violence'.

   152. *Forbear*] let me go; cf. l. 156.

   153. *'Tis ... it*] i.e., I want you to remain and your rage to depart.

   154. *It ... me*] i.e., if you pull me back, you pull back my rage upon
yourself.

   156.] The metrical irregularity, which serves no apparent purpose, invites
emendation. 'Crudelity' (cruelty) was in current use till at least 1707 (*OED*),
and a d/e misreading is easy.

   159. *Thy knees are*] your kneeling is; cf. *Cor.*, V.iii.56–7: 'What's this? /
Your knees to me, to your corrected son?'

   more] worse.

   160. *worse than sick*] i.e., dead (with grief).

   knees follow me] Cf. *Tro.*, V.iii.10: 'Pursue we him on knees.'

   161. *that*] that which.

Evadne. Receive me, then.

Amintor.   I dare not stay thy language;
          In midst of all my anger and my grief,
          Thou dost awake something that troubles me,
          And says I loved thee once. I dare not stay;   165
          There is no end of woman's reasoning.   *Leaves her.*

Evadne. [*Rising*] Amintor, thou shalt love me now again.
          Go, I am calm. Farewell, and peace for ever.
          Evadne, whom thou hat'st, will die for thee.   *Kills herself.*

Amintor. I have a little human nature yet   170
          That's left for thee, that bids me stay thy hand.   *Returns.*

Evadne. Thy hand was welcome, but it came too late.
          O, I am lost! The heavy sleep makes haste.   *She dies.*

Aspatia. O, O, O!

Amintor. This earth of mine doth tremble, and I feel   175
          A stark affrighted motion in my blood;
          My soul grows weary of her house, and I
          All over am a trouble to myself.
          There is some hidden power in these dead things
          That calls my flesh unto 'em; I am cold.   180
          Be resolute, and bear 'em company!
          There's something yet which I am loth to leave;
          There's man enough in me to meet the fears
          That death can bring, and yet would it were done!
          I can find nothing in the whole discourse   185

167. *Rising*] *Dyce; not in Q1, Q2.*   173. *She dies.*] *Q2; not in Q1.*
180. flesh] *Q2;* selfe *Q1.*   unto] *Q1;* into *Q2.*

---

162. *stay thy language*] stay here and hear you speak. The repetition of 'I dare not stay' (l. 165) is for emphasis. Gurr (attaching too much importance to the comma between 'stay' and 'thy language' in Qq) regards 'I dare not stay, thy language' as an uncorrected false start or an unnoticed cancellation.

166. *There . . . reasoning*] This sounds proverbial, but is not in Tilley.

169. Kills herself.] The direction, though appropriately printed at the end of Evadne's speech, does not mean that she strikes the fatal blow *before* Amintor's ll. 170–1 but *during* them. It is important that Amintor should almost have got off-stage before Evadne's ll. 167–9.

173. *lost*] at my life's end.

175. *earth*] flesh.

176. *stark*] stiff, i.e., freezing.

177. *her house*] i.e., the body.

179. *dead things*] bodies.

182. *something*] i.e., in the world.

185. *discourse*] treatise (*OED*, 5); figuratively for the exhaustive consideration of the subject.

Of death I durst not meet the boldest way,
Yet still betwixt the reason and the act
The wrong I to Aspatia did stands up.
I have not such another fault to answer.
Though she may justly arm herself with scorn　　　190
And hate of me, my soul will part less troubled
When I have paid to her in tears my sorrow.
I will not leave this act unsatisfied
If all that's left in me can answer it.

Aspatia. Was it a dream? There stands Amintor still,　　　195
Or I dream still.

Amintor. How dost thou? Speak; receive my love and help.
Thy blood climbs up to his old place again:
There's hope of thy recovery.

Aspatia. Did you not name Aspatia?

Amintor.　　　　　　　　　　　　I did.　　　200

Aspatia. And talked of tears and sorrow unto her?

Amintor. 'Tis true, and till these happy signs in thee
Stayed my course, it was thither I was going.

Aspatia. Thou art there already, and these wounds are hers.
Those threats I brought with me sought not revenge,　　　205
But came to fetch this blessing from thy hand.
I am Aspatia yet.

Amintor. Dare my soul ever look abroad again?

Aspatia. I shall sure live, Amintor; I am well;
A kind of healthful joy wanders within me.　　　210

Amintor. The world wants loveliness to excuse thy loss;

---

211. loveliness] *This ed.;* lines *Q1, Q2;* lives *Theobald, conj. Seward;* limits
conj. Theobald.　　excuse] *Q1, Q2;* expiate *Theobald, conj. Seward.*

---

187. *the reason . . . act*] the thought and the deed (i.e., of suicide).

188. *stands up*] i.e., as an impediment; perhaps with a figurative sense, i.e.,
like an opponent (*OED*, stand, 103. n.; cf. *Lr.*, III.vii.79: 'A peasant stand up
thus!').

193. *unsatisfied*] not settled by payment (*OED*, 4.f); figuratively for the
moral debt.

207. *I . . . yet*] i.e., I am the same Aspatia that I always was (i.e., loving and
forgiving); cf. *Ant..*, III.xiii.92–3: 'I am / Antony yet.'

208. *look abroad*] look out (from my body), i.e., face the world.

211. *loveliness*] Q1's 'The world wants lines to excuse thy losse' (reprinted
by Q2) is corrupt. Theobald's emendation 'lives' has obscured for later editors
(whether or not they accept his further emendation 'expiate' for 'excuse') the
nature of the corruption, which I think is as follows. The original read
'louelines', and the compositor (either through regarding the first four letters

Come, let me bear thee to some place of help.
Aspatia. Amintor, thou must stay; I must rest here;
My strength begins to disobey my will.
How dost thou, my best soul? I would fain live   215
Now, if I could; wouldst thou have loved me then?
Amintor. Alas,
All that I am's not worth a hair from thee.
Aspatia. Give me thine hand: mine hands grope up and down,
And cannot find thee; I am wondrous sick.   220
Have I thy hand, Amintor?
Amintor. Thou greatest blessing of the world, thou hast.
Aspatia. I do believe thee better than my sense.
O, I must go; farewell!   [*Dies.*]
Amintor. She swoons. Aspatia! Help, for God's sake! Water,   225
Such as may chain life ever to this frame!
Aspatia, speak! What, no help? Yet I fool;
I'll chafe her temples. Yet there's nothing stirs.
Some hidden power tell her Amintor calls,
And let her answer me! Aspatia, speak!   230

217–18. Alas … thee] *so Theobald*) Alas … haire / From thee *Q1, Q2*.
219. hands grope] *Q2*; eyes grow *Q1*.   224. *Dies.*] *Theobald; not in Q1, Q2*.
225. swoons] *Q1, Q2* (sounds).   228. there's] *Q4*; there *Q1, Q2*.

---

as an uncancelled error for the second five, or through eye-skip from the first
to the second 'l' set only the latter part of the word. Spellings in 'nes' and
'nesse' are both common in the period (e.g., in Sidney's *Arcadia*), and though
in Q1 the latter heavily predominates the former is found in IV.ii.117
(smoothnes') and 309 ('madnes'). The sense of the emended line is 'The world
lacks sufficient loveliness to serve as an excuse for (OED, excuse, v., 5) thy
death;' i.e., Aspatia's death, if it happens, will take from the world most of its
loveliness, which it cannot spare.

213. *thou … here*] you must stop (trying to lift me); I must stay here (on
the ground).

215. *soul*] a term of endearment (*OED*, 6); cf. *Rom.*, III.v.25: 'How is't, my
soul? Let's talk—it is not day.'

223. *better … sense*] better than I believe my sense of touch.

226. *frame*] body.

227. *Yet*] still; cf. l. 228.

fool] stand idle (*OED*, 2.a).

228. *there's*] Q4's emendation (i.e., still there's nothing that stirs; i.e., I can
feel no pulses) is idiomatic and fits the versification. The reading of Q1 and
Q2 cannot be understood in this sense; it has to mean 'still nothing stirs there',
and when so spoken it does not fit the versification.

229. *hidden*] i.e., within her insensible body.

I have heard, if there be any life, but bow
The body thus and it will show itself.
O, she is gone! I will not leave her yet.
Since out of justice we must challenge nothing,
I'll call it mercy if you'll pity me,   235
You heavenly powers, and lend forth some few years
The blessèd soul to this fair seat again.
No comfort comes; the gods deny me too.
I'll bow the body once again. Aspatia!
The soul is fled for ever, and I wrong   240
Myself, so long to lose her company.
Must I talk now? Here's to be with thee, love!

                                                    Kills himself.

                        Enter Servant.

Servant. This is a great grace to my lord, to have the new King
    come to him; I must tell him he is entering. [*Sees Amintor's
    body.*] O God! Help, help!   245

    Enter LYSIPPUS, MELANTIUS, CALIANAX, CLEON, DIPHILUS,
                        [*and*] STRATO.

Lysippus. Where's Amintor?
Servant. O, there, there!

244–5. *Sees Amintor's body.*] *Theobald (subst.: (Sees the bodies.)); not in Q1,
Q2.*   245.1. CLEON] *Q2; not in Q1.*   247. *Servant.*] *Colman; Strat. Q1, Q2.*

───

231. *bow*] bow down, i.e., bend it forwards from the waist, to bring the
blood to the head.
    233. *leave her*] give her up for dead.
    234. *challenge*] lay claim to (*OED*, 5). The point is that human beings have
no right ('justice') to any help from the gods, and must ask it as a favour
('mercy').
    236. *lend ... years*] lend out (like money, *OED*, 1.e, 'to lend forth') for
some few years.
    237. *seat*] dwelling (i.e., the body).
    238. *too*] as well as mortals; cf. l. 227.
    242. *talk*] i.e., waste time in talking; cf. *Arcadia*, bk. III, chap. 22, p. 483:
'And have I seen *Philoclea* dead, and doo I live? and have I lived, not to help
her, but to talke of her? and stande I still talking?'—after saying which
Pyrocles attempts suicide.
    Here's ... love!] Cf. *Rom.*, V.iii.119: 'Here's to my love!'
    242.1. Kills himself.] Perhaps by falling on his sword with which he killed
Aspatia; alternatively, with a dagger.
    247. Servant.] That the Servant should say this is the natural sequel to his

Lysippus. How strange is this!
Calianax.   What should we do here?
Melantius. These deaths are such acquainted things with me
    That yet my heart dissolves not. May I stand   250
    Stiff here for ever! Eyes, call up your tears:
    This is Amintor! Heart, he was my friend:
    Melt! Now it flows. Amintor, give a word
    To call me to thee.
Amintor. O!   255
Melantius. Melantius calls his friend Amintor. [*Embracing him*]
        O,
    Thy arms are kinder to me than thy tongue.
    Speak, speak!
Amintor. What?
Melantius. That little word was worth all the sounds   260
    That ever I shall hear again.
Diphilus.   O brother,
    Here lies your sister slain! You lose yourself
    In sorrow there.
Melantius.   Why, Diphilus, it is

256–7. Melantius ... tongue] *so Theobald; Melantius*... armes / Are ...
tongue *Q1, Q2*.   256. *Embracing him*] *This ed.; not in Q1, Q2*.   260. worth]
Q1, Q2; worthy *conj. this ed.*   261–2. O ... there] *so Theobald;* Oh ...
slaine, / You ... there *Q1, Q2*.

---

previous speech (note the resemblance between 'Help, help!' and 'there,
there!') and to the question put by the entering Lysippus. Colman points out
that 'Strato is following Lysippus into the room'. Q1's assignment of the
speech to Strato must be an error induced by the compositor's having just set
the direction in which Strato's name appears as entering with the others. The
speech prefix 'Ser.' could have been taken as being (or meaning) 'Str.'
    248. *What ... here?*] Whether this means 'Why should we have come here?'
or 'What use are we here?' I do not understand why Calianax says it, unless the
authors mean to prepare us for his discovery of his dead daughter. It is possible
that 'we' is an error for 'he' and that Calianax is asking 'What should he [i.e.,
Amintor] do here [i.e., on the ground]?'.
    249. *these deaths*] deaths in general; cf. I.ii.170.
    253. *flows*] Cf. 'dissolves', l. 250. That sorrow or sympathy causes the heart
to melt, or to bleed, is a common figurative expression.
    254. *to thee*] i.e., in death.
    260. *worth*] possibly an error for 'worthy' (*OED*, 1.b: 'of the value of, worth
(so much)'), which would restore the metre, as it would in *Cupid's Revenge*,
III.iv.81: '"Worth a Fathers Thanks." "Syr, I cannot."'
    262. *lose yourself*] are distracted, lose your senses (*OED*, 10.c).

A thing to laugh at in respect of this:
Here was my sister, father, brother, son,   265
All that I had. Speak once again;
What youth lies slain there by thee?
Amintor.   'Tis Aspatia.
My last is said; let me give up my soul
Into thy bosom.   [*Dies.*]
Calianax. What's that? What's that? Aspatia?
Melantius.   I never did   270
Repent the greatness of my heart till now;
It will not burst at need.
Calianax. My daughter dead here too! And you have all fine
new tricks to grieve, but I ne'er knew any but direct
crying.   275
Melantius. I am a prattler; but no more. [*Offers to stab himself.*]
Diphilus.   Hold, brother!
Lysippus. Stop him!
                [*Diphilus and Strato hold Melantius.*]
Diphilus. Fie, how unmanly was this offer in you!
Does this become our strain?
Calianax. I know not what the matter is, but I am grown very   280
kind, and am friends with you all now. You have given me
that among you will kill me quickly, but I'll go home and
live as long as I can.   *Exit.*
Melantius. His spirit is but poor that can be kept
From death for want of weapons.   285

266. again;] *Q1* (againe), *Q2* (againe,); again, Amintor; *conj. this ed.*
269. Dies.] *Theobald; not in Q1, Q2.*   270-1. I never ... now] *so Weber;*
as one line, Q1, Q2.   271. of my] *Q2;* of *Q1.*   276. Offers to stab himself.] *Theobald (subst.); not in Q1, Q2.*   277.1.] *This ed.; not in Q1, Q2.*
280-3. I know ... can] *so Theobald;* I know ... am / Growne ... now / You
... me / Quickly ... can *Q1, Q2* (Growne ... with you. / You]).   281. with
... now] *Q1;* with you *Q2.*   283. Exit.] *Q1; not in Q2.*

264. *in respect of*] in comparison with.
266. *All ... again*] a defective line, unless a pause is intended while
Melantius subdues his emotion. Possibly 'Amintor' was omitted after 'again'
(Q1 ends the line without punctuation, but it is so badly punctuated a text that
little can be inferred from this fact).
274. *tricks*] clever devices (*OED*, 3).
278. *offer*] attempt.
279. *strain*] family; cf. III.ii.270; IV.ii.285.
282. *will*] which will.

Is not my hands a weapon sharp enough
To stop my breath? Or if you tie down those,
I vow, Amintor, I will never eat,
Or drink, or sleep, or have to do with that
That may preserve life: this I swear to keep.   290
Lysippus. Look to him, though, and bear those bodies in.
May this a fair example be to me
To rule with temper, for on lustful kings
Unlooked-for sudden deaths from God are sent;
But curs'd is he that is their instrument.   [*Exeunt.*]   295

FINIS

295. *Exeunt.*] *Langbaine; not in Q1, Q2.*

---

291. *bear ... in*] Apart from Cleon and Amintor's servant there are no
named characters on stage who are free to obey this order. The carrying off
of the bodies has to be done by supernumeraries, who either enter with the
named characters at l. 245.1 or enter now through one of the stage doors
(which will probably have been left open at l. 245.1).
    293. *temper*] self-control (*OED*, 3).
    295. *he*] that person.

APPENDIX A
Sidney's *Arcadia* and *The Maid's Tragedy*

As Dyce first pointed out, the death of Aspatia (V.iii) was suggested by the death of Parthenia in *Arcadia*, bk. III, chap. 16. The chapter is reprinted here from the first edition (London, William Ponsonby, 1590) with corrections, including the epitaph omitted in 1590, from the second edition (London, William Ponsonby, 1593).

The fight being ceased, and ech side withdrawne within their strengthes, *Basilius* sent *Philanax* to entertaine the straunge Knights, and to bring them unto him, that he might acknowledge what honour was due to their vertue. But they excused themselves, desiring to be knowne first by their deedes, before their names should accuse their unworthinesse: and though the other replied according as they deserved, yet (finding that unwelcome curtesie is a degree of injury) he suffered them to retire themselves to a tent of their owne without the campe, where they kept themselves secrete: *Philanax* himself being called away to another straunge Knight; straunge not onely by the un-lookedfornesse of his comming, but by the straunge maner of his comming.

For he had before him foure damosels, and so many behind him, all upon palfreys, & all appareled in mourning weedes; ech of them a servant of ech side, with like liveries of sorrow. Himselfe in an armour, all painted over with such a cunning of shadow, that it represented a gaping sepulchre, the furniture of his horse was all of Cypresse braunches; wherwith in olde time they were woont to dresse graves. His Bases (which he ware so long, as they came almost to his ankle) were imbrodered onely with blacke wormes, which seemed to crawle up and downe, as readie alreadie to devoure him. In his shielde for *Impresa*, he had a beautifull childe, but having two heades; whereof the one shewed, that it was alreadie dead: the other alive, but in that case, necessarily looking for death. The word was, *No way to be rid from death, but by death.*

This Knight of the tombe (for so the souldiours termed him) sent to *Basilius*, to demaund leave to send in a damosel into the towne, to cal out *Amphialus*, according as before time some others had done. Which being granted (as glad any would undertake the charge, which no bodie else in that campe was knowne willing to do) the damosell went in, and having with tears sobbed out a brave chalenge to *Amphialus*, from the Knight of the Tombe, *Amphialus*, honourably enterteining the gentlewoman, & desiring to know the Knights name (which the doolefull Gentlewoman would not discover) accepted the chalenge, onely desiring the Gentlewoman to say thus much to the strange Knight, from him; that if his minde were like to his title, there were more cause of affinitie, then enmitie betweene them. And therefore presently (according as he was woont) as soone as he perceyved the Knight of the Tombe, with his Damosels and Judge, was come into

the Iland, he also went over in accustomed maner: and yet for the curtesie
of his nature, desired to speake with him.

But the Knight of the Tombe, with silence, and drawing his horse backe,
shewed no will to heare, nor speake: but with Launce on thigh, made him
knowe, it was fitte for him to go to the other end of the Career, whence
wayting the starte of the unknowne Knight, he likewise made his spurres
claime haste of his horse. But when his staffe was in his rest, comming
downe to meete with the Knight, nowe verie neere him, he perceyved the
Knight had mist his rest: wherefore the curteous *Amphialus* woulde not
let his Launce descende, but with a gallant grace, ranne over the heade of
his there-in friended enemie: and having stopped his horse, and with the
turning of him, blessed his sight with the Windowe where he thought
Philoclea might stand, he perceyved the Knight had lighted from his
horse, and throwne away his staffe, angrie with his misfortune, as having
mist his rest, and drawne his sworde to make that supply his fellowes fault.
He also lighted, and drew his sworde, esteeming victorie by advantage,
rather robbed then purchased: and so the other comming eagerly toward
him, he with his shield out, and sword aloft, with more braverie then anger,
drew unto him; and straight made their swords speake for them a pretie-
while with equall fearcenes. But *Amphialus* (to whom the earth brought
forth few matches) having both much more skill to choose the places, and
more force to worke upon the chosen, had already made many windowes
in his armour for death to come in at; when (the noblenes of his nature
abhorring to make the punishment overgoe the offence) he stept a little
backe, and withall, Sir Knight (said he) you may easely see, that it pleaseth
God to favour my cause; employ your valour against them that wish you
hurte: for my part, I have not deserved hate of you. Thou lyest false traytor,
saide the other, with an angrie, but weake voyce. But *Amphialus*, in whome
abused kindnesse became spitefull rage, Ah barbarous wretch (said hee)
onely couragious in discourtesie; thou shalt soone see whether thy toonge
hath betrayed thy harte, or no: and with that, redoubling his blowes, gave
him a great wounde upon his necke, and closing with him overthrew him,
and with the fall thrust him mortally into the bodie: and with that went to
pull off his helmet, with intention to make him give himselfe the lye, for
having so saide, or to cut off his head.

But the head-peece was no sooner off, but that there fell about the
shoulders of the overcome Knight the treasure of faire golden haire,
which with the face (soone knowne by the badge of excellencie) witnessed
that it was *Parthenia*, the unfortunatelie vertuous wife of *Argalus*: her
beautie then even in despight of the passed sorrow, or comming death,
assuring all beholders, that it was nothing short of perfection. For her
exceeding faire eyes, having with continuall weeping gotten a little rednesse
about them; her roundy sweetly swelling lippes a little trembling, as though
they kissed their neighbour death; in her cheekes the whitenesse striving
by little and little to get upon the rosinesse of them; her necke, a necke indeed of Alablaster, displaying the wounde, which with most daintie blood
laboured to drowne his owne beauties; so as here was a river of purest redde,
there an Iland of perfittest white, each giving lustre to the other; with the
sweete countenance (God-knowes) full of an unaffected languishing: though
these thinges to a grosly conceaving sense might seeme disgraces; yet indeed

were they but apparailing beautie in a new fashion, which all looked-upon thorough the spectacles of pittie, did even encrease the lynes of her naturall fairenes, so as *Amphialus* was astonished with griefe, compassion, & shame, detesting his fortune, that made him unfortunate in victory.

Therfore, putting off his headpeece & gauntlet; kneeling down unto her, & with teares testifying his sorow, he offred his (by himselfe accursed) hands to helpe her: protesting his life and power to be readie to doo her honour. But *Parthenia* (who had inward messingers of the desired deathes approch) looking upon him, and streight turning away her feeble sight, as from a delightlesse object, drawing out her wordes, which her breath (loath to parte from so sweete a bodie) did faintly deliver, Sir (saide she) I pray you (if prayers have place in enemies) to let my maides take my body untouched by you: the onely honour I now desire by your meanes, is, that I have no honour of you. *Argalus* made no such bargaine with you, that the hands which killed him, shoulde helpe me. I have of them (and I doo not onely pardon you, but thanke you for it) the service which I desired. There rests nothing now, but that I go live with him, since whose death I have done nothing but die. Then pawsing, and a little fainting, and againe comming to herselfe, O sweete life, welcome (saide she) nowe feele I the bandes untied of the cruell death, which so long hath helde me. And O life, O death, aunswere for me, that my thoughts have not so much as in a dreame tasted any comfort; since they were deprived of *Argalus*. I come, my *Argalus*, I come: And, O God hide my faultes in thy mercies, and graunt (as I feele thou doost graunt) that in thy eternall love, we may love eche other eternally. And this O Lorde: But there *Atropos* cut off her sentence: for with that, casting up both eyes and hands to the skies, the noble soule departed (one might well assure himselfe) to heaven, which left the bodie in so heavenly a demeanure.

But *Amphialus* (with a hart oppressed with griefe, because of her request) withdrewe himselfe, but the Judges, as full of pitie, had bene al this while disarming her, and her gentlewomen with lamentable cries, laboring to stanch the remediles wounds: & a while she was dead before they perceived it; death being able to divide the soul, but not the beauty from that body. But when the infallible tokens of death assured them of their losse, one of the women would have killed her selfe, but that the squire of *Amphialus* perceaving it, by force held her. Others that had as strong passion, though weaker resolution, fell to cast dust upon their heads, to teare their garments: all falling upon the earth, and crying upon their sweet mistres; as if their cries could perswade the soul to leave the celestiall happines, to come again into the elements of sorrow: one time calling to remembrance her vertue, chastnes, sweetnes, goodnes to them: another time accursing themselves, that they had obeyed her, they having bene deceaved by her words, who assured them, that it was revealed unto her, that she should have her harts desire in the battaile against *Amphialus*, which they wrongly understood. Then kissing her cold hands and feet, wearie of the world, since she was gone, who was their world. The very heavens semed, with a cloudie countenance, to loure at the losse, and Fame it selfe (though by nature glad to tell such rare accidents, yet) could not choose but deliver it in lamentable accents, & in such sort went it quickly all over the Campe: &, as if the aire had bene infected with sorow, no hart was so hard, but was subject to that contagion; the rarenes of the accident, matching together (the rarely matched together) pittie with admiration, *Basilius* himselfe came foorth, and brought the faire *Gynecia* with him who was come into the campe under colour of visiting her husband, and hearing of her daughters: but indeed *Zelmane* was the Sainct, to which her pilgrimage was entended: cursing, envying, blessing, and in her harte kissing the walles which imprisoned her. But both they with *Philanax*, and the rest of the principall Nobilitie, went out, to make Honour triumph over Death, conveying that excellent body (wherto *Basilius* himself would needes lend his shoulder) to a church a mile from the campe, where the valiant *Argalus* lay intombed; recommending to that sepulchre, the blessed reliques of faithfull and vertuous Love: giving order for the making of marble images, to represent them, & each way enriching the tombe. Upon which, *Basilius* himself caused this Epitaphe to be written.

> *His being was in her alone:*
> *And he not being, she was none.*
> *They joi'd one joy, one griefe they griev'd,*
> *One love they lov'd, one life they liv'd.*
> *The hand was one, one was the sword*
> *That did his death, hir death afford.*
> *As all the rest, so now the stone*
> *That tombes the two, is justly one.*

Four Plays in One and The Maid's Tragedy

It is necessary to begin by summarising the plot of *The Triumph of Death* in order that the quotations from it may be seen in their context. Thereafter passages from *The Triumph of Death* will be related to passages from *The Maid's Tragedy*, and the relationship between the tragic playlet and the tragedy will be explored.

The Triumph of Death opens with Gabriella reproaching the lord Lavall for neglecting her since their secret marriage. His insincere excuses are interrupted by the arrival of an old lord, Gentille, who was the friend of Gabriella's father and whose daughter Casta is Gabriella's friend. He summons Lavall to court where his bride-to-be, Hellena, awaits him. Gabriella and her maid Maria lament her marriage to Lavall and her earlier loss of Gentille's son, Perolot, who was too poor to be her suitor, and who was reported killed in warfare. In Scene ii two courtiers discuss Lavall's proud, deceitful, intemperate and lustful disposition, and declare that the devil often appears to him and torments him. In Scene iii Gabriella and Maria, at a window, witness Lavall's wedding procession. Gabriella exclaims

> just such a flattery,
> With that same cunning face, that smile upon't
> Oh mark it, *Marie*, mark it seriously,
> That Master smile caught me.   (p. 339)[1]

(Compare *The Maid's Tragedy*, II.ii.42, 51–2.) She invokes the justice of heaven:

> I am abus'd,
> She that depended on your Providence,
> She is abus'd: your honor is abus'd.
> That noble piece ye made, and call'd it man,
> Is turn'd to Devil: all the world's abus'd: (p. 339)

(Compare *The Maid's Tragedy*, IV.i.169.) Maria begins to encourage her revengeful feelings.

Scene iv opens with Gentille proposing to recommend Casta as a waiting-woman to Hellena; Casta, fearful of corruption at court, declines:

Teach not your child to tread that path, for fear (Sir)
Your dry bones after death, groan in your grave
The miseries that follow.   (p. 340)

(Compare *The Maid's Tragedy*, IV.i.86–90.) Lavall enters, sees
Casta, learns her identity, covets her, and is urged by his evil Spirit
to pursue her. He resolves to do so. Maria now enters and invites
him to supper at Gabriella's house. He accepts the invitation and
bribes Maria to get Casta to go there too by pretending that Gabriella
is ill. Maria, alone, declares that she sees his wicked intent. She is
suddenly confronted by Perolot, who has not been killed after all,
and whose confidence Lavall has betrayed in marrying Gabriella
after falsely maintaining his death. Maria promises to admit him
to Gabriella's house.

In Scene v Gentille, bearing an invitation to Lavall from the Duke,
discovers that he has left his house for the night. Scene vi, the final
scene, is at Gabriella's house where she is greeting Casta. Lavall's
arrival is announced. Gabriella, in an aside, exclaims

I am resolv'd, and all you wronged women,
You noble spirits, that as I have suffer'd
Under this glorious beast insulting man,
Lend me your causes, then your cruelties;
For I must put on madness above women.   (p. 348)[2]

(Compare *The Maid's Tragedy*, IV.i.169–70; II.ii.27; V.i.12–22.)
Lavall enters, and begins vaingloriously courting Casta and insulting
Gabriella, who retorts indignantly, while Maria, with Gabriella's
knowledge, drugs his wine. Casta flees, and Lavall sinks into a sleep.
Gabriella is about to revenge her wrongs on him when Perolot appears
and, after a brief explanation, asks her

What do you mean to do? for I'll make one.
Gab. To make his death more horrid (for he shall dye)—[3]
Per. He must, he must.
Gab. We'll watch him till he wakes,
    Then bind him, and then torture him.
Per. 'Tis nothing.
    No, take him dead drunk now without repentance,
    His leachery inseam'd upon him.
Gab. Excellent.   (p. 351)

Perolot stabs Lavall, who wakes and wounds Perolot, who immediately dies. As Gabriella grieves over him, the Spirit enters and exults
over Lavall:

Thy hour is come; succession, honor, pleasure,
And all the lustre thou so long hast look'd for,
Must here have end: Summon thy sins before thee.   (p. 352)

Enumerating them, he vanishes, leaving Lavall in the agonies of a
guilty conscience and visions of damnation. Gabriella, her attention
drawn to him by Maria, now stabs him repeatedly:

> *Gab*. This for young *Perolot*.
> *Lav*. Oh, mercy, mercy.
> *Gab*. This for my wrongs.
> *Lav*. But one short hour to cure me! [*Knock within*.
>   Oh be not cruell: Oh! oh.
> *Mar*. Heark, they knock.
>   Make hast for Heavens sake, Mistris.
> *Gab*. This for *Casta*.
> *Lav*. Oh, O, O, O!   [*He dies*.   (p. 353)

(Compare *The Maid's Tragedy*, V.i.110–12.) Gabriella and Maria
carry his body upstairs as the Duke and his courtiers burst in. Gentille
discovers his son's body, and Gabriella, above with Maria, produces
Lavall's body, denounces him as Perolot's murderer, throws down
a paper relating her other reasons for killing Lavall, throws down
Lavall's heart, and stabs herself, in which action Maria immediately
follows her. Hellena and Casta determine to enter a religious house,
and Gentille to leave the court and pray at home. The Duke briefly
concludes:

> Now to ourselves retire we, and begin
> By this example to correct each sin.   (p. 355)

The absence of external evidence as to the date of *Four Plays in
One* and as to its authorship (other than its inclusion in the Folio
of 1647) makes it difficult to establish whether *The Triumph of Death*
preceded or followed *The Maid's Tragedy*.[4] The internal evidence
suggests that *The Triumph of Death* came first. Its plot, unlike that of
The Maid's Tragedy, has a steady dependence on a source: the secret
marriage, the second marriage, the invitation, the murder, the dis-
closure, all derive from Bandello and his followers. Three of the
similar passages, furthermore, look as though they originated in *The
Triumph of Death*: a treacherous smile becomes Lavall more obviously
than it becomes Amintor; Gabriella was abused, but Evadne was
corrupted rather than abused (it was Amintor and Aspatia who were
abused); and the formula accompanying the repeated stabbings is
much improved by being concentrated into one speech in *The Maid's*

Tragedy rather than interspersed with interjected speeches as in *The Triumph of Death*. In addition, Evadne's lines

> I'll shape his sins like furies till I waken
> His evil angel, his sick conscience (V.i.33–4)

are more likely to have been suggested by the actual appearance of Lavall's evil Spirit than to have inspired it.

NOTES

1 References are to the Folio text (1647) of *Four Plays, or Moral Representations, in One* in Glover and Waller, x, 287–364.
2 The Folio text has 'beast-insulting'.
3 The Folio text has 'dye.'
4 The most helpful discussion of the arguments about date and authorship is by E. H. C. Oliphant, *The Plays of Beaumont and Fletcher* (New Haven, 1927), pp. 369–83. As he says, 'The date is altogether doubtful' (p. 371), particularly since it cannot be assumed that all four playlets were written at one time. Various dates between 1608 and 1625 have been at various times proposed. Fletcher's authorship of the last two plays is not in doubt. Of the first two plays, some give both to Beaumont, some give him only *The Triumph of Love*, and some give both to Nathan Field (1587–1620). Cyrus Hoy, 'The Shares of Fletcher and his Collaborators in the Beaumont and Fletcher Canon (IV)', *Studies in Bibliography* XII(1959), pp. 91–116, regards Field as Fletcher's sole collaborator in *Four Plays*, a view at which Oliphant had also arrived; Oliphant proposed a date of about 1614 for the collaboration (p. 378).

APPENDIX C
Valerius Maximus and *The Maid's Tragedy*

William Dinsmore Briggs (*Modern Language Notes*, XXXI (1916), 502–3) cited the following passage as the source of the incident in *The Maid's Tragedy*, IV.ii, in which Melantius continues to solicit Calianax's assistance against the King when they are both in the latter's presence and Calianax is accusing Melantius of treasonable intentions. The passage is here reprinted from the edition by C. Kempf of Valerius Maximus, *Valerii Maximi Factorum et Dictorum Memorabilium Libri Novem* (Valerius Maximus' Nine Books of Memorable Acts and Sayings), Stuttgart, 1888, reprinted 1966. An English translation has been appended to the original Latin.

Conplura huiusce notae Romana exampla supersunt, sed satietas modo uitanda est. itaque stilo meo ad externa iam delabi permittam. quorum principatum teneat Blassius, cuius constantia nihil pertinacius: Salapiam enim patriam suam praesidio Punico occupatam Romanis cupiens restituere Dasium acerrimo studio secum in administratione rei publicae dissidentem et alioquin toto animo Hannibalis amicitiae uacantem, sine quo propositum consilium peragi non poterat, ad idem opus adgrediendum maiore cupiditate quam spe certiore temptare ausus est. qui protinus sermonem eius, adiectis quae et ipsum commendatiorem et inimicum inuisiorem factura uidebantur, Hannibali retulit. a quo adesse iussi sunt, ut alter crimen probaret, alter defenderet. ceterum, cum pro tribunali res gereretur et quaestioni illi omnium oculi essent intenti, dum aliud forte citerioris curae negotium tractatur, Blassius uultu dissimulante ac uoce summissa monere Dasium coepit ut Romanorum potius quam Karthaginiensium partes foueret. enimuero tunc ille proclamat se in conspectu ducis aduersus eum sollicitari. quod quia et incredibile existimabatur et ad unius tantum auris penetrauerat et iactabatur ab inimico, ueritatis fide caruit. sed non ita multo post Blasii mira constantia Dasium ad se traxit Marcelloque et Salapiam et quingentos Numidas, qui in ea custodiae causa erant, tradidit.

(bk. III, chap. viii, ext. 1)

Several Roman examples of this kind remain, but one should try to avoid giving too many. Therefore I will now allow my pen to stoop to foreign examples. Blassius must be given the first place among them; nothing could be more unyielding than his determination. For, in his desire to restore to the Romans Salapia, his native land, which was occupied by Carthaginian troops, he ventured, more from desire than hope, to urge Dasius to undertake the same task (though Dasius

207

was vehemently opposed to him in matters of state administration and in other respects wholly open to the friendship of Hannibal), without whom the proposed plan could not be put into effect. Dasius immediately reported his words to Hannibal with additions which seemed likely to make himself more favoured and his enemy more hated. Hannibal summoned them both, so that the one could make good the charge and the other defend himself. But, when the matter came before the tribunal and all eyes were following the cross-examination, while they were dealing with another affair of more immediate concern Blassius, disguising his expression and lowering his voice, began to advise Dasius to embrace the Romans' cause rather than the Carthaginians'. Dasius then announced that he was being incited against the general before his very eyes. The accusation did not have the ring of truth, because it was considered incredible, and had reached the ears of only one person, and was asserted by an enemy. But not so very long afterwards the amazing determination of Blassius won over Dasius, and delivered to Marcellus both Salapia and five hundred Numidians who were there on guard duty.

Glossarial Index to the Commentary

Words and phrases are listed in the form in which they appear in the text. An asterisk before a word indicates that the note contains information which may supplement that given in *OED*.